The Sapphire Cross

by

George Manville Fenn

The Sapphire Cross
by George Manville Fenn

ISBN: 978-93-59959-88-7

Published by

DOUBLE 9 BOOKS

2/13-B, Ansari Road
Daryaganj, New Delhi – 110002
info@double9books.com
www.double9books.com
Tel. 011-40042856

ABOUT THE AUTHOR

George Manville Fenn was a very productive author of novels, a writer, an editor, and an educator from England. He was born on January 3, 1831, in Pimlico, London. He mostly learned on his own; he taught himself Italian, French, and German. During the years 1851-1854, he went to Battersea Training College for Teachers and then became the head of a state school in Alford, Lincolnshire. In the early 1850s, Fenn started to write short stories and pieces for newspapers and magazines. The Old Forest Ranger, his first book, came out in 1856. Afterward, he wrote more than 100 books, many of them for teenagers and young adults. He was one of the most famous writers of his time, and his books were well-liked and read by many people. I also worked as a reporter and writer for Fenn. Among the newspapers and magazines, he worked for was The Boy's Own Paper, which he ran from 1866 to 1874. He worked hard to make children's books better and was a strong supporter of education and reading. The Englishman Fenn passed away on August 26, 1909, in Isleworth.

CONTENTS

In the Old Fen-Land

"Oh, how sweet the pines smell, Marion! I declare it's quite bliss to get down here in these wilds, with the free wind blowing the London smoke out of your back hair, and no one to criticise and make remarks. I won't go to the sea-side any more: pier and band, and esplanade and promenade; in pink to-day and in blue to-morrow, and the next day in green; and then a bow here and a 'de-do' there; and 'how's mamma?' and 'nice day;' and all the same sickening stuff over again. There! I won't hear fault found with the Fen-land ever any more. I don't wonder at that dear old Hereward the Wake loving it. Why, it's beautiful! and I feel free—as free as the air itself; and could set off and run and jump and shout like a child?"

"Dangerous work, running and jumping here," said a tall, pale girl, the speaker's companion, as she picked her way from tuft to tuft of heath and rushes, now plucking a spray of white or creamy-pink moss, now some silky rush, and at last bending long over a cluster of forget-me-nots, peering up from the bright green water plants, like turquoise set in enamelled gold.

"What lovely forget-me-nots!" cried her blonde companion, hurrying to her side, the oozy ground bending beneath her weight, as she pressed forward. "True blue—true blue! I must have a bunch as well."

"Poor Philip's favourite flowers," said the other, sadly. "I have the little dried bouquet at home now that he gave me—six years ago this spring, Ada. Forget-me-not!"

She stood, sad and thoughtful, with the flowers in her hand, the tears the while dropping slowly upon the little blue petals, that seemed like eyes peering up at her. They were standing together upon the edge of a wide stretch of uncultivated marsh, which commenced as soon as the grove of whispering pines through which they had come ceased to flourish; though here and there, just as they had been dragged forth from the boggy depths, lay, waiting for carriage, huge roots of pines, that had been growing, perhaps, two thousand years before, and now, probed for and dragged to the surface, proved to be sound—undecayed, and crystallised with the abundant turpentine, forming a fuel much sought after by the country people.

"Marion, darling," whispered the fair girl, passing her arm round the other's waist, and speaking in soft, deep tones—a perfect contrast to her gay accents of a few moments before—"try not to mourn now: it is hardly loyal, and it is of no avail. I too have wept for the dead, many and many a time."

"Yes; we all weep for our passed away," said Marion, sadly.

"Yes, true; I mourned, too, for poor Philip, Marion."

"You, Ada?"

"Yes; why not? I feel no shame in owning that I loved him, too—warmly as ever you could, though I saw his preference and bore it in silence."

"You, you—Ada?"

"Yes, dear, I. You think me light and frivolous, but may not that be merely on the surface? I wept long when I found that he loved and was engaged to you; but I hid my secret, for my only wish was to see him happy; and you cannot say that I ever failed in my friendship."

"Never—never, dear," said Marion, gazing with troubled eyes at her friend, but clinging to her the while; and then, making their way to the pine grove, they sat down amongst the soft shed needles to rest, dreamily pondering over the past, till, starting from her reverie, Ada Lee exclaimed lightly:

"There, this will not do. Poor Philip has gone to his soldier's grave, honourably fighting for his country. May Heaven rest him! for he was a brave fellow; but life is not long enough for much time to be spent in weeping. There, Marion, darling, rouse your self; this is not a thing of yesterday. Come! we must get back. Think of the wooing and wedding, and be as merry and light-hearted as I am. Heigho! I wish, though, that some one would marry me, and bring me to live down here in these dear old solemn marshes. How nice for me to be always close to you, wouldn't it? There's a house across there amongst the trees that would do capitally. Who lives there?"

"No one, Ada," said the other, sadly. "That is Merland Hall, where poor Philip should have dwelt."

Ada started, and again her arm was pressed round her companion's waist, when, almost in silence, they walked back to the parsonage, where Ada Lee was staying with her friend, having come down from London to fulfil the office of bridesmaid at Marion's wedding.

But on reaching her bedroom Marion threw herself in a chair, letting the botanical specimens she had been gathering fall upon the carpet beside her, as she leaned her head upon her hand, and remained silent and thoughtful.

"Oh, come—come, darling; this will never do," cried Ada. "Mrs Elstree said that I was to do all I could to cheer and enliven you, and here have I been making you worse with my ill-chosen chatter. Why, you ought to be as happy as the day is long: a fine, handsome husband, young as well as rich; a castle to live in, and he as devoted as possible. Why, I declare I'm almost in love with him myself. Look at the presents he has sent you. Why, one would think, to see that doleful face, that you did not like him!"

"But I do, Ada. I esteem and respect, and I think I love him."

"Think, indeed! why, of course you do. Didn't I see you give him a kiss last night when he asked you as he was going?"

"And I believe that I shall be very happy with him," continued Marion, not heeding her companions words; "but, just now, as I am going to take this irrevocable step, the past all seems to come back, and it almost seems as if I were going to be faithless to poor Philip; and, in spite of all I can do, my poor heart is filled with forebodings."

"Oh dear—oh dear! What a girl it is!" cried Ada. "This won't do, you know. What am I to do with you? Oh! look here! Why, here's a note on the dressing-table, and a case—a jewel-case, I'm sure! Why, it's another present from that dear Sir Murray. Why, you happy, lucky darling! There, pray read your note, and do show me what's in the case, there's a dear sweet girl."

As she spoke, she seized a note lying by a large morocco case upon the dressing-table, and eagerly placed it in her friend's hand, laying the case in her lap, at the same time stroking the hair from her forehead, and kissing her tenderly, though a shade of care and anxiety was plainly visible upon the face she strove to make appear mirthful.

Marion read the note, the colour mantling faintly in her cheek the while.

"He is most kind and affectionate," she said, sadly. "I would that he had chosen one more worthy of his love!"

"How can you talk like that?" cried Ada, reproachfully. "There, do pray chase away this horrible low-spiritedness! It is not right to Sir Murray, dear—it isn't, indeed; and I'm sure you have no cause to blame yourself. But there, my own handsome darling, I know what it is: you feel the step you are going to take, and no wonder; but try—pray try—for his sake, to be brighter. He's coming to dinner, you know; and he's a dear, nice fellow, in spite of his pride and so much of the Spanish grandee. Think, too, how happy it makes Mr and Mrs Elstree to see you so well provided for!—and without going right away. They're as proud as can be, and the dear old rector is making out that he is condescending wonderfully in letting Sir Murray have his darling. But all the time he's reckoning upon your being

Lady Gernon, and so is dear aunt. But come, you have not shown me your present; and, look here, if all your specimens are not lying upon the floor! I suppose you will give up botany now you are taking to husbandry."

"The joke is old, Ada," said Marion, smiling, and, making an effort, she rose from her chair, gathered together her flowers and mosses, and laid them on the table, before turning the handsome gilt key of the morocco case, to display, glittering in the light, a gorgeous suite of sapphires: necklet, bracelets, earrings; and a large cross, a mingling of the same gems with brilliants.

"Oh, what a lovely piece of vanity;" cried Ada, rapturously. "Oh, my darling, how proud I shall feel of my friend Lady Gernon—that is, if she does not grow too stilty for her old friend."

"For shame, Ada!" cried Marion.

"Oh, I don't know," said Ada. "I have my forebodings, too, and I think I may as well say good-bye for good when you start to-morrow for your tour."

"Do you wish to make me more unhappy?" said Marion, reproachfully.

"No, of course not," said Ada, kissing her. "But, mark my words, it will be so," she continued, dreamily, as she clasped the jewels upon her friend's arms and neck. "There, I declare they are quite regal, and must have cost hundreds of pounds! I love sapphires; they are so much like forget-me-nots—true blue, you know. There, how stupid I am, setting you off again! But look, darling, are they not lovely? I never saw a more beautiful suite. That cross, too—it's magnificent! But you must take care not to lose it. The ring is slight, and it might come detached. Now, then, bathe those eyes, while I put the present away. Really I've a great mind to let you wear them at dinner to-night."

Marion said nothing, and Ada slowly replaced the gems, lingering long over the cross, little thinking it was to be the bane of her cousin's life.

Under the Shadow

Ada Lee was right: there was a good deal of the Spanish grandee in the aspect of Sir Murray Gernon, who traced back his pedigree to the old Norman days, when, as a recompense for the service of the stout knight, Sir Piers Gernon, his squire, and so many men-at-arms, William gave him the pleasant lands whereon he built his castle, overlooking many an acre of Lincolnshire fen-land—a castle that gave place, in Tudor days, to the fine, square, massive, and roomy building, which still retained the name as well as the broad moat. Sir Murray entered the rectory drawing-room, tall, swarthy, and haughty of bearing, and was chatting graciously to the parents of his intended bride, when she entered the apartment.

To a careless observer the morning's sadness had all departed, and courtly lover could not have been better satisfied with his greeting as Marion crossed the room to meet him, placing both her hands in his, and looking up in his proud face as much as to say, "I am soon to be yours—be gentle with me."

Sir Murray took the hands with quite a protective air, smiling down upon the face, which he saluted with a lordly kiss upon the white forehead; and then, apparently well satisfied with the lady so soon to grace his table, he led her to a chair beside Ada, and in a somewhat cumbersome fashion began to chat about the morning's proceedings.

"Studying dress I presume we should have been?" said Ada. "But we were away by the edge of the marsh, botanising, for half the day. Poor Marion has been taking a farewell of her favourite pursuit," she added, laughingly.

"I don't see that at all," said Sir Murray. "I admire natural history, and shall hope that Lady Gernon will prove a kind and patient instructress."

"I think it was reserved for us at our return to find our brightest specimens, though," said Marion, turning her large, dreamy eyes upon the baronet. "I have to thank you for your present, Murray."

"Oh, don't talk about it—wear it," was the response. "They are the old family jewels reset. I thought you would like them better modernised."

The dinner passed off quietly. Sir Murray Gernon, who prided himself upon his birth, lineage, and wealth, taking matters in a courtly manner, considering that it would be unbecoming, even upon the evening preceding his marriage, to forget his dignity. Hence there was a something that seemed almost verging upon coldness in his farewell that night, even when he whispered the words, "Till to-morrow, dearest." There was no apparent ardour, although he was, certainly, contented and proud; and he rode home that night at a very respectable hour, telling himself that he was one of the happiest men in the kingdom.

When Marion was once more alone with her cousin, the emotion, crushed down, hidden beneath a mask of cheerfulness, asserted itself in a way that alarmed even herself: sobs and hysterical cries seeming to tear themselves from her breast, to be succeeded, though, at last by a calm, as, evidently by a great effort, she overcame the weakness to which she had given way.

"Don't be angry, Ada!" cried the agitated girl, as she clung to her friend. "I am very—very weak, I know; but to-morrow I must be strong, and put weakness aside. To-night, I feel that if I did not give way, my agony would be greater than I could bear. I cannot dissimulate!" she exclaimed, passionately. "I do not love this man as I should; he is cold and haughty, and does not try to make me love him. I have tried—tried hard, for they have set their mind upon it, and what can I do? But the old, old love will come back, and I seem to see poor Philip beckoning to me from the other side of the great black gulf, calling me, as it were, to him; and to go on with this—to keep faith to-morrow, is like being false, when I recall all my vows made before he went away."

"But, Marion, darling," exclaimed Ada, "does not death solve all those ties? Come, dear, be tranquil, and do not give way to all this weakness. You do not do Sir Murray justice: he is proud and haughty; but look at the pride he has in you. There!" she cried, "I shall be glad when to-morrow is here, and the wooing ended by the wedding. I will not say, fight back all these sad memories, because I know you have tried; but pray, pray think of duty, of what you owe to your betrothed, as well as to your parents. Come, to bed—to bed, or I shall be blamed for the sad, pale face that will be under the orange blossoms to-morrow."

"Do you think the dead have power to influence us, Ada?" said Marion, who had sat with her hair pressed back from her temples, and had not apparently heard a word her cousin had said.

"The dead!—influence!" said Ada, looking almost with fear in her companion's face.

"Yes, influence us; for it seems as if Philip were ever present with me, drawing me, as it were, to him, and reproaching me for my want of faith. Shall I always feel this?—always be haunted by his spirit, unseen but by myself? Ada, do you believe in foresight—in a knowledge of what is to be?"

"No, certainly not, you foolish, childish creature!" exclaimed Ada, making an effort to overcome the strange thrill of dread her cousin's words engendered. "How can you be so weak? It's cruel of you—unjust."

"I shall not live long, Ada. I feel it—I am sure of it. If there is such a thing as a broken heart, mine is that heart. But I will do my duty to all, hard as it may be. And now, kiss me, dear, and go to your own room; for I am going to pray for strength to carry me through the trial, and that Heaven will make me to my husband a good and earnest wife."

What could she say?—how whisper peace to this troubled breast? Ada Lee felt that peace must come from another source, and, kissing tenderly the cold pale cheek, she went softly, tearfully to her own room.

A Glance at the Substance

The moon shone brightly through the window of Ada Lee's bedroom as she seated herself thoughtfully by her dressing-table. She had extinguished her light, and, attracted by the soft sea of silvery mist spread before her sight over the marsh, she gazed dreamily out, watching the play of the moonbeams upon the wreathing vapour, now musing upon the past, now upon the present, and at last letting her eyes fall upon the green lawn beneath the window—one of about half-a-dozen, looking out upon that side of the old ivy-covered rectory. The trees cast dark, massive-looking shadows here and there, while patches of the grass, and now and then a flower-bed stood out, bathed in the soft light.

How long she sat there musing she could not tell, but her reverie was rudely broken by the sight of a dark figure coming forth from amidst the shrubs upon her left, to stand for a moment gazing up at the house.

Her heart beat violently, and a strange swimming sensation made blurred and indistinct the moonlit scene; but when, approaching more nearly to the window-pane, she gazed anxiously out, the dark figure had disappeared; there was nothing visible but the shadows cast by tree and shrub, and, hastily casting aside her fears, she smiled, telling herself that it was but fancy.

What could any one want there at that time of the night? Burglars? Absurd, they would not openly show themselves while there were lights about the house, and even then it was not likely that they would cross the lawn. If not a creation of her brain, it was most probably one of Sir Murray Gernon's keepers out upon his rounds, and taking a short cut to some copse or preserve.

But for all that, Ada Lee sat long watching from her window. The painful beating of her heart was still there, and a cloud of fancies kept flitting through her brain. Strange, wild fancies they were, such as she could not have explained; but, in spite of her efforts, troublous enough to make the tears flow silently from her eyes as she recalled, she knew not why, the heart-aches of the past, and the battle she had had with self to hide from every eye the suffering she had endured.

Again and again, as she rose from her seat by the window and paced up and down the room, she tried to drive away these troubled thoughts, but they were too strong for her, and at last, raging against her weakness the while, she burst into a passionate flood of tears—passionate as any shed by her friend that night, as she threw herself, sobbing, by the bedside.

"There! now I hope you'll be better!" she exclaimed, apostrophising herself in a half-sad, half-bantering spirit. "What we poor weak women would do without a good cry now and then, I'm sure I don't know. Well, it's better to have it now than to break down to-morrow at the altar. But a nice body I am to be preaching to poor little Marion about being weak and childish, for there really is a something at these times that is too much for our poor little weak spirits. I wonder whether men are nervous, or whether they feel it at all!"

Ada Lee's words were light, and she knew that she was trying to deceive herself as she lay down to rest with a smile upon her lip; but when, towards dawn, sleep did come, it was to oppress her with wild and confused dreams, from one of which she awoke, trembling as if from some great horror, but trying vainly to recall the vision. It was of trouble and danger, but she knew no more; and it was with sleep effectually banished from her pillow that she lay at last, waiting for the coming of that eventful day.

The Happy Pair

People came from miles round to see that wedding, for the morning was bright and genial, and there were to be grand doings up at the castle as soon as the happy pair had taken their departure. It was not often that a wedding took place at Merland church, and this was to be no ordinary affair. Hours before the time appointed the people from the village and outlying farms began to assemble. The school children, flower-laden and excited, had rehearsed their part of throwing flowers in the bride's path, and had picked them up again; the ringers were having a preliminary "qu-a-a-art" of the very bad ale sold at the village inn preparatory to looking over the ropes of the three bells, all that Merland tower could boast. Sir Murray Gernon's tenants, and the farmers' daughters, were in an acute state of excitement, and dresses that had been in preparation for days past were being carefully fitted on.

"There could not have been a brighter and happier morning for you, my darling," exclaimed Marion's mother, as she kissed her affectionately, holding her with the clinging fondness of one about to lose a household treasure; proud of the position her child was to take, but, now that it had come to the time, tearful and hard pressed to hide her pain.

"And no bride ever looked better, aunt, I'm sure," said Ada Lee, merrily, as she adjusted a fold here, and arranged some scrap of lace there.

"She'd have had to look strange and fine, if she did, mum, that she would!" exclaimed Jane, handmaiden in ordinary at the rectory, but now to be promoted to the honourable post of maid to Lady Gernon. Jane had first entered the room very red of cheek, due to a salute placed thereon by Mr Gurdon, Sir Murray's gentleman, who had but a few moments before arrived with the bouquet Jane bore in her hand, and a note. But note and flowers, and even the impudence of "that Gurdon," were forgotten in Jane's genuine admiration, as, catching Ada's words, she had delivered her own opinion.

Till now, though pale, Marion's face had been bright and animated as that of her cousin, and to have seen the two girls, no one would have imagined that they had each passed a troubled and almost sleepless night.

The forebodings of the past seemed to have been dismissed, and Ada, seeing how bright and happy her cousin appeared, forbore even to hint at last night's tears.

But now came a message from the anxious rector, respecting time, and the last touches were given to the bridal apparel; when, turning round, after hastily adjusting her own veil, Ada exclaimed:

"Oh, Marion! Is that wise?"

"Oh, Miss!" exclaimed Jane. "Not wear that beautiful bookey, as Sir Murray sent?"

Marion made no answer, but quietly arranged the bunch of forget-me-nots, culled the previous day in the fen, and utterly regardless of her cousin's words, pinned them on her breast, with a sad smile. Then, turning to Ada, she said, gaily: "You must have that bouquet, Ada."

"But there's ever so many more downstairs, miss, on purpose for the bridesmaids," said Jane, excitedly. And then she raised her hands, as if mutely exclaiming, "What obstinacy!" as she saw Ada take the bouquet and hold it, gazing curiously at Marion's pale, sweet face, and then glancing at the little blue flowers upon her breast.

Marion interpreted her looks, and leaning forward, kissed her tenderly.

"Don't grudge me that little satisfaction, dear," she said. "You see how I am this morning. Are you not satisfied with the way in which I have taken your advice to heart?"

"Oh, yes—yes, dear," exclaimed Ada, clinging to her; "but was this wise?" And she pointed with Sir Murray's bouquet to the simple marsh flowers.

"Wise!" said Marion, "perhaps not; but I placed them there *in memoriam*. Should we forget the dead?"

"There, do pray, for goodness gracious' sake, Miss, mind what you're a doing! You're cramming Miss Marion's veil all to nothing, and I know you'll be sorry for it after."

"Jane's right," said Ada, merrily. "I won't 'cram' you any more. Come, dear, there's uncle going out of his wits because we're so long. He won't be happy till the knot is tied. I know he's afraid that Sir Murray will repent at the eleventh hour, aren't you, uncle?" she continued, as, on opening the door, she found the anxious father on the landing.

"Come, my dears—come, my dears!" he cried; and then, "Heaven bless you, my darling!"

"Ah—ah! mustn't touch! Oh, sir, please don't!" exclaimed Ada and Jane in a breath; for the father was about to clasp his child to his breast.

"There! Bless my soul, I forgot!" exclaimed the rector; and, handing Marion down, in a few minutes more the party were walking across the lawn to the gate in the great hedge, which opened upon the churchyard, where they were saluted by a volley of cheers—heartiest of the hearty; cheers such as had saluted Sir Murray Gernon and his friends, when, a quarter of an hour before, his barouche and four had come along the road, dashed up to the gate, and, proud and elate, the bridegroom had strode into the church, hit, in the process, on the hat, back, and breast with cowslips, hurled at him by the over-excited school children. They could not be restrained till the proper time by their equally excited mistress, who, like the rest of the feminine community present, was ready to fall down and worship the proud handsome man who had just passed into the church.

The cheering ceased, as the rectory party were seen to cross over to the chancel door, and the people crowded into the building. There had not been such a congregation—"no, not since Sir Murray's father and mother—Heaven rest 'em!—were married in that very church," said the oldest inhabitant, who wiped his eyes on the sleeve of his smock-frock as he recalled the day.

"And how drunk you did get that day, up ta castle, Joey!" said a crony.

"Well, yes, lad, I did—I did," said the oldest inhabitant. "But, then, castle ale is stark drink, lad, and old Barnes Thorndike used to brew good stuff."

"Nought like what they have there now, lad," said the other old lad, both speakers being over eighty; and comfortably seated as they were upon a tombstone, patiently waiting the conclusion of the ceremony, with one exception, they were now the only occupants of the churchyard.

"Well, I don't know, lad; but we'll try it, by and by—by and by. We'll get a lift up ta castle, some gate or other, and see how things are, for such days as this don't come often."

"Nay, not often," said the other. "But it's open house up there to-day, and there's to be fine doings after the squire's gone with his lady."

"Where are they going, lad?"

"Oh, furren parts, sure; so my boy Jack tells me."

"And he's agoin' too—ain't he?"

"Ay, lad. He's Sir Murray's head man now, and he's to be butler when they come back; and butlers keep keys, and there'll be a rare taste or two—eh?"

"Ay; and my Fan's gal, Jenny, she's going, you know—my grandchild as has been at parson's. She's going with her young missus; and strikes me, neighbour, as young Jack Gurdon's thinking about her a good deal. Jane's mother twitted her with it, and the gal laughed; and there might be more strange things come to pass than for they two to come to be butler and housekeeper up ta old place."

The old men chuckled and blinked at one another upon the tombstone, for a few minutes, and then one spoke:

"Ain't they a long time getting of it done?"

"Two parsons, lad," said the other. "Takes two to do these grand weddings. But they'll be a-coming out directly, for here's Miss Minson putting the bairns straight with the flowers. But who's yon?"

The first old man shaded his eyes with his hands, as a tall figure, in a brown travelling suit, crossed the churchyard hastily from the rectory garden-gate, hurried up to the chancel door, peered in, and then, as if struck a violent blow, he reeled back against a tombstone, to which he clung for a few moments, till, recovering himself, he made his way in a blind, groping fashion, towards the south door, close to whose porch sat the two old men. There was a fair gravel-path, but he saw it not; but walked straight forward, stumbling over the mounds of the dead in his way, and feeling with outstretched hands the tombs—passing himself along, till, clear of the obstacles, he again pressed on to the great railed vault of the Gernon family, hard by the porch, where, holding by one hand to the iron rails, he tore off his broad soft felt hat, and stood gazing into the church.

The school children, flower-basket in hand, shrank back; for there was something startling in the strangers appearance. For though quietly and gentlemanly dressed, his face was wild—his eyes staring. At first sight a looker-on would have raised his eyebrows, and muttered, "Drunk!" But a second glance would have shown that the owner of that bronzed face, handsome once, but now disfigured by the great scar of a sabre-slash passing obliquely from temple to jaw, was suffering from some great emotion, one which made his breast to heave, as his teeth grated together, one hand tearing the while at his handkerchief, as though he wanted air.

A few seconds, though, and the stranger grew apparently calm, as the people began to flock out, and the children excitedly grasped handfuls of flowers; while, though the newcomer took a step forward, so as to be in front of the double line of children, through which the bridal procession was to pass, he was unnoticed; for now the cry rose of "Here they come!" and the three bells struck up their sonorous chime—sweet, though wanting in proper cadence; for the old bells dated from days when the monks blessed, and threw in their silver offering to the molten metal.

"Now, lads! hooray!" piped one of the old fellows, climbing, by his companion's aid, to the tombstone, where he stood, bent of back, feebly waving his stick. "Hooray! and long life to Sir Murray and his lady!"

"Hooray!" cheered the crowd, in broken but hearty volleys. Handkerchiefs were waved, flowers thrown, the buzz of excitement was at its height when the proud bridegroom strode forward with his blushing bride, bright, almost radiant in her white drapery, as, slightly flushed, she smiled and bowed in acknowledgment of the greetings of the little ones whom she had often taught, now casting their simple flowery offerings at her feet; or with gentle glance thanked some old villager for the blessing invoked upon her head. Progress was made but slowly: they had advanced but a couple of yards from the porch, and Sir Murray, hat in hand, was intending to wave it in response to the greeting he was receiving, when he felt his wife's arm snatched from his, and turned to see her with her hands clasped together and raised to the height of her face; the smile gone; a deadly stony pallor overspreading her features; her eyes starting, lips apart—it was as though death had smitten her in an instant; for with one stride the stranger had confronted her, his hand was upon her breast, and he had torn away the bunch of forget-me-nots, to dash them upon the ground, and crush them beneath his heel.

There was no word spoken: the language was of the eye; and the crowd around, who could see the incident, seemed paralysed, as was the bridegroom; but at that instant a wild and piercing shriek rang out from the porch, and there was a sharp movement in the group.

But that cry was not from Lady Gernon, who stood as if turned to stone; for as Sir Murray, recovering himself, had, pale with rage and mortification, exclaimed, "How dare you!" Ada Lee had sprung forward, and almost thrown herself upon the stranger's breast, pressing him back from her cousin, as she glided between them.

It was but in time; for, mad with rage and hatred, roused by his words, the newcomer had half-turned now to Sir Murray; but Ada clung to him tightly, her bridesmaids veil torn, her flowers crushed, but a bright wild look of joy and eagerness in her countenance, as she exclaimed—

"Back, Philip! Are you mad?"

Too Late

"Now just you put that back where you took it from, Mr Impudence, or I'll tell your master."

"There you are, then, my dear; that's as near the spot as I can recollect," said the person addressed, giving Jane Barker a hearty smack on her rosy cheek, such a liberty being a little excusable on a wedding-day.

"Take your arm from round me, then; you can tell me without that, I'm sure," said Jane, shrinking back into the rectory kitchen.

"No, I can't; and how do I know but what perhaps, after I've been loving you with all my might, and saving up so as we may be married, there mayn't come a foreign lover, a currier, or something of that sort, and cut me out?"

"Don't be a fool, John!" exclaimed Jane, "and do adone there. I do declare—and serve you right, too! Such impudence!"

There was the sound of a smart slap received upon his cheek by John Gurdon, from the sole of one of the Rector's very broad old slippers, a weapon held in Jane's hand at the moment; and now she stood arranging her ruffled plumes, and gazing very defiantly at the red-cheeked gentleman before her.

"Well, that's pretty, certainly," he said, half in anger. "What are you doing with that shoe?"

"It's to slap the other side of your face with, if you're saucy," cried Jane, "now then; and if you're not, it's to give to cook to throw after the carriage when we go, for luck, you know; and it's bad enough we need it, I'm sure, for I never saw such a set-out. There's young missus looking that stony and dreadful and never speaking, it quite frightens me. I wouldn't care if she would only cry; but she won't. But do tell me."

"Well, you won't let me," said John Gurdon. "I didn't see it all; but them two nearly come to a fight, when Miss Lee jumped forward and held Mr Norton, and master carried her ladyship—you mustn't say 'young missus' now—on to the Rectory. Regular row and confusion, you know. I do wish they'd be off. All the company's gone; and there's that beautiful breakfast going a-begging, and all because two people want the same woman. Just as if there weren't plenty of women in the world ready to jump at a husband! I never see such fools!"

"Didn't you, Mr Greatgrand?" exclaimed Jane, firing up. "You're a nasty, unfeeling good-for-nothing—there! You're worse than that Mr Norton himself, shamming dead all these years on purpose to come back and break that poor dear angel's heart. There, it's no use; I hate you! that I do; and if I'm to sit in that rumble with you, hour after hour, I shall be ill, that I shall, so now. Keep your hands to yourself, for I have done with you quite. There, go and answer that bell."

Jane flounced out of the kitchen, and John Gurdon, who was at the Rectory, to help wait at the wedding-breakfast, hurried into the hall, for there had come the loud ringing of a bell, succeeded by a clamour of voices.

"I tell you I will see her!" exclaimed Philip Norton, angrily, as he stood in the hall, with Ada clinging to his arm.

"Come in here, pray!—for Heaven's sake, come in here, Norton," cried the Rector, opening the drawing-room door. "This is not seemly—we are all grieved; but do not insult my child."

"Insult, old man!" exclaimed Norton angrily, as he followed him into the room; and then he uttered a cry of rage, for, unwittingly, the Rector had asked him into the very room where, angry and mortified, his newly-wedded wife up-stairs with her mother, Sir Murray Gernon was striding up and down.

In a moment the young men had each other by the throat, and stood glaring into each other's eyes, heedless that Ada and the Rector clung to first one and then the other, in a vain attempt to separate them.

"Murray! for my child's sake!" exclaimed the Rector.

"Philip! oh, for Heaven's sake, stop this madness!" whispered Ada.

Sir Murray Gernon cooled down in an instant, though still retaining his grasp.

"I am quite calm, Mr Elstree," he said; "but this man must leave the house at once."

"Calm!" shouted Philip Norton, mad almost with rage. "Thief! robber! you have stolen her from me. She is mine—my wife—sworn to be mine; and you, amongst you, have made her false to her vows."

"Mr Norton," said Sir Murray, "are you a gentleman?"

"How dare you—you dog—ask me that?"

"Leave this house, then; and I will meet you at any future time, should you, in your cooler moments, wish it. I did intend to leave for the Continent this afternoon; but I will stay. I pity you—upon my soul, I do—but you must know that no one is to blame. You are, or ought to be, aware that the *Gazette* published your death nearly four years ago, and that you have been truly mourned for. No one has been faithless, but your memory has been respected as well as cherished. You have come in a strange and mad way; but we are ready to overlook all that, as due to the excitement and bitterness of your feelings. I now ask you, as a gentleman, for the sake of her parents, for your own sake—for the sake of *my wife*—to leave here quietly, and to try to look calmly upon the present state of affairs. I have done."

As Sir Murray ceased speaking he suffered his hand to fall from Norton's throat, and stood calmly facing him, gazing into the other's fierce, wild eyes unblenched, while, as if the calm words of reason had forced themselves to his heart, he, too, allowed his hands to fall, and as the fierce rage seemed to fade out of his countenance, a strange shiver passed through his frame, and he looked in a pitiful, pleading way from face to face, as if seeking comfort, before speaking, in a cracked, hollow voice:

"Too late!—too late! But no, not yet! You," he exclaimed, turning to Sir Murray, "you will be generous. You will waive this claim. See here!" he cried excitedly, as with outstretched hands he pleaded to the husband: "I was cut down, as you know, in hard fight, and I woke to find myself a prisoner amongst the hill tribes; and ever since, for what has seemed a lifetime, I have been held a slave, a captive—beaten, starved, ill-used in every conceivable way; but look here!" he cried, tearing from his breast a little leather purse, and opening it. "See here!" he cried, taking out a few dry flower-stalks: "her flowers, given me when, young and ardent, we plighted troth—forget-me-nots; true blue—and we swore to live one for the other. Man! man! those few withered blossoms have been life to me when, cut and bruised, I could have gladly lain down beneath the hot Indian sun and gasped out my last breath. I believe my captors tried to kill me with ill-usage; but I said I would not die—I would live to look once more upon her face, even though it were to breathe my last at her feet. And now—now, after hardships that would make your blood run cold, I escape, and reach home, what do I find? Her, worse than dead—worse than dead! But no! it cannot be so. You, sir—I ask you humbly—I ask you as a supplicant— forgive my mad words, and tell me that you waive your claim. You will be generous towards us; the law will do the rest. You, sir," he cried, turning to the Rector, "plead with me. I am no beggar. I come back to find myself rich. Help me, for poor Marion's sake! Do not condemn her to a life that must be only such a captivity as mine! Am I right? You will both be generous, and this horrid dream of despair is at an end!"

He advanced a step nearer to Sir Murray; but the latter turned from him.

"Speak to him, sir," he said to the Rector. "It will be better that I should go."

Sir Murray's head was bent as he left the room, not daring to trust himself to gaze again upon the wild, appealing face turned towards him; while, as the door closed, Philip Norton turned to the Rector, who, poor man, stood wringing his hands, hardly knowing what to do or say. But the next moment, with a groan of despair, Philip Norton let his head drop upon his breast, for he read his sentence in the old man's eyes. But again, with an effort, he roused himself, and caught Ada's hands in his, sending a wild thrill through the poor girl's frame, as she averted her head, and listened, with beating heart, to his words.

"You turn from me too," he said, bitterly; and he did not retract his words, though Ada started as if stung, and met his gaze, her face breathing, in every lineament, love and sympathy, though he could not read it then. "You know, young as you were then, how I loved her. Plead for me. Ask her to come to me, if but for a minute. But, no—no—no!" he cried, despairingly, "it is too late! I thought to have gained heaven, and the door is shut in my face. Too late—too late!" and then, with the same hopeless, groping, half-blind look in his countenance, he reeled towards the door, seeing nothing, hearing nothing, but, mad with grief, striving blindly to leave the house, his hopes crushed, his life seeming blotted out by the blackness of despair. He passed into the hall, and there stood for a minute; but only to mutter to himself: "Weak—weak—broken—too late!"

There was no one in the hall, and he passed out on to the lawn, making his way towards the little wicket-gate which led into the churchyard, and, passing through, he stumbled over grave after grave, till unseen, with a deep groan, he fell heavily, to lie, with his face buried in his hands, weeping like a child, the strength of his nature crushed out of him by the terrible blow he had received, and for hours after he heard, felt, saw, nothing external.

Meanwhile, struggling hard with herself, Ada Lee had watched Philip as he staggered from the room, the tears welling down her cheeks, and a strange, wild feeling mingled with the compassion she felt for his sufferings. It was only by a violent effort that she restrained herself from running to his side, as she saw his blind, hopeless exit; but, as she heard the door close, the place seemed to swim round, and then, overcome by the excitement of the past hour, she threw out her hands and would have fallen, had not her uncle caught her in his arms.

Two hours later, cold, pale, and without a word in reply to her parents' farewell, Marion, Lady Gernon, took her place in her husband's carriage.

"It is still your wish, then?" said Sir Murray to the Rector, as he stood upon the doorstep.

"Yes, yes!—for Heaven's sake, yes! Go, by all means."

"Give him that note, then, should he make inquiry?" said Sir Murray. "I have your word for that?"

"Yes—yes; indeed you have," said the Rector; "but I have known Philip Norton from a boy. He was my pupil; and when calm, I have no doubt I shall have some influence with him. That and time will do the rest. Heaven bless you! be gentle with her. Marion, my child, good-bye!"

The wheels grated loudly over the gravel; but the heart-broken man, lying prone in the churchyard, heard them not; and five minutes after, when the old Rector had seen the carriage disappear at a turn of the road, he turned to encounter the agitated countenance of Ada Lee.

Amidst the Pines

"Going out, my child?" said the Rector. "Where is your aunt?"

"Gone to lie down," said Ada; "she feels this excitement."

"No wonder—no wonder," said the old gentleman. "Pray Heaven that it may turn out happily!"

The Rector's prayer was echoed by Ada Lee, as she passed out into the garden and stood thinking for a few minutes upon the lawn. Where should she go? she asked herself, for her mind was strangely agitated, and it seemed to her that to be at rest she must go right away from human habitation, and seek for calm in solitude. The events of the past four-and-twenty hours had been too much for her, she said, and a long quiet walk would restore her.

But, even to herself, Ada Lee could not confess all. She knew that her heart seemed at times to beat wildly, and that though she crushed down such thoughts with all her might, a strange feeling of elation would strive to assert itself; and even while upbraiding herself for her cruelty, she felt that she did not grieve as she should for the sufferings of her friends. She could stay no longer in the house, though she felt that her place should have been at her aunt's side; and now, hastily crossing the garden, her heart again commenced its tumultuous beating, as she passed over the very spot where she had seen the dark figure the night before—a figure which, she now felt convinced, must have been that of Philip Norton, who had come over from the town too late to see any of the family, while on his arrival at the Rectory that morning he had learned the news which had sent him, reeling, to the church.

If Ada Lee's intention had been to escape her thoughts by rapid walking, she soon found that her efforts were useless. She sought the wild open moorland where she had walked the previous day with her cousin; but every step seemed to recall some portion of their conversation. Philip Norton's name was constantly repeating itself in her ears, even out there in the free open waste where she had told herself that she could find peace. She hurried into the pine grove, walking amidst the tall, sombre pillars of the great natural temple, whose darkly interlacing roof was far above, and where her footsteps were silent amidst the pine needles. There was the tree upon which they had rested when they had talked of the past; and had she not there avowed her own love?

It was cruel—most cruel, she told herself, to feel as she did when two hearts were breaking; growing every moment more agitated in her vain efforts to flee, as it were, from self. She had wished for solitude, but the silence of the wood, only broken now and again by the faint whispering roar amidst the pine tops, frightened her. There was a dread solemnity in the place that she could not bear, and hurrying once more to the edge of the marsh, she stopped, gazing across it for a few minutes, with the soft summer wind playing pleasantly upon her heated cheeks, toying with her hair, and fluttering the light dress which draped her form. For the wedding-garments had been hurriedly put aside, and at times it almost seemed that the sorrows of the morning, her troubled night, and gloomy forebodings were things of months ago, while this hurried beating, this anxiety of mind, were things only of the present.

She turned to hurry in another direction, hoping that by thoroughly tiring herself sleep would come to her early, bringing with it calm, when her eyes fell to the ground, but only to fill with tears, as once more the morning scene rushed through her mind; for, with her feet each crushing some of the simple blue flowers, she was standing in the midst of the forget-me-nots, and, recalling Philip Norton's words, in spite of herself, she knelt down to gather a bunch.

True blue! the flowers that had seemed to give him life in those sore perils; the little bunch that he had so treasured—and for what? To come back to find her wedded to another. But then, had not she herself counselled that Norton should be forgotten, since they believed him dead?

Ada Lee bent over the flowers she had gathered, weeping bitterly—foolish, vain tears, she said; and then, hastily rising, she walked towards the Rectory.

On reaching the village it seemed as if deserted, for, in spite of the damp thrown upon the morning's proceedings, there was high revelling at the Castle. People could not see why the sorrows of one man should interfere with their pleasure: the Squire was married, the feast had been prepared; and, under the management of a relative of Sir Murray, the happy pair were toasted, and the morning's scene was about forgotten.

Ada reached the churchyard, where the flowers scattered by the children lay withering in the hot sun. The blood rushed to her cheeks as she recalled the scene in its every detail; and then, as if anxious to avoid the place which brought back so much, she turned off to reach the Rectory gate, when, right in her path, rising from amidst the graves, she saw Philip Norton.

More than once the question had arisen, where had he gone? A question that she had tried to avoid, merely hoping that there might be no further encounter between him and Sir Murray Gernon. But now, so unexpected was the vision before her, that she stopped short, trembling violently, and she would have turned and fled, she knew not why, had not her limbs refused their office.

But it soon became evident that he saw her not, for groping along from amidst the graves, he reached the path, and making his way out into the road, turned in the direction from which she had so lately come.

Ada stood for a few minutes, too agitated to form a coherent plan; but soon her thoughts began to shape themselves, and it seemed to her that it was not right for Philip Norton to be left at such a time. Judging from his acts, he did not seem to be master of himself; and a shudder passed through her frame, galvanising her, as it were, into action, as she thought of what men had done when under the pressure of some great trouble. Sorrowful and despairing, of what rashness might not Philip Norton be guilty? She shuddered as she evaded the question, and hurrying into the Rectory, she sought, with a sensation as of a hand grasping her heart, for her uncle.

He had gone up to the Castle half an hour ago, when a message had come for him, she was told by one of the servants, while Mrs Elstree was still in her bedroom.

Ada hurried out into the village, seeking for help there, but not a soul was visible; the public-house even was closed; and of the only person she could find, a bedridden old crone, she learned that no one was left.

"Only me, miss—only me. They wanted to carry me up too, but I wouldn't let 'em."

Ada was in despair. Judging from his state of mind, Philip Norton could have taken the direction of the marsh for no good purpose; he was not likely to have gone there at such a time merely for the sake of the walk, and the road soon became lost in dangerous, impassable quagmires, pits, and treacherous morasses, thoroughly known only to the seekers for pine roots and the diggers of peat. In the wild, half-mad condition in which he then was, it would be suicidal to take such a course; and feeling this, Ada's heart sank as she thought of the dangers that would beset a man, reeling blindly about amidst tuft and moss, rush-bed, and black peaty hole full of amber water, whose depths were unknown, save as being the home of huge, slimy, serpent-like eels.

What should she do? — run up to the Castle for aid? It would take her a quarter of an hour to get there, as long to return with help, even if she found it directly; and in half an hour what might not have happened?

"Heaven grant me strength!" exclaimed the agitated girl; and fear lending her wings, she darted along in the direction taken by Norton but a few minutes before, her heart beating wildly, and an undefined dread of something about to happen increasing in strength each moment.

The road wound about past the outlying cottages, so that it was some time before she caught sight of Norton. Once she fancied that he must have struck off to the right or left, or else she must before this have overtaken him; but at the end of another hundred yards she could plainly see him, a good half mile in advance, not reeling and staggering along now, but walking swiftly, straight forward towards the marsh, when, trembling with dread, Ada hurried on, following rapidly upon his track, pausing not to think of imprudence, but led ever by the feeling that she might be able to avert some terrible impending danger.

Where could he be going? What was his aim? Ada paused and shuddered as she saw him suddenly stop by one of the black water-pits, the spots favoured by the shooting fraternity in winter, as the resort of wild goose, poachard, and divers of rapid flight. Her breath came more easily, though, as she saw that her horrible dread was without foundation, for Norton struck off to the left at a headlong rate, over heath and rush tuft, apparently making for the wildest part of the marsh, so that Ada's powers of endurance were hardly tried as she struggled on, her spirit rising with the difficulties she had to encounter.

But now, as if moved by a fresh impulse, Norton changed his course in a way that enabled Ada to gain ground, for he paid not the slightest heed to his pursuer, making now for the great pine grove, starting off into a run as if to reach the goal he had in view, but falling heavily, twice over, upon the soft, trembling soil, which yielded more or less to every step.

Panting and almost exhausted, Ada pressed on till she saw Norton reach the edge of the pine wood, when, as he dashed in, be coming in an instant lost to sight amidst the tall, bare trunks, her heart for a few moments failed her, and sinking upon her knees, with a faint wail of misery, the hot tears coursed one another down her cheeks. But the next minute she was up again, and hurrying to the edge of the wood, whose gloom cast a chill upon her as she entered its precincts.

Peering anxiously in every direction, her breath drawn in hysterical, laboured sobs, Ada pressed on farther and farther into the great dim, shadowy solitude, trembling horribly the while, and with her imagination picturing some dreadful tragedy taking place. In the vast wood she knew that it was by the merest chance that she could find him, for he had become lost to sight when he entered; while, even if she could discover him alone, mad almost, and with no help at hand, how dared she go near? Her heart whispered, though, that she must proceed, and she still panted along, her eyes ever wandering amidst the dim aisles spread out on every side, but in vain—she could not see him; and again the weak, despairing tears forced themselves from her eyes.

It was, then, useless: she had done everything possible to a human being, and all that was now left was for her to pray; and sinking, with clasped hands, to her knees, she again gave way to the despair of her heart, when a short, sharp snap on her right made her leap to her feet and run hurriedly over the slippery pine needles in the direction from which it had come. For from that sound she felt that her worst fears were realised, and that he had indeed sought this solitude for the horrible purpose she dreaded. But the pistol had missed fire, and she might yet be in time, though so dreadful was the feeling upon her that her energies felt frozen, and to her it seemed that she was barely crawling over the ground. There he stood, not fifty yards from her, fitting a cap upon the pistol he held, and then, every stroke jarring upon her heart, so distinctly in the strained state of her faculties was it heard, she could make out that he was tapping the pistol that the powder might ascend the nipple. But it was all like some horrible nightmare: she could see every act with almost a clairvoyant power—she could hear with a fearful distinctness; but she could not shriek—she could not call to him to desist. It was as though certain of her faculties were chained, while others were goaded into unnatural activity.

A few seconds longer, and she felt that she would be too late—that the dread deed would be accomplished, and she alone with a still, dreadful corpse—when, panting, half-mad with fear and the horror which gave her strength, she ran to Norton's side, grasped at his arm, and then her powers of utterance returned. As she seized his arm he turned upon her fiercely, dashed her to the ground, and raised his pistol; but in an instant Ada was again upon her feet, and grasped the fatal weapon, when there was a bright, blinding flash, a loud report, and then, for Ada Lee, the present became a blank.

Balm

It seemed as though that report awakened Philip Norton from the fit of mad despair that had prompted him to seek in oblivion the rest he could not find here—awakened him to the sense that he must be a murderer; for there, stretched at his feet, her light muslin dress already deeply stained by the blood flowing from her shoulder, lay the brave girl who had struggled to his side to suffer, almost with the loss of her own, for her successful endeavour to save his life. For some minutes, as he stood there in that dim pine arcade, Philip Norton's brain was giddy; he felt as though awakening from some horrible dream, and it was only by an effort that he could recall the present; when, throwing the pistol aside, he knelt down by the fainting girl, and by means of his handkerchief succeeded in staunching the blood flowing from a long, jagged wound torn by the bullet in its passage along her shoulder.

The sight of the wounded girl, as she lay pale and insensible at his feet, and the knowledge that it was his work, seemed to drive back the horrible thoughts of self, forcing him into action; and the next minute, trembling in every limb with anxiety for her safety, he was running to the nearest pit for water, bringing it in his soft hat, a little at a time, to sprinkle her stern marble face. Again and again he ran to and fro, growing more and more excited, but with a healthy excitement that moved his better impulses; for, forgetting his own pain, interest was excited in the deliverer whom he told himself that he had slain, to recompense her for her bravery in his behalf. But it was long before animation began to reappear, and the colour to return to Ada Lee's face. Twice, though, Norton had been encouraged to persevere in his efforts by a sigh; and he had chafed her cold hands, torn off his coat to fold and place beneath her head, seen to, and tightened the bandage so that the blood was staunched, and had at last determined to bear her back into the village at all hazards. Then her soft blue eyes slowly unclosed, as he kneeled by her side, his arms gently supporting her against his breast, preparatory to rising and carrying her over the treacherous ground to the footpath.

But the sight of those soft eyes gazing into his so wonderingly, arrested him, and for a few minutes no word was spoken, till by slow degrees, realising all that had passed, Ada's eyes lost their strange wondering look, a shudder ran through her frame, and the old aspect of horror came back.

"Are you hurt?" she gasped.

"No," he said, gently; and there was pity for her in his tones.

"Not hurt?" she gasped again. "But the pistol?"

"Hush!" he said, sadly. "You must not speak. You are wounded, and I am a soldier, and have seen and known many wounds. You must be quiet until I can get you back to the village."

"But you are safe—not hurt?" she said.

"No—no!" he exclaimed, impetuously. "I—I—"

"Yes—yes, I know. I remember all," she said, eagerly. "I startled you—the pistol went off by accident—it struck me."

She smiled in his face as she spoke, while, burning with grief and shame, he cried:

"Oh, Miss Lee, Miss Lee, has it come to this? Good Heaven! am I fallen so low that I must screen myself in this way? I am a coward—a pitiful—"

"Hush—hush!" she cried, and her little hand was laid upon his lips. "I know how you suffered. I was in dread lest you should do anything rashly, and I followed; but it is our—your secret. Let it be hidden for ever. You may trust me."

Philip Norton groaned. "Hidden! How can it be hidden?" he said, as he pointed to her wounded shoulder, when, with the hot blood suffusing her face, she dragged the scarf she wore over the deep stain, and essayed to sit up, but fell back weak, and half fainting.

Laying her gently down, he again fetched water, and bathed her face, when, reviving somewhat, she lay with her eyes half closed, and lips moving gently.

"Did you speak?" he said, as he bent over her.

"No," she said, after a few moments. "I was praying. Will you try to lift me up?"

Philip raised her a little, but she winced from the sharp pain caused by the movement, upon which he desisted; but, with a smile, she begged him to help her to her feet. A few moments' trial, though, showed that she was utterly incapable of walking, when, taking her in his arms, Norton slowly and carefully bore her amidst the pine trees to the edge of the marsh, whence, after a brief rest, he again proceeded, bringing her over the soft, springy ground, till, during a longer rest, he said to her, in sad tones:

"I thought the age of miracles was past, but an angel was sent to stay my hand." Then, heedless of her remonstrance, he continued: "How am I ever to repay you for the injury I have done?"

"By acting as a man should," she said, softly; "by ceasing to be a coward. You," she exclaimed excitedly, "a soldier—a man whom we loved—to fly from suffering like that! It was cruel to all—to Marion—to yourself! How could—"

"For Heaven's sake, spare me!" he groaned. "The sight of what I have done seems to have brought me back to a life of greater suffering. But you need not fear; I will bear it."

What Followed

It was an accident—so people said at Merland, and from being a wonder for a time, it was soon forgotten; and when, pale and weak from many months of illness, Ada Lee was seen out, with the tall bronzed soldier pushing her invalid chair, or reading to her from some book, the gossips of the village used to prophesy. And yet no word of love had passed between the invalid and her companion. Ada's prolonged stay at the Rectory had resulted in Mrs Elstree wishing her to make it her home, on the grounds of her own loneliness, now that Sir Murray Gernon had, on account of his wife's health, decided to remain in Italy, where he had taken a residence on the shores of Como. While Ada, continuing weak and ill, accepted Philip's attentions with a smile of pleasure, though there was sorrow at her heart, which bled daily for the sufferings of her companion.

For time seemed to bring no healing to the wounds of Philip Norton, who, apparently disgusted with life, had sold out from the army, to settle down at his own place, Merland Hall, seeing no one, visiting nowhere save at the Rectory.

But the result was what might have been expected. Philip Norton awoke one day to the fact that there was happiness for him yet in this world, and he told himself it would be his duty to devote his life to the suffering invalid—to the blighted woman who paid penalty for his sin. And one evening, when the sun was glowing ruddily in the west, Philip Norton rested his brown hand upon the thin transparent fingers, and then, in the stillness of the evening, he asked her, in low, earnest tones, if she would take him as her protector.

"Ada," he said, calmly, "I cannot love. You know all; but I owe you my life. Will you take that life now, with such devotion as I can attach to it, such tenderness as time will enable me to weave with it? I know I am but a broken, disappointed man; but you know my weaknesses and sufferings; you can help me to get through my journey, and, perhaps, in time you may learn to love me."

Ere he had finished speaking another trembling, fluttering hand was raised, to be placed upon his strong arm, and then, leaning forward, Ada's poor thin pale lips were pressed upon his hand, as one might salute a king, and then softly whispering to herself the words, "At last! At last! Thank God!" the invalid sank back in her chair, fainting from the wild tumult of joyful feelings that, in her then weak state, seemed almost more than she could bear.

For Ada Lee was dying; not, perhaps, in the ordinary sense of the word, for she might have lived on for years; but, none the less, she was fading away. One disappointment she had fought down; but the news of Norton's death had preyed heavily upon her. Then had come his return, the shock, the adventures of the wedding-day, and, lastly, the wound. Her by no means strong constitution had given way beneath this, when, in addition, there had ever been the pang of hope deferred, and the sick heart finding no ease.

It was a strangely unimpassioned wooing, that of Philip Norton; but Ada was content; and at the end of five years, bright, happy of face, and only slightly more matronly, she came one day into her husband's study, to find him stern and thoughtful—looks which passed away as if by magic, as the sturdy little fellow she led by the hand ran to him and climbed upon his knee.

"Is there anything the matter?" exclaimed Ada anxiously, as she leaned upon her husband's shoulder.

"Matter! No, love!" said Norton, heartily—another man now, his face lighting up with pleasure as his child snatched first at pens, then at paper, everything within reach—"unless it is with this young rebel; but what made you ask?"

"Philip," she said, softly, "you keep nothing from me, dear: do not begin now."

"Well, there," he said, "I won't;" and he drew her nearer towards him. "Heaven forbid that I should from the woman to whom I owe life and happiness such as no other man could enjoy. But you see," he said, slightly hesitating, "I have been over to the Rectory this morning."

"Yes," said Ada, anxiously.

"And they have had a letter from Italy."

"Well, Philip?" she said, laying her head against his cheek, as one arm drew her nearer and nearer, while the other toyed with the boy's curls.

"Well, darling, it is nothing; but I could not help it: the news seemed to cause me a vague feeling of uneasiness—nothing but a passing cloud—for thoughts will go backwards sometimes. Not complimentary, that," he said, laughing; "but I meant no more, love, than a general reference to old troubles."

"I know—I know," she said, with unruffled countenance; "but what was the news?"

"Well, dear, it was that workmen are to be sent up to the Castle directly; and there's to be painting, and paper-hanging, and re-furnishing, and Heaven knows what beside; and I was thinking that Merland has done for years past now uncommonly well with the Castle in its present state, and that, if I had my will, it should remain as it is."

"And all this means, dear?" said Mrs Norton, quietly.

"Yes, of course," laughed Norton. "Now, did you ever see anything like the dog? Both his fingers in the ink! Yes, it means, of course, that after five years of absence the Gernons are coming home."

Ada's Promise

The old love of change and adventure, which in earlier life had led Philip Norton into seeking a commission in the Indian army, clung to him still, and sometimes for days—sometimes even for weeks together, he would absent himself from home, journeying north or south, or even going abroad without making the slightest preparation. He would laugh on his return, and own that it was eccentric; but, perhaps, before many weeks had elapsed, he would again take his departure, while Ada never complained, for by constant study of his character, she felt that to some extent she now knew him well. He had given up all his former pursuits; ambition, too, had been set aside, and he had buried himself in the old Lincolnshire retreat, apparently content with his wife's companionship—for visitors seldom crossed the steps of Merland Hall. "I am not fit for society," Norton used to say, with a smile; and seeing how at times an unsettled, feverish fit would come upon him, resulting in some far off, aimless journey, from which he would return happy and content, Ada quietly forbore all murmurings, accepting her fate, thankful for the quiet, tender affection he displayed towards her. She used at last to laugh about his hurried departures, and long, purposeless trips, telling him that they acted as safety-valves for letting off the pent-up excitement of his nature, and he, taking her words in all seriousness, would earnestly accept her definition.

"I know it seems strange and wild, and even unkind to you, dear; but I think sometimes that if I were chained down entirely to one place I should lose my reason. These fits only come on at times; perhaps during a walk, and then the inclination is so strong that I do not feel either the power or desire to battle with it."

Ada Norton felt no surprise, then, the morning after that on which the news respecting the Gernons had been received, when asking one of the servants if she had seen her master, she learned that he had been driven across to the town, and that the groom had just come back with the dog-cart.

It was nothing new, but taken in conjunction with the last night's conversation, it caused no slight uneasiness in her breast, and as she sat watching the gambols of their child, the weak tears began to course one another down her cheeks. For she felt that he was unsettled by the tidings they had heard; and for a few moments her heart beat rapidly as she recalled the past, trembling for her own empire when thinking of Marion Gernon's return.

Would not the old feeling of love come back, and would they not both hate her? Marion, for her possession of him who should have been her husband; Philip, for her ceaseless efforts to enlace herself round his heart. For, after all, he could not truly love her: he had been gentle, tender, affectionate, ever ready to yield to her every desire, almost worshipping his boy. In short, upon reviewing calmly her married life, with the sole exception of those occasional absences, she was obliged to own that she had all that she could desire, and that, however wanting in the wild, passionate, and romantic, Philip Norton's love for her was imbued with that tender gentleness, based on admiration, trust, and faith, which was far more lasting and satisfying to the soul—a love that would but increase with years; and at last, with an impatient stamp of the foot, she wiped away her tears, upbraiding herself for her want of trust and faith in her noble husband, accusing herself of misjudging him. Catching up her boy, she covered him with kisses, her face lighting up with a joyful maternal pride in the strong link which had been sent to bind them together.

"Heaven helping me," she muttered, "I'll never doubt him."

It was a grave promise—a vow hard to keep, as circumstances wove themselves in the future; and more than once Ada Norton had the excuse of sore temptation; but how she bore herself, how she kept faith in her husband under circumstances that might well raise doubts in the most trusting woman's heart, will be seen in the sequel.

Sir Murray's Gentleman

There had been busy doings at the Castle, and Merland village was in an intense state of excitement. Old Chunt—Jonathan Chunt, who kept the "Black Bull"—said that there was to be some life in the place at last. He knew, for he had it from Mr Gurdon—old Gurdon's lad, but *Mr* Gurdon now, and an awfully big man in his master's estimation. He was butler now, and had come over to superintend the getting in order of the place, for Sir Murray was fond of company, and there were to be no end of gaieties at the Castle. Mr Gurdon was setting the old servants to rights and no mistake, for he'd got full power, and they hadn't had such a waking up for long enough. Why, what with company's servants coming down to the "Bull," and post-horses now and then, and one thing and another, it would be a little fortune to him, Chunt said. Time there was a change, too: keeping a house like that shut up for the rats to scamper across the floors, was injuring the trade of the village, where there was no one else but the old people at the Rectory, and them Nortons, who might just as well be a hundred miles off, shutting themselves up as they did.

Chunt knew, and he imparted his knowledge, with no end of nods and winks, to his fellow-tradesmen, as he termed them—to wit, Huttoft, the saddler, who made nothing but harness, and Mouncey, the baker, when they came in for a glass.

"And if here ain't Mr Gurdon himself!" exclaimed Chunt, one evening, when he had been distilling information to a select knot of customers. "Take a chair, Mr Gurdon, sir. Glad to see you this evening. Very curious coincidence, sir: we were just talking about you and your people;" which was indeed most remarkable, considering that nothing else had been talked of in the village for weeks past. "What'll you take, sir? only give it a name. Quite an honour to have you distinguished furreners amongst us."

Mr Gurdon smiled and rubbed his hands; but, evidently considering that he had mistaken his position, he frowned the next moment, and nodded condescendingly to the tradesmen and little yeomen present. Certainly they had, several of them, known him as a boy; but then he had risen in the world, and deserved their respect; besides which, look at the patronage he could bestow. So Mr Gurdon frowned, coughed, and looked important; but, finding that room was made for him, and that incense in abundance was being prepared in his behalf, he condescended to take a seat, and gave what he would take the name of sherry, with which he smoked a cigar, whose aroma whispered strongly of the box from which it had been taken.

Mr Gurdon's presence, though, did not tend to the increase of comfort in the party assembled, for the gentleman's gentleman seemed to have imbibed a considerable portion of his master's dignity, sitting there very haughty and reserved, while, the flow of conversation being stopped, the rest sat still, smoked, breathed hard, and stared.

But Chunt was satisfied, and he winked and nodded, and whispered behind his hand most mysteriously as he took orders from one and another. He expected that Mr Gurdon would thaw in time with a little management, and, putting on his diplomatic cap, he set to work by asking his advice.

"That sherry's not much account, Mr Gurdon, sir," he said, in a whisper; "but it's the best I've got to offer you. The long and short of it is, sir, we can't order enough, in a little house like this, to make a wine-merchant care about sending it good; but I've got a few gallons of brandy down now that I should just like you to try, and give me your opinion. You see, it isn't every day as one has a gent in as understands such things; but you, being used to your cellar, and having good stuff in your bins, yours is an opinion one would like to have. There, sir, now just taste that," said Chunt, filling a liqueur-glass from a big stone bottle; "that's, between ourselves, just as it comes—untouched, you know. I'll mix you a glass hot; but just give me your opinion on it as it is."

Mr Gurdon was touched in a weak place, for, though his cellar knowledge was almost nil, it was not worth while to say so. Incense was nice—almost as nice as brandy, so accepting Chunt's glass, and confidential wink, he tasted the brandy—tasted it again, and then agreed that it wasn't bad, only it wanted age.

"The very words as my spirit-merchant says to me, sir," said Chunt. "If that brandy had age, sir, it wouldn't be surpassed anywhere."

Mr Gurdon felt better, and agreed with one of the visitors present that they wanted rain. Then, after finishing the neat brandy, he commenced the stiff tumbler of hot grog placed before him by Chunt, toyed with the end of his cigar; and, finding a general disposition to pay him respect, and to call him "sir," he gradually unbent—more swiftly, perhaps, than he would have done—under the influence of the brandy and water, for which he had a decided weakness, the potent spirit unlocking, or, as Chunt told his wife, oiling the butlers tongue, so that he gratified the curiosity of the Merlandites that evening to a considerable extent. And there was no lack of brandy and water that night: every one drank it, doing as Mr Gurdon did; and there was quite a struggle amongst the little traders for the honour of "standing" Mr Gurdon's next glass, the most eager of them, so as not to be outdone, requesting Chunt to fill it again, while it was yet but half empty.

"And do you like furren parts, Mr Gurdon, sir?" said Chunt, setting the ball rolling.

"Pretty well—pretty well," said Gurdon. "On the whole, perhaps, better than England. Society's higher there—more titles."

"I suppose Mr Gurdon ain't brought home a Hightalian wife," said Huttoft.

Mr Gurdon did not quite approve of this; and Huttoft had to suffer the frowns of the whole company.

"And so, after all these years, Mr Gurdon, sir," said Mouncey, who was in high spirits with the prospect of bread supplying, "you haven't brought us home a heir to the Castle."

"No," said Mr Gurdon; "and it's my opinion as there'll never be one."

"Turned out a happy match, and all that sort of thing, though, I suppose?" said Mouncey.

"Happy! yes, I should think so. Sir Murray worships her, and she's never happy unless he's along with her, or else going hunting weeds and grass and moss in the hills. Lor' bless you! it's wonderful what a happy pair they are. Awfully jealous man, though, Sir Murray—nearly had a duel with a foreign Count, who wanted to be too attentive to my lady; but when my gentleman found as master meant fight, he cooled down, and made an apology."

"Ladyship changed much?" said Chunt.

"Well, no; not much," said Gurdon. "We all look older at the end of five years. She always was pale, and perhaps she is a bit thinner than when she went away. But there, you'll see her safe enough before long; they'll be home to-morrow, and she'll be always out, either riding or walking."

"I used to fancy that things wouldn't turn out happily after that set-out at the church door," said Huttoft, venturing another remark. "Of course you know as Mr Norton's settled down at the Hall?—married Miss Lee, you know. Good customer of mine, too."

"Ah, yes; we know all about that," said Gurdon, sarcastically. "Her ladyship was frightened, of course; and enough to frighten any lady, to see a mad-brain fellow rush at her like that. Boy and girl love affair, that's what that was. Them sort of things never come to nought; and look how soon he got over it and married. Her ladyship was upset about it, though, when she got the news. She was fond of her cousin, you know, Miss Lee, and you may say what you like here, but we got the right tale over abroad about that Captain Norton shooting her; while, when her ladyship heard that her cousin had been foolish enough to marry him, she had a brain fever, and was bad for weeks. No wonder, neither. He must be half-cracked with sunstroke or drink. They do say them Indy officers drink hard. Well, just one more, gents, and this must be the last."

Mr Mouncey could not help siding with the butler, for he happened to know that Captain Norton was a bit queer at times, as the servants had told him more than once, going rushing off to all parts without saying a word to anybody, not even to Mrs Norton; and he couldn't quite see through it, unless it was, as Mr Gurdon said, the Captain was, after all, a bit touched.

"By the way, though," said Chunt, "isn't he taking up with that Iron Company?"

"Iron!" said Gurdon, thickly. "No iron about here."

"Oh yes," said Huttoft; "they've found a bed, and there's some talk of trying to work it, bringing coal by canal, but I can't see as it will answer."

Soon after this the conversation became general upon the future of the iron, the company being divided, some declaring for riches to those who took shares in the company, others prognosticating that the shareholders would find the iron too hot to hold, and would burn their fingers in a way not to be forgotten. But, at last, remembrances of frowning wives sitting up for absent lords brought the hour into serious consideration, and, after glasses round, the enthusiastic party insisted upon seeing Mr Gurdon home, which they did to the lodge gates, parting from him most affectionately, though it might have been better had they continued their escort until he reached his normal bed, the one he chose, when left to himself, being a bed of verbenas, where he was found, covered with dew, at early morning, by Alexander McCray, one of the under-gardeners, who did not fail to treasure up the circumstance against the next time he might be snubbed.

Husbands and Wives

The Gernons had returned to the Castle for some days before Philip Norton came home, his wife anxiously scanning his countenance, to find him apparently quite happy and untroubled of mind. She had something she wished to say to him, but she shrank from her task, hardly knowing how to commence; her difficulty, though, was ended by Norton himself, who, as they were seated at tea, turned the conversation in the required direction.

"So the Castle folks are back," he said, quietly.

"Yes; they arrived last Thursday," said Mrs Norton, uneasily.

"Busy times there'll be there, then, I expect," said Norton. "Do the old place good."

Mrs Norton looked searchingly at him, but not a muscle of his countenance was moved.

"Do you know, love, I've been thinking over their return," he said, after a few moments' silence, "and I fancy that, perhaps, it would be better if the intimacy between you and Lady Gernon were not resumed. Time works wonders, we know, but I cannot think that there could ever be the cordiality that one would wish to feel towards one's friends."

"Can you read my thoughts, dear?" said Mrs Norton, kneeling at his feet, so as to rest her elbows on his knees, and gaze up in his face.

"Well, not all," he said, laughing. "A great many, though, for you are horribly transparent. But why?"

"Because you have been thoroughly expressing my wishes. Do not think me foolish, but I do, indeed, think it would be better that there should be no intimacy between the families."

"Foolish!" he laughed. "Why, that would be like blaming myself. But there, I don't think we need trouble ourselves; for I suppose they will be very grand, and take up only with the county families and grandees from London; they will not want our society. And do you know, dear, we shall have to pinch and save no end, for I have been investing heaps of money in a speculation—one, though, that is certain to pay. Iron mines, you know, that were found last year at Blankesley. Capital thing it is to be, so they tell me."

"But was it not foolish?" said Mrs Norton. "Had we not enough, dear?"

"Well, yes," he said, rather impatiently; "enough for ourselves, but we have the child to think of. You do not suppose he will be content to lead his fathers dreary life."

"Dreary, Philip?"

"Well, no—not dreary. I don't mean that; but quiet, retired existence; and besides, a little to do with this iron affair—a little occupation—will be the making of me. I've grown so rusty," he said, laughing, "that I have run to iron to polish it off."

That same night a similar conversation took place at the Castle, where, in quiet, well-chosen words, Sir Murray expressed a wish that there might be no communication held with the inmates of the Hall.

"Do you doubt me, Murray?" said Lady Gernon, rising, and standing looking down upon her husband, as he leaned back in his chair.

"Doubt you!" he said, almost angrily. "My dear Lady Gernon, what a question!"

"Then why should you ask me, now that at your wish we have returned to the Castle, to give up the love, sympathy, and companionship of my cousin? Why did we not stay abroad, if such coldness is to be preserved. I ceased corresponding with her at her marriage, but with what pain and cost you only know. Do not ask more of me."

"There—there," he said, "what a trouble you are making of this trifle. It is my wish that the old acquaintanceship should not be renewed. No good can result from it; but, perhaps, for all parties a great deal of heartburning and pain. Be guided by me, Marion."

"Not in this," she said, firmly. "Murray, I never yet in anything opposed your wishes, but in this I do. It is my intention to drive over and call upon Ada to-morrow, and I ask you to accompany me. To be distant now would be like disinterring old griefs and sorrows that should before this have been forgotten. Let the past be buried in the past, and let us be, with these our nearest neighbours, upon intimate terms. You do not know Philip and Ada as I know them; and I love them both too dearly to slight them even in thought."

"As you will," he said, with a shrug of the shoulders.

"And besides," she continued, "your wish is almost an insult to your wife, Murray; it is cruel in tone, cruel in wording—harsh as it is unjust—unfair."

"Do I not say," he exclaimed, angrily, "do as you will? I gave you my opinion as to what I thought would be best, and you differ. Very well; one of us must give way, and I have yielded. What more would you have? Do I ever play the domestic tyrant? Am I ever unreasonable?"

Lady Gernon was silent, and stood pale and motionless, looking at the table upon which she rested her hand. She was still very beautiful; but there was a sharpness about her features that told of suffering, and the workings of a troubled heart. It was evident that she wished to speak, but the words would not come, and at last, fearing to display her agitation, she glided back to her seat.

But she had gained her end: there was to be reconciliation, and a friendly feeling preserved between the two families. And why not? she asked herself. Were they to be always enemies on account of the past?

Sinking thoughtfully back in her chair, she rested her forehead upon her hand, dreaming over the incidents of the past few years, and even while feeling a dread of the impending meeting, she felt a longing desire to look once more upon her old lover—upon the man who, upon her wedding-day, had seemed, as it were, to cast a blight upon her future life, as he appeared like one rising from the dead to upbraid her with her falling away.

Lady Gernon did not see the curious way in which her husband sat and watched her, marking every change in her countenance, noting every sign. He had been startled by the earnestness with which she had combated his wishes. Her manner had been so new, her eager words so unusual; for during their married life her actions had been of the most subdued nature, and, as if resigning herself to her fate, she had been the quiet, uncomplaining wife, to whom his word had been law, while, proud of her beauty and accomplishments, he had been content.

But no words passed till, rousing herself, Lady Gernon sought to remove any strange impression her utterances might have made—sought, but in vain, for she had unwittingly sown seeds that had already begun to germinate, striking root deeply in her husband's breast, soon to flourish for ill in a way that should defy her utmost efforts to uproot them.

Food for Suspicion

"Who?" exclaimed Mrs Norton, aghast, as her servant hurriedly made an announcement.

"Sir Murray and Lady Gernon. I saw the carriage come in at the lower gate. There they are, ma'am," said the girl, as the grating of wheels upon the drive preceded a loud peal at the bell.

"For Heaven's sake be calm, Philip!" exclaimed Mrs Norton, as she saw him turn ghastly pale, all save the great scar upon his face, which seemed to glow and throb.

"Not at home! We can't see them!" he exclaimed hoarsely.

"Too late," she said, unwittingly giving him another pang, as she quoted his despairing words of the day when he had last seen Marion. "But, Philip, love, dear husband, recollect yourself," she whispered imploringly; and then, trying to recover her composure, she rose as Sir Murray and Lady Gernon entered the room—the former courtly and at ease, the latter to run to Ada, throw her arms round her neck, and kiss her fondly, holding her for a few moments to her throbbing breast, while, overcome by the warmth of the greeting, Mrs Norton as lovingly returned the embrace.

To her great delight, though, as she raised her eyes from her cousin, it was to see that, quite composed and courteously, Philip Norton had advanced to meet his guest, they had shaken hands, and Norton had now turned to greet Marion.

Ada's heart palpitated, and she hardly dared watch her husband, but turned to look at Sir Murray, who was narrowly scanning every glance and act. But Lady Gernon's greeting of her old lover was graceful, kind, and yet dignified; her every word and look was unimpeachable, and Ada Norton's agitation gave place to a feeling of thankfulness as she saw her husband take Marion's hand without a shade crossing his countenance, press it slightly in a frank greeting, and then place for her a chair; when, apparently himself relieved, Sir Murray engaged his wife's cousin in conversation, his old stiff, courtly manner being more proud and polished than ever, as he talked of their long absence, the changes that had taken place, expressing, too, a hope that he should see her often at the Castle.

"Will you take me into the garden, Captain Norton?" said Lady Gernon, in a low tone. "I have something to say to you." Then aloud: "Do you not find the weather very oppressive? I am always longing for the fresh air."

The remark was too pointed to escape observation, for Lady Gernon was no way skilled in subterfuge, while Norton hesitated for an instant, and there was a slight change in his countenance as he rose, saying:

"You have probably not seen our poor place, Lady Gernon; will you walk round?" She rose on the instant and took his arm, and they passed through the French window on to the lawn, while, half rising, Ada Norton looked anxiously in Sir Murray's face.

"No," he replied calmly, as, with a bitter smile on his lip, he read off her unspoken words. "I think we will stay. They will probably return directly;" and then he started, in a cool and indolent way, a fresh topic of conversation, to which, in the agitation she could not conceal, Ada could but reply in monosyllables.

"Well, Marion," said Norton, calmly, as they stood amidst the flower-beds of the little parterre, "you wish to speak to me?"

"Yes, yes," she said, eagerly. "I know that it may seem strange, but, Philip, I could not rest till I had spoken to you. Heaven willed that we should not be one, and I am now another's. You loved me once; will you, for the sake of that old love, make me a promise?"

"Loved you once—promise!" said Norton, bitterly.

"Yes," she cried, eagerly; "promise me, and then let the past be dead."

"What would you have me promise?" he said. "Though you fail with yours."

"Hush!" she said, imploringly; "do not be cruel. Now, at once, promise for the sake of our old dead love, that the past shall all be forgotten, and that you will treat my husband as a friend."

"The man who robbed me of all my hopes!"

"Oh, hush! Do not speak so, Philip. There was some talk, before we left England, of a meeting—of angry words between you, and it was for this that I fostered Sir Murray's desire to live abroad. But you will promise me, will you not—on your word—yours, Philip—that there shall never be a quarrel between you?"

"Lady Gernon," said Philip, coldly, "your husband is safe from me. My madness is at an end, and I am now your cousin's husband. There, for Heaven's sake!" he cried, a change coming over him, "never let us refer to the past, and let us meet but seldom. Come back into the house. Forgive me if I speak bitterly, but the sight of your happiness would drive me to forget the duties I owe to others. Why did you come?"

"For my husband's sake," said Lady Gernon. "And now, from my soul, I thank you. I know how worthless are my promises," she said, bitterly; "but I can confide in yours. Now let us return."

The blood was mantling in Philip Norton's forehead, and he was about to speak, when an end was put to the painful interview by the merry, prattling voice of a child, and Philip's bright little fellow came running up, but only to draw back shyly on seeing the strange lady, who sank upon her knees with outstretched hands, as if hungering to clasp the child to her breast.

"Yours?—your boy, Philip?" she said.

"Mine, Lady Gernon," said Norton, coldly, for he had once more regained control of himself. Then, stooping over the child, "Go to that lady, Brace," he said; and in obedience the child suffered himself to be caressed, Lady Gernon kissing his bright little face eagerly, a tear or two falling the while upon his sunny hair.

Lady Gernon was still on her knees, holding the boy, who, forgetting his fear, was playing with her watch-chain, when slowly, and with courtly grace, conversing loudly the while, Sir Murray led Ada Norton into the garden, when the dread and undefined feelings in the latter's heart were chased away, and a happy light beamed in her eye as she caught sight of the group before her; but there was an ill-concealed, angry glance directed at his wife by Sir Murray, and another at the child—an angry, jealous, envious look, but it was gone in an instant, and, stooping down, he too sought to take the child's hand, but only for it to shrink from him hastily.

"Oh, Ada!" exclaimed Lady Gernon, with swimming eyes, as she laid her hand upon her cousin's arm; and in those two words there seemed sufficient to disarm every doubt and suspicion—to break off the points of the thorns that had been ready to enter into her soul; and Ada, as much at rest as now seemed Lady Gernon, turned to her smilingly, ready to listen to her praises of the child's beauty, and her prayers that they might be as of old.

"I have been so lonely abroad, Ada," said Lady Gernon, sadly. "You will renew the old days, will you not?"

Ada Norton paused for a moment before she answered, looking steadfastly in her cousin's face, to see there now a calm, sad serenity, that she could hardly understand, when, the words being repeated almost imploringly, the reply was, "Yes."

"I am at your service, Lady Gernon," said Sir Murray at that moment, when, once more, embracing the child, Lady Gernon kissed her cousin with the same old tenderness as of yore, turning the next moment to offer her hand, with a sad, quiet smile, to Philip Norton, who led her to the carriage; and then it all seemed to him to have been a dream, while the sound of the carriage-wheels, fast subsiding into a murmur, were but a part of the imaginings of his troubled brain. But the next instant he had started back to the reality, for his wife was gazing anxiously in his troubled face, when, as his eyes met hers, his old quiet smile came back, and, catching the boy in his arms, he made the little fellow shout with glee as he galloped him round the garden, to return with flushed face and tumbled hair to his watching wife.

"Philip?" she said, looking up at him inquiringly.

"My love," he said, tenderly.

"You have something to say to me, have you not?"

"No," he said, quietly; "unless it is—better friends than enemies."

Mrs Norton said no more; but there was a pang at her heart, for she felt that her husband was keeping something from her.

Brooding

People said that Lady Gernon had benefited by the change—that Italy could not have agreed with her—for day by day she seemed to be casting off the dull, heavy languor that oppressed her. There was still a quiet sadness pervading every movement; but Sir Murray, without hearing people's remarks, noted for himself that she took more interest in the affairs of daily life: in place of disliking company, she now gladly met his wishes, concerning dinner or breakfast party. In fact, there was a complete change; but it gave no pleasure to her husband, for he watched her with jaundiced eyes, saying nothing, but followed her every movement uneasily. Even the apparent increase of affection she displayed towards him was distasteful; and he grew in private moody and dissatisfied. But only in private, for he told himself that he had a duty to perform—one which demanded all watchfulness and care, and sternly he set himself to that duty.

The intimacy with the Nortons grew daily more close, and they dined several times at the Castle, the old warm affection between the two cousins growing stronger than ever. Both Lady Gernon and Mrs Norton viewed with satisfaction the quiet, unobtrusive courtesy of Sir Murray; while Captain Norton grew more and more dreamy, just waking up into an animated smile when spoken to, and joining for a few minutes in the conversation; but only to subside again directly after.

No stranger could have imagined that there had ever been more than the simplest of friendly ties between the families, and Sir Murray Gernon again and again owned to himself that his wife's conduct was unimpeachable; but, at the same time, it troubled him, that from the day of the visit to the Hall, and Lady Gernon's unconcealed efforts to obtain a few words with her old lover in private, she had been an altered woman; and he felt that it was not on his account, else why had not the change come during the past five years. It troubled him, too, that there was nothing that he could complain of; and, as he sat one day in his library, thoughtfully brooding, he passed over in review the conduct of those in whom he was most interested. Captain Norton called but seldom, and then with his wife; he was absent, too, a great deal, report said, at the iron mines; and when at the Castle his attentions to Lady Gernon were always of the most formal nature, while, after rendering the duties incumbent on her towards her guest, Lady Gernon seemed to avoid him. Mrs Norton was evidently much attached to her cousin, while

Lady Gernon—yes, there was the knot: Lady Gernon was another woman, growing daily brighter and more elate, while his spirit refused to let him believe that it was all due to the change of scene and return to the society of parents and friends.

But he wanted some clue. He was, he told himself, wandering in the dark, for, musing upon imaginary wrong, he had grown into the belief that there was a plot against his happiness—that there were matters in progress that perhaps all but Mrs Norton and himself saw and mocked at. He was too proud to ask confidence, while a hint from any one would have been repulsed with indignation. He knew that others remarked the change in his wife; frequently, in fact, he had grimly thanked friends who had congratulated him. But all his brooding resulted in nothing, and at the end of six months he was soured and angry to find that his labours had been in vain. At times, he almost resented the gentle advances of Marion, telling himself that they were not genuine, but used as a blind; and often and often Lady Gernon went in tears to the Hall to ask her cousin's sympathy—an act which only widened the breach daily growing between husband and wife. And this, too, at a time when Lady Gernon's heart had begun to leap with new hopes—hopes of that happiness which she had envied in others; when the world gave promise to her of a happier future, with fresh cares and interests; so that, even now that this hopeful state lent brightness to her eye, and colour to her cheek, she had new cause for sorrow in her husband's coldness.

Sir Murray Gernon persuaded himself that his suspicions merely wanted confirmation, and, waiting that confirmation, he shut himself up, as it were, within his cold, proud hauteur, and waited—waited, for he would not stir an inch to find proof of his suspicions; it should come to him, and blankly stare him in the face before he would take step or speak word; and so the months glided on at the Castle, company coming and going, parties following one another rapidly, and Sir Murray Gernon a very pattern of courtly politeness to all. His greatest intimates congratulated him upon his domestic happiness, and he smiled his thanks, and then subsided again into his saturnine gloom, waiting—waiting for what he told himself would some day come.

There was to be a grand party at the Castle, at Sir Murray's wish, on the anniversary of the marriage. The idea had proceeded from Mrs Elstree, during a visit to the Rectory, and Sir Murray had immediately taken it up, though, upon receiving a meaning glance from the Rector, who had seen a shadow cross his daughter's brow, the proposer would gladly have recalled her words.

Great preparations were in progress; but after making his decree that there should be a grand affair, one that should do honour to his name, Sir Murray Gernon took no further interest in the matter.

He was seated, as was his wont, one morning in his library, turning over his letters, and thoughtfully brooding over his wrongs. It was cruel, he said, that he, rich, powerful, and well endowed by nature, should suffer in this way. But he could wait; and he turned to think of what he should do to drive away the ennui which oppressed him. Suddenly a thought came, and ringing sharply, the summons was answered by a footman.

"Send Gurdon here," said the baronet; and then, adopting his most magisterial air, he sat waiting the coming of the butler, upon whom the thunders of his wrath were about to descend.

Mr Gurdon, rather red of nose and pasty of face, soon appeared, wearing on the whole rather a limp expression. But John Gurdon had not improved in appearance; prosperity had not agreed with him. He said that it was his digestion; but Jane Barker—Mrs Barker now, my lady's maid—shook her head at him and sighed, as she thought of the smart young fellow who used to come courting her at the Rectory, laughingly telling her that he'd caught the complaint of his master.

"I think, Gurdon," said Sir Murray, "that this is the third time that I have sent for you into the library."

"Yes—yes, Sir Murray," said Gurdon, with a cough behind his hand.

"It is the last time, then. But for your being an old servant, and son of an old tenant of my late father, I should discharge you at once!"

"Oh, for Heaven's sake, don't, Sir Murray," said the man piteously. "It shall never occur again; it shan't, indeed!"

"You had been drinking again, last night!"

"Only the least drop, Sir Murray—the least drop. I was a little out of order yesterday."

"And you were not fit to come before her ladyship, in the drawing-room?"

"Perhaps not quite, Sir Murray—not quite; but—but—"

"And mind this is the last time. No servant of mine shall be a disgrace to my establishment."

"I humbly beg your pardon, Sir Murray, I do, indeed; and it shall never occur again, it shan't, indeed. I know your ways, Sir Murray, and I should die, if you was to turn me off. Please look over it this once."

"I have looked over it, Gurdon, or I should have given you your wages when you entered the room. Now go and ask her ladyship if she can see me for a few minutes."

"Her ladyship isn't in, Sir Murray."

"Not in?"

"No, Sir Murray; I wanted to see her about the blue-room chandelier, and went up, but she was not there; and Barker said, sir, she had just put on her things and gone out."

"Did she order the pony-carriage?"

"No, Sir Murray; her ladyship often goes out walking."

In spite of himself, Sir Murray Gernon started; for after months of waiting, it seemed to come to him with a sudden light flashing in upon his mind that he had found that which he had sought. He looked up the next moment in his servant's face, trembling for his pride. Did that sallow, shivering creature who took his pay, and who had been trembling for fear of his frown, read his thoughts? Did he share his suspicions? For a moment, as he caught his eye, Sir Murray felt as if he could strangle him. It seemed to him that this man would henceforth possess a hold upon him, and assert himself upon the strength of his knowledge.

The baronet could hardly arrest a groan; but he sat there, stern and immovable, fighting behind his mask of pride, to regain his composure before again speaking.

"Let me know when her ladyship comes in—at least," he said, correcting himself, "ask her if she will see me upon her return."

"Yes, Sir Murray."

"That will do. You can go," said the baronet, for the man still lingered as if about to speak; but the next moment he made a low bow and left the room.

As the door closed upon the servant, the strength which had been sustained by Sir Murray's pride collapsed, and letting his head fall upon his hands, he groaned bitterly. The lines in his face grew more deeply marked; his lips became parched; and at last he rose from his seat to pace the room with hasty strides, as he turned over and over the thoughts that had flashed upon him.

Yes, she was often out; her old passion for botany had returned, and, it had never struck him before, she did take long, very long walks. And now it was all plain enough: he was the laughing-stock even of his servants—he had read it in that man's eye. True, he might dismiss him, but it was sure to be known throughout the house. But wait awhile; he would not be rash and hasty; he would think matters over.

He smiled as he took his seat once more, but the smile faded into a look of the most bitter misery, and, as he sat there hour after hour awaiting Lady Gernon's return, years seemed to have passed over his head, and not without leaving their marks.

Man and Maid

"Curse him!" muttered Gurdon, as he left the room; "a purse-proud, haughty brute! looks upon a servant as if he were a dog. I know him, though—read him like a book—turn him inside out like a glove. Waited on him, served him as I have all these years, and yet, because a man can't help giving way just a trifle to his weakness, he's to be threatened always with the sack. He won't send me away, though, not he—he knows better. Read him like a book I can, and he knows it too. Pride must have a fall, and he's full of it—running over with it. Just as if one man wasn't as good as another. Discharge me, will he? Perhaps I'll discharge myself before he has the chance. Sitting and sulking there in his old library, day after day. I haven't forgotten the old affair. I ain't blind, and I'll tell him so as soon as I look at him. Here, hi! Jane!"

Mr Gurdon's legs had conveyed him, as he went on muttering, as far as the housekeeper's room, when, seeing the flutter of a garment just turning a corner at the end of the passage, he called out, and Jane Barker, rather red of eye, turned round and confronted him.

"Here, come in here, Jenny, I want to talk to you," he said, catching her by the hand, when, without a word, she followed him into the housekeeper's room, and he closed the door.

"I knew he hadn't," said Jane, who had been watching him from a distance, and had seen him enter and leave the library, "you wouldn't have looked cross like that, John, if he had."

"He don't dare!" said Gurdon, insolently. "It's all smoke, and he knows now that I'm not blind. Discharge me, indeed! I'll discharge myself, and have something for holding my tongue into the bargain! Don't tell me: I can read him like a book, and his pride will humble itself before me like a schoolboy's. Now, look here, Jenny: there's been enough nonsense now. We've been courting years enough, and you've saved up a bit of money. Let's go at once. I've saved nothing; but I've had my eyes open, and if I don't leave the Castle a hundred pounds in pocket it's a strange thing to me. I'm sick of it, I am; and I know of a decent public-house to let over at Blankesley, where the iron-pits are. There'll be no end of trade to it, so let's get married and take it. Now, what do you say?"

"Say?" exclaimed Jane Barker, whose face had been working, while her lips were nipped together, and her arms crossed over her breast, as if to keep down her emotion—"say? Why, that sooner than marry you, and have my little bit of money put in a public-house, for you to be pouring it down your throat all day, I'd go into the union! I'll own that I did, and I have, loved you very, very much; but you've half broke my heart with seeing you, day after day, getting into such sotting ways. You know you wouldn't have been here now if it hadn't been for me going down on my knees to my own dear, sweet lady, to ask her not to complain, when you've gone up to her, time after time, not fit to be seen, and smelling that horrid that tap-rooms was flower-gardens compared to you! And now, after all her kindness and consideration, you talk like that! I'm ashamed of you—I'm ashamed of you!"

And Jane burst into tears.

"Now, don't be a fool, Jenny! What's the good of being so squeamish, and talking such nonsense? We've both had enough of this place, and, without anything to trouble me, I should never touch a drop from month's end to month's end."

"No, John—no, John," she said, disengaging herself from the arm that he had put round her. "I'll never marry a man who drinks. I'd give you my bit of money if I thought it would do you good; but you've drunk till it's made you hard, and cruel, and suspicious, and wicked; and, though I've never said nothing, I've thought about all your wicked hints and suspicions. And as to being tied up to a man who was going to get money by telling lies of other people, I'd sooner go down and jump into the lake—that I would!"

"'Tisn't lies," said Gurdon, sulkily: "it's truth, and you know it is."

"It is not, you bad, wicked fellow!" cried Jane, firing up, and stamping one foot upon the floor.

"'Tis truth, and he knows it too, my fine, fierce madam!"

"What! have you dared to say a word, or drop one of your nasty, underhanded hints?" cried Jane.

"Never mind," said Gurdon, maliciously. "I've not studied him all these years for nothing. Perhaps I know something about letters—perhaps I don't; perhaps I've seen somebody savage about somebody else taking long walks, after being sulky and upset about what's to happen now after all these years; perhaps I haven't seen anything of the kind, but I ain't blind. I haven't forgotten what took place six years ago, and now we're going— good luck to us!—to have an anniversary. I hope everybody will be there to keep it, that's all I've got to say."

"Oh, you serpent!" cried Jane, pale with rage. "You bad, wicked fellow! You're like the scorpion in the Holy Bible, you are, that turns to rend the hand that fed it. Oh!" she cried, growing gradually more and more furious, "to think that I've wasted all my best days about such a traitor—such a cruel, malicious, spiteful, dirty story-teller! Shame on you! How dare you, you villain, hint at such wickedness about my poor dear sweet mistress, whose dear heart is as pure as an angel's—a sweet, suffering lamb?"

"A sweet, suffering lamb, indeed!" cried Gurdon, savagely. "Yah! There's a pair of you—she-wolves, more likely."

"Then I'll be the wolf that shall shake such a nasty lying cur as you!" cried Jane, furiously. "Go down on your knees, you wicked—wicked—nasty—story-telling—villain—you, or I'll shake all the breath out of your body!"

In effect, beside herself with rage, Jane had caught the butler by the collar with both hands, and at every word she had given him a furious shake, till, utterly confounded at the suddenness of the attack, he had really, to avoid the onslaught, sunk upon his knees, enabling her, though, to deliver the correction more effectually.

"Say it was all stories—say it was all stories," cried Jane.

"I won't: it's all as true as true, and her—"

"Take that, you wicked villain!" shrieked Jane; and with the full force of her by no means weak arm, she slapped him across the mouth just as the door opened, and a knot of eager, curious servants appeared.

"What is the matter?" was the cry.

"Let him say a word if he dares," cried Jane, ending her punishment by a tremendous box on the butler's ears, to the intense delight of the lookers-on. "He told lies about me, and I hit him—there!" said Jane defiantly, "and let him say it isn't true if he dares."

Then, utterly exhausted by her efforts, poor Jane threw herself, sobbing, into a chair.

"Oh, take me away!—take me away!" she cried; and two of the sympathising women ran to her, declaring that it was a shame, that it was; while the stout cook delivered her opinion that it would be a blessing if there wasn't a man left on the face of the earth, "breaking poor women's hearts as was faithful unto death."

Whereupon one of the footmen winked at a very smart and aspiring kitchen-maid, who had whispered to him her suspicions respecting cook's possessing a similar weakness to Mr Gurdon's, and requiring stimulants for the due invention of fresh dishes.

"It's a pity that people don't know their places," said Gurdon, sulkily, "and keep to the kitchen and hall, instead of pushing themselves into the housekeeper's room, where they're not wanted."

But somehow, the butler's words had but very little effect, for in spite of their knowledge of his engagement to Jane Barker, and her great influence in domestic matters with her mistress, John Gurdon's tenure at the Castle was held to be in a very insecure state.

Nobody therefore stirred—Mr Gurdon's hint evidently not being sufficiently potent; so, with a scowl at the sobbing woman, he turned and left the room, to don a fresh cravat—the present one being limp, crumpled, and displaying very clearly the encounter in which he had been engaged.

"Let them look out, some of them," he cried, wrathfully, as soon as he was alone. "If I'm to be dragged down, I'll pull somebody with me, so let them look out, that's all I've got to say;" and with a savage scowl upon his face, he brought down his fist with a heavy blow upon the table by which he stood.

The Sapphire Cross

"How well Marion looks," said Ada Norton to her husband, as, seated in one of the brilliantly-lighted drawing-rooms at the Castle, they watched her receiving fresh guests, on the night of the party. The Nortons had dined there, and all had gone off, so far, most successfully; people coming from a great distance just for an hour in the evening,—an invitation to the Castle being something not to be slighted.

"Yes, she looks well," said Norton, calmly. "The old weary air seems to have passed away entirely. I used to think that Gernon did not use her well, but, thank Heaven, I believe I misjudged him."

"Oh yes, I think so," said Mrs Norton, hastily. "I am so much in her confidence that I think something of the kind would have oozed out, if such had been the case. And yet I don't know," she continued in a tone of reproach; "Marion has, like other people, her secrets."

Norton turned sharply round; but Lady Gernon approaching, the conversation ceased.

"Mamma says you have not spoken to her to-night, Ada," said Lady Gernon, whose face was flushed with excitement; and never had Norton thought her beauty more regal than now, as she stood before him with a brilliant tiara of sapphires and diamonds in her hair, while the large cross of pure and costly gems rose and fell with the soft heaving of her bosom.

"You extravagant woman!" laughed Ada, in reference to her cousin's jewels. "If I had those sapphires I should never dare to wear them."

"Murray always likes me to wear them on these particular occasions," said Lady Gernon, carelessly; and, after exchanging a pleasant smile with Norton, she moved away towards where Mrs Elstree was seated.

In spite of himself, Sir Murray Gernon frowned at the sight of that smile; but he turned away the next moment, to encounter his butler, at whom he gazed for a moment, and then, walking close up to him, he said, severely, "I told you I should not look over the next occasion, sir. Come to the library for your wages at ten to-morrow morning."

John Gurdon's face broke out into a profuse perspiration as he heard that sentence—one from which he knew there was no appeal—and he darted a scowling look of hatred at his master as he turned away. For Gurdon knew the justice of the decree: he had been drinking again. He had fought with the temptation, but the fine old wines, constantly to his hand, had been too much for him; and he had again succumbed, so that, as he stood there that moment beneath one of the brilliant chandeliers, in the midst of wealth and splendour, he saw himself beggared and wretched—a poor, out-of-place servant, whom no one would employ on account of his potent vice.

But a feeling of rage and hatred filled his breast the next instant, as he turned to single out his master; but he had disappeared, and with lowering brow the butler left the room to attend to some call.

Sir Murray Gernon had entered the blue-room, one of the handsome suite of drawing-rooms at the Castle, where he came upon a knot of his male friends, amongst whom stood Mr Elstree. He would have avoided them, but for some earnest mention of Norton's name, that was made in a low tone, and in spite of himself he said hastily:

"What's that about Captain Norton?"

"Ruined, I fear," said Mr Elstree. "Those mines have collapsed—perfect crash—heavy calls on the shareholders, I'm told. We were remarking how calmly the poor fellow takes it. Poor Ada cannot know, for she is laughing happily with my wife."

"These things are better kept from the ladies, I think," said a friend. "I'm sorry for them, though."

"Unworldly man!"—"foolish speculation!"—"perfect madness!" were amongst the remarks Sir Murray then heard made, when he turned to gaze at his stricken guest, who, apparently quite calm and untroubled by a care, had risen from his seat and crossed to where Lady Gernon was standing. A minute after, she had left Mrs Norton with her mother, placed her arm in Captain Norton's, and with him crossed towards the conservatory, where, amidst the golden-fruited oranges, the heavily-scented exotics, and the soft light diffused from flower-encircled and shaded lamp, a few of the guests were seated, or wandering in what seemed to be a fragment of some tropic land.

It was hard work for Sir Murray to preserve his calm and smiling aspect amidst his guests when such thoughts as troubled him were struggling in his breast. But he was determined to show no anger, and, with the intention of walking quietly into the conservatory, he passed through the drawing-room, where Gurdon was handing tea to the party conversing at one of the tables.

The Sapphire Cross | 61

Just then a gentleman arrested him, and kept him in conversation upon some political matter for quite a quarter of an hour, his courtly politeness even now preventing him from hurrying away; but at length, with a sinking at his heart, he stepped into the conservatory to see several friends enjoying the soft coolness of the flower-scented place; but those whom he sought were not there.

He turned to leave—a strange feeling of excitement making his breast to throb, and the blood to flush giddily to his head. He passed through the different well-lit rooms, but without seeing the pair of whom he was in quest; and, scarcely in command of his actions, he was about to make some eager inquiry, when Gurdon approached, bearing a small tray with tea.

"Looking for my lady, Sir Murray?" he said. "She's at the back of the orangery with Captain Norton."

John Gurdon's eyes glittered as he spoke, for he was sobered now by the former meeting with his master, and the excitement of what was in his mind. Sir Murray knew that the man saw his emotion, but he could not hide it then; and with a muttered oath he once more entered the conservatory, but had not advanced more than a few paces when he became aware that he was followed.

Turning upon the instant, he found that Gurdon was close behind him with the tray.

"Go back into the drawing-room!" he said, sternly, though he repented his speech the next minute, for, with a meaning smile, the man met his eye, and then stopped short, but made no movement to return.

Gurdon was right; for on turning a corner, Sir Murray came suddenly upon Lady Gernon seated by Captain Norton's side. Her head was bent, and the tears were falling fast, while he was speaking to her earnestly. There was no one near: the voices from the crowded rooms came only in a murmur. They, too, were speaking in soft and subdued tones. But one word fell upon Sir Murray's ear, and that word was "love!" He heard neither the preceding nor the concluding spread over the brightly-tiled floor—he was standing by their side before they were aware of his approach, when, with a start of dread, Lady Gernon half rose from her seat, but only to sink back, gazing at her husband.

For a few moments Sir Murray stood, unable to speak in the calm tones he desired; for even then he dreaded a scene and the comments of his guests, when—approaching quite unheard, so that he, too, was in the midst of the group before his presence was noticed—Gurdon appeared, to look full in his master's face as he handed the tray he bore.

"Tea, sir?" he said.

"Stand back!" exclaimed Sir Murray, fiercely, and with his raised hand he struck the man heavily across the chest, causing him to stagger back, and the tray fell with a crash upon the floor.

"You shall pay for this!" muttered the man, rising, but only to drop on one knee, napkin in hand, the next moment, and commence gathering up the fragments.

"Leave this place, sir, this instant!" exclaimed Sir Murray, fiercely; and muttering still, but with a supercilious leer at all present, Gurdon slouched off, passing between the assembled guests, who, alarmed by the crash and loud, angry words, were now inquiring the cause.

"Nothing—nothing wrong," exclaimed Sir Murray, with a ghastly show of being at ease. "A drunken servant, that is all. Lady Gernon, let me take you into the drawing-room."

Glances were exchanged; but the sullen countenance of Gurdon, the spilled tea, and the broken cups and saucers, afforded sufficient explanation, and the visitors slowly filtered back into the different rooms, in one of which another accident had taken place.

As Sir Murray, trembling with suppressed anger, entered the inner drawing-room, known as the blue-room, he saw Gurdon, napkin and tray in hand, standing as if waiting his coming, his face breaking into a mocking smile upon his master's entrance, closely followed by Captain Norton, who, so far, had not spoken a word.

"Go to your mother, Marion," said Sir Murray. "I must have a few more words with this man."

"With whom?" exclaimed Lady Gernon. "With my servant, madam," said Sir Murray, loudly. "Not with Captain Norton now. But where is your cross?"

"My cross!" stammered Lady Gernon; and her hand involuntarily sought the place where it had hung. "I had it when I—when—"

"Yes, when you entered the conservatory," said Sir Murray, a suspicion crossing his breast; "but where is it now?"

"I do not know!" exclaimed Lady Gernon, whose agitation became extreme.

The rumour of the failing mines; Captain Norton's poverty; his own jealousy; thought after thought flashed across Sir Murray Gernon's brain in an instant of time.

"Go to your guests," he said sternly. "There are people coming this way, and I wish to avoid a scene. James," he said, beckoning to a footman, "see that man, Gurdon, into the little garden-room, lock him up, and then fetch a constable."

"What for—what for?" said Gurdon, loudly. "You don't think, do you, that I've got the cross?"

"Silence, sir! Take him away!" exclaimed Sir Murray, sternly. Then, turning to Captain Norton, he said in a whisper, "There are two things in this world, Philip Norton, that I value: my honour and those old family jewels."

"I am attending to your words," said Norton, coldly; for he had just met an imploring look from Marion.

"I told you, Lady Gernon, to go to your guests!" said Sir Murray, in an angry whisper.

"No, Murray," she said. "I shall stay!"

"In Heaven's name, then, stay!" he said, angrily, "and hear what I would say. I value my honour and those family jewels, Captain Norton," he continued, facing his guest; "and the man who filches from me one or the other does so at the risk of his life!"

"What!" exclaimed Lady Gernon, with a horrified aspect, "do you for a moment suppose, Murray, that Captain Norton—"

"Where is that sapphire cross?" exclaimed Sir Murray.

"Indeed—indeed—"

"Silence, madam! I will have no scene!" hissed Sir Murray, angrily. "You, as my wife, hold those jewels in trust for me; and I should hold him who took them, even as a gift, as a robber of what is mine."

"Sir Murray Gernon, you are mad!" exclaimed Norton—"you know not what you say, and—Hush! sir, no words. Lady Gernon has fainted!"

An Encounter

Sir Murray Gernon had expressed a desire that there should be no scene, but his wish was of no avail, for in a few moments an excited group had collected round his wife. Salts, vinegar, and cold water were sought and applied; but, fortunately, one of the guests was the medical adviser of the family.

"Bed, Sir Murray—empty house—quiet—and," he said, meaningly, "all going well, I may be able to offer you congratulations before morning."

Half an hour after, the house was vacated by the last guest, and before morning had dawned the tidings were borne to Sir Murray Gernon that his lady had given birth to a daughter, but that from her ladyship's critical state Dr Challen wished for further advice, and for a fellow-practitioner to share the burden of his responsibility.

Messages were sent; and in the course of a few hours there was a consultation held respecting Lady Gernon's state—a consultation over which the medical practitioners shook their heads solemnly. The child was healthy; but its mother still existed, that was all.

Mrs Norton was at her side, where she insisted upon staying for days, in spite of a request from Sir Murray that she would leave; and now it was that for the first time she heard of the loss of the jewels from Jane Barker, who told her, with many sobs, that Gurdon had been suspected by Sir Murray, who had sent for a constable; but after having him searched that morning, his wages had been paid him, and he had been discharged, "threatening horrible things."

"And oh! ma'am," whispered Jane, "you were always like my dear lady's sister; if you should hear anything said about her, it isn't true. You won't believe it, I'm sure."

"You know I should never believe words uttered by an angry servant, Jane," was the reply; "and if you take my advice you will be silent."

"I would, ma'am; and I should not have said a word now, only Gurdon went away full of such threatenings, and talked so loudly, that I was afraid it might come to your ears without preparation, for he spoke of Captain Norton, and—"

"Silence, woman!" exclaimed Ada, fiercely, as she caught the startled maid by the arm. "How dare you bandy about such talk! I will not hear another word."

Jane stopped, gazing aghast at her mistress's cousin, as, with her hands pressed upon her bosom, she seemed to be striving to keep back the painful emotion which oppressed her.

"Don't be angry with me, ma'am, please." Jane whispered humbly. "I would not have spoken had I known."

Mrs Norton made her a motion to be silent; and for awhile the girl stood watching her agitated countenance, as she strove to conquer her emotion. She was herself unsuspicious to a degree. She had full faith in her husband, but now thick and fast came blow after blow. She found how calumny was at work—how Sir Murray Gernon's name was talked of in connection with her husband's, and at last she felt that for his sake, much as she loved her cousin, her place was at his side; for once more in her life there came the shuddering dread of a great evil, and obtaining from Jane a promise that if her mistress grew worse she should be informed, she returned to the Hall.

It was evening when she reached home, to find the servant looking excited, while, as soon as she entered the house, the sound of a loud and angry voice reached her ear.

"Who is in the drawing-room?" she hastily inquired of the servant.

"Oh'm, I'm so glad you've come," ejaculated the girl. "It's Sir Murray Gernon."

For a moment Ada felt as if she could not proceed. Her heart accused her of neglecting home for the past few days, and she told herself that, with the rumours she knew of floating around, she ought not to have stayed away. But at last, with an effort, she hurried forward, opened the door, and entered the room just as, with a cry of rage, Sir Murray Gernon raised the hunting-whip he held in his hand, and struck her husband furiously across the face.

"Dog!" he exclaimed. "I gave you the chance of meeting me as a gentleman, and you refused, driving me to horsewhip you as the scoundrel and thief you are. Ha!"

He paused, for Ada Norton was clinging to the arm that held the whip, while her husband—

Was he a coward? Was that the man of whose daring she had heard in India, performing deeds of valour that had been chronicled again and again in the despatches sent home? She was no lover of strife, but it was with something akin to shame that she saw her husband stand motionless, with one hand pressed to the red weal across his face. He was very pale, and the old scar and the new seemed to intersect one another, the latter like a bar sinister across honourable quarterings. He was trembling, too, but it was with a sigh of relief that she heard him break the silence at last.

"Sir Murray Gernon," he said, in a cracked voice that she hardly knew, "when your poor dying wife came here with you, we walked through that window into the garden, where, in memory of our old love, she made me swear that I would never injure you, a promise—I hardly know why—that, though I made, I never even mentioned to my wife."

Sir Murray laughed scornfully.

"I tell you now again, in the presence of my wife here, that your suspicions are baseless, that you wrong Lady Gernon most cruelly; and that, but for the fact that you dared call me—a poor, but honourable soldier—thief, your last charge is so contemptible that it would not be worthy of an answer. Go now and try to undo the wrong you have done. Thief! robber!" he exclaimed, excitedly. "Who was the thief of my love—of my life? But there; I have done," he said, calmly. "I thought," he continued, tenderly, "that hope was crushed out of my existence; that there was to be no future for me. That day, when I cast myself down in the churchyard with the feeling of despair heavy upon me, it seemed as if, with one harsh blow, my life had been snapped in two. And it was nearly so; but Heaven sent his angel to save me, and to prove that there was hope, and rest, and happiness for me yet in this world."

Ere he had finished speaking Ada had thrown herself into his arms, and was looking proudly in his scarred face.

"Sir Murray Gernon," he continued, after an instant's pause, "I refused to meet you, and I have now told you the true reason for my having done so. In this world we shall probably never meet again. Our paths lie, as they ought, in different directions. It is fit they should. But once more, I swear before Heaven that your base charges are false. Go, and by honest, manly confession, try and win her back to life, and obtain her forgiveness. Tell her that I kept my word, even to making myself for her sake a coward in the eyes of the world."

As he ceased speaking, he turned from Sir Murray to gaze down in his wife's face. There was a sad, despairing look in his countenance, though, that troubled her; it was the same drawn, haggard aspect that she had looked on years before; but as she clung to him closer and closer, twining her arms more tightly round him, and trying to draw that pale, scarred face to hers, the wild, scared aspect slowly faded away, for from her eyes he seemed to draw life and hope, and at last, with a sigh that seemed torn from his breast's utmost depths, he pressed his lips upon her forehead, and then turned once more to confront his accuser.

But they were alone; for, after listening with conflicting thoughts to Norton's words, Sir Murray Gernon had slowly turned upon his heel, leaving the room, unnoticed.

Jane's Heart

"Oh, dear!—oh, dear! what shall I do?—what shall I do?" sobbed Jane Barker. "What a wicked set we must all be for the troubles to come bubbling and rolling over us like this in a great water-flood. There's poor Sir Murray half-mad with grief, shutting himself up in his library, and never hardly so much as eating or drinking a bit. There's my own dear, sweet lady lying there day after day, with the lids shut down over those poor soft eyes of hers, never moving, and nobody knowing whether she's living or dead, only when she gives one of those little sobbing sighs. And then there's the poor old Rector, coming every day over and over again to see how she is, and looking as if his heart would break; and poor Mrs Elstree wandering up and down the passages like a ghost. Oh, dear!—oh, dear!—oh, dear! the place isn't like the same, and I don't know what's to become of us all. One didn't need to have jewels missing, and poor servants suspected of taking them, and sent away without a month's warning, and not a bit of character. But oh, John!—John!—John! it wasn't a month's warning you had, but many months' warning; and it wasn't you stole the cross, but let something steal away all your good heart and good looks too."

Here Jane Barker burst out into a passionate fit of weeping, sobbing as though her heart would break. She was sitting by her open window—one looking over a part of the shrubbery which concealed the servants' offices from the view of those who strolled through the grounds. It was not the first night by many that Jane had sat there bewailing her troubles, for it had become a favourite custom with her to sit there, thoughtful and silent, till her passionate grief brought forth some such outburst as the above. Busy the whole day at her work about the sick-chamber of her lady, Jane told herself that at such times there was something else for her to do beside sorrowing; but when at midnight all about was wrapped in silence, the poor girl would sit or kneel at her window, mourning and crying for hour after hour.

"Oh, my poor dear lady! If it should come to the worst, and her never to look upon the little soft face of that sweet babe, sent to be a comfort to her when she's been so solitary and unhappy all these years; for she has been. Oh! these men—these men! They break our poor hearts, they do! Why didn't the Captain come back sooner and make her happy? or why didn't he die in real earnest over in the hot Ingies, where they said he was killed, and not come back just then to make her heart sore, as I know it has been ever since? though, poor soul, she loves, honours, and obeys her husband as she should. There didn't never ought to be any marrying at all, for it's always been an upset to me ever since I thought about it; and him such a proper man, too, as he used to be—such a nice red and white face, and always so smart till he took to the drink; as I told him, he got to love it ever so much better than he loved me, though he always coaxed me round into forgiving him. I always knew it was weak; but then I couldn't help it, and I didn't make myself; and if poor women are made weak and helpless, what can they do?

"I always told him it would be his ruin, and begged of him to give it up—and oh! the times he's kissed me and promised me he would! And then for it to come to this. He'd never have said such cruel things about my lady if it had not been for the drink; and though I'd forgive him almost anything, I couldn't forgive him for speaking as he did. I do think he likes me, and that it isn't all for the sake of the bit of money, which he might have and welcome if it would do him any good. If he would only leave off writing to me, and asking me to meet him when he knows I daren't, and every letter breaking my heart, and at a time, too, when I've got nowhere to go and sit down and cry. No; let him mend a bit, and show me that he's left off the drink, and my poor dear lady get well first, and I'll leave directly, as I told him I would, and work and slave for him all my life, just for the sake of a few kind words; for I know I'm only a poor ignorant woman; but I can love him very—very much, and—"

Jane stopped short, listening attentively, for at that moment there was a faint rustling sound beneath the window, and then, after a few minutes' interval, another and another; a soft rustling sound as of something forcing its way gently amongst the bushes and low shrubs, for at times a step was audible amongst the dead leaves, and once there came a loud crack, as if a foot had been set upon a dry twig which had snapped sharply.

Then there was utter silence again, and the girl sat listening with pale face, lips apart, and her breath drawn with difficulty, as her heart beat with a heavy throb, throb, throb, at the unwonted sound. It could not be one of the dogs, for they were all chained up; and if it had been a strange step she felt that they would have barked, and given some alarm. The deer never came near the house, and it was extremely doubtful whether any of the cattle in the great park could have strayed into the private grounds through some gate having been left open. Her heart told her what the noise was, and accelerated its beats with excitement, so that when, after a renewal of the soft rustling, she heard a sound as of hard breathing, and then a husky voice whispering her name, she was in no wise surprised.

"Tst—tst, Jane!" seemed to come out of the black darkness below—a darkness that she in vain tried to penetrate.

"Oh, why did you come—why did you come?" sobbed Jane. "Somebody will be sure to hear you, and then you'll be in worse trouble than ever, besides getting me turned out of my place. Oh, John!—oh, John! how can you be such a cruel fellow!"

"Hold your tongue, will you, and don't be a fool," was the husky reply. "I'm going to have you away from here, Jenny, in a few days, and then his proudship shall have some letters as shall make him pay me to hold my tongue, or else have all his pride tumbling about his ears."

"Oh, you wicked wretch!" muttered Jane to herself, for his words roused her slumbering resentment, and drove her troubles away for the present.

"Can you hear all I say?" whispered the voice from below.

"Yes," whispered Jane again; "but what do you want? Oh, pray, pray go!"

"Yes," said Gurdon. "I'll go when I've done; but I want to talk to you first. Who's at home? Is he here?"

"Who? Master? Yes," whispered Jane, "and the doctor, and my lady's pa: they're all here, for she's been very bad to-night."

"But are they all gone to bed?" whispered Gurdon.

"Yes, all but Mrs Elstree, who's sitting up in my lady's room."

"Come down then, softly, into the passage and open the lobby door; you can let me in then, through the billiard-room."

"That I'm sure I'm not going to!" exclaimed Jane, indignantly, "and you ought to be ashamed of yourself for asking me such a thing. It isn't like you, John."

"Hold your tongue, will you!" he exclaimed, gruffly. "Do you want to be heard, and have me shot by one of the keepers, or some one fire at me from one of the windows?"

"N-n-no," gasped Jane; "but pray do go; pray, dear John, go away!"

"Ah, you're very anxious to get rid of me now," said Gurdon, sneeringly, for he could hear that Jane was sobbing; "I may go now, just because I made a slip, and you want to see me no more. It's the way of the world."

"No—no; don't talk like that," cried Jane, "for you know I don't deserve it; but pray, for both our sakes, go away at once. Write to me and say what you want."

"I shan't do nothing of the kind!" hissed Gurdon, angrily. "You do as I tell you: come down and let me in, or it'll be the worse for you. I want to talk to you so as I can't talk here. I've got a deal to say about the future."

"I don't care, and I won't!" said Jane, excitedly, for anger roused in her anger in return. At such times she did not at all feel afraid of John Gurdon, nor of his threats, but was ready to meet him with open resistance. "I'm not going to do any such thing, so there now! It's more than my place is worth, and you know it, John. And besides, it wouldn't be seemly and modest."

"Oh, you've grown very modest all at once, you have," sneered Gurdon, angrily. "It's all make believe; and if you don't do as I tell you, I'll pay you out in a way as'll startle you! Come down this minute," he hissed, "and do as I tell you! I will speak to you!"

"You won't do nothing of the kind," said Jane, angrily; "you've been drinking again, or you wouldn't have come here to ask such a thing, nor you wouldn't have thrown them nasty, sneering, jeering words at one that no one can say a word against, so there, now. And now, good night, Mr Gurdon," she said, frigidly; and he heard the sash begin to close.

"Oh, Jane—Jane, darling! please—please stop, only a minute," he whined, for he knew that he had played a false card, and that it was time to withdraw it. "Don't be hard on a poor fellow as is fallen, and who's put out of temper by his troubles. I didn't think that you'd turn your back upon me—I didn't, indeed."

John Gurdon paused, and gave vent to a snuffle, and something that was either a hiccup or a sob. Jane Barker, too, paused in her act of closing the window, for somehow John Gurdon had wound his way so tightly round her soft heart, that she was ready to strike him one moment, and to go down on her knees and beg forgiveness the next.

"It's very hard," sobbed Gurdon, in maudlin tones. "Even she has turned upon me now, even to closing the window, and denying me a hearing—I didn't think it of her. A woman that I've worshipped almost—a woman as I'd have died for a dozen times over; but it isn't in her nature."

Gurdon stopped and listened attentively.

"She isn't a bad one at heart," he continued, in the same whining, lachrymose tones, "but she's been set against me, and it's all over now; and I may as well make an end of myself as try and live. I did think as she'd have come down to listen to me; but no, and it's all over. The whole world now has shut its doors and windows in my face!"

"Oh, John—John, pray, pray don't talk so!" sobbed Jane.

"What! not gone?" he exclaimed, in mock ecstasy.

"No, no! How could you think I should be so cruel?"

"Oh, I don't know," he whined. "But pray, pray come down: I want to have a few words about what's to be done. I don't want to take a public-house now, Jane, but to go into the grocery and baking; and there's a chance before me, if I could only point it out."

"Well, tell me now," sobbed Jane.

"No; how can I?" said Gurdon—"I shall be heard. Ah! Jenny, you don't care for me as you used, or you wouldn't keep me out here like this!"

"Oh, what shall I do?" sobbed Jane. "I can't do as he asks, and he knows it; and yet he's trying to break my heart, he is!"

"Now, then, are you going to listen to me, Jenny?" whispered Gurdon, imploringly.

"Oh, I can't—I can't: I daren't do it!" sobbed poor Jane.

"Oh, please, if you love me, don't drive me to desperation!" cried Gurdon. "I—"

"Hush!" whispered Jane, in affrighted tones, for at that moment there was a loud knocking at her bedroom door, and the voice of Mrs Elstree was heard.

"Jane—Jane! Quick! Call Sir Murray! My darling is dying!"

Beneath the Shadow

As, muttering a savage oath, John Gurdon crept through the yielding shrubs, Jane Barker softly closed the window, and then glided to the door.

"Not gone to bed?" exclaimed Mrs Elstree. "Thank Heaven! Rouse Sir Murray and my husband while I run back."

"Have you called Dr Challen, ma'am?" said Jane, in agitated tones.

"Oh yes: he is in the bedroom," sobbed Mrs Elstree; and she hurried back.

In a few minutes husband and father were by the bedside, watching with agitated countenances the struggle going on, for truly it seemed that the long lethargy into which Lady Gernon had been plunged was to be terminated by the triumph of the dread shade. As Mrs Elstree had sat watching her, she had suddenly started up to talk in a wild, incoherent manner; and as Sir Murray Gernon stood there in his long dressing-gown, with brow knit, a shade that was not one of sorrow crossed his brow upon hearing some of his stricken wife's babblings.

"Philip," she said—and as she spoke her voice softened, and there was a yearning look of gentleness in her countenance—"Philip, the cross: where is the cross? Have you hid it?—have you taken it away? Pray, pray restore it! He will be angry. They are favourite old jewels, that I wear for his sake. You loved me once; for the sake of the old times give it me back! He will ask for it. Where is the cross? Do you see: blue sapphires, each like a little forget-me-not peering up at you. Your flowers—true blue, Philip. But the cross—I must have the cross!"

She was silent for a few minutes, and then, wildly turning to her husband, she caught his hand in hers.

"Philip," she cried, addressing him, "it is all madness—something of the past. It was not to be, and we have each our path to follow. I heard the rumours: trouble—failure—your income swept away—dearest Ada. But you must not come to want. You will give me back the cross, though; not the forget-me-nots. Keep them, though they are withered and dry—withered and dry as our old love—something of the past. Let me see," she said—and her eyes assumed a troubled, anxious expression—"you cannot claim me now. I am another's—his wife. How blue the lake looks! and how plainly it mirrors the mountains! Fair blue waters—blue—true blue. If I could have died then—died when you plucked the flowers from my breast—but it was not to be. I have a duty to fulfil—a burden—a cross"—she said, dreamily—"a cross? Yes—yes—yes, the cross. You will give it me back, Philip," she whispered, with a smile; "it lies, you see, where once your forget-me-nots lay. I cannot wear them now, but the colour is the same—true blue. But you will find them for me, those bright gems, and all will yet be well."

She raised Sir Murray's hand to her lips, and kissed it reverently, as she continued:

"Always true and noble, Philip. You will respect my husband for the sake of the old days. It has been like a cloud always hovering above my life: that great dread lest you should ever meet in anger. Go now—let me sleep—I am weak and weary. But remember your promise."

Pride, misery, despair, shame, and grief, seemed to have mingled for him a cup of bitterness, forcing him to drink it there in the presence of those who were gathered round the sick woman's couch; and it was with a step that tottered in spite of all his self-command, that when Lady Gernon loosed his hand, Sir Murray strode slowly from the room, to seek the solitude of the library, where, alone through the rest of that night, he could sit and brood upon his misery. She did not love him—she had never loved him; and he told himself that he could not stay to hear her words—to hold her hand, when her last sigh was breathed. Had not that man risen, as it were, from the dead to blast their wedding, she would have clung to him with a softened, child-like affection; but now—"how could he stay when her thoughts all seemed another's?"

The tearful eyes of father and mother met across the bed, as Sir Murray left the room, and then as the doctor sat silent and averted of gaze by the bedside, the broken voice of the father rose, as, sinking upon his knees, he prayed long and earnestly that Heaven of its goodness would grant the renewal of life to his child, if but for a short time, that she might prove to her husband that the words he had that night heard were but the vain babblings of her distempered brain. That she might live for his, for her child's, for her parents' sake, and during her life, however short, sweep away the cruel mists of doubt and suspicion that clung to her hearth.

Fervent and low did that prayer sound in the silence of the sick-chamber, where all that wealth could spread in profusion was waiting to minister to the owner's wants. But to those present it seemed as if the splendour were but a mockery; and the story of Lady Gernon's life, well known to all, pointed ever to one great void—a void that no wealth could supply.

Fervent and low grew that prayer in the silence of that night, till, as the Rectors lips parted to give utterance to those sublime words of humility and resignation, "Thy will be done!" a sob choked his utterance, and, save a low, weary wail from the stricken mother, all was for a long space still.

The shaded lamp made the hangings of the bed to disport themselves in strange shadows upon wall and carpet; and at times, when the night breeze softly swept round the house, it was as though the spirits of air were waiting in gathering levée to bear away the newly-freed essence to a happier realm. No word was spoken; only at times the Doctor bent over the bed to moisten his patient's lips from a glass in his hand. The pendule ticked softly upon the mantel-piece, every second beaten off finding its echo in the listeners' hearts, as it seemed to tell of the rapid flight of time, and the few brief minutes left to the wretched sufferer upon the bed. Her wanderings had long since ceased, and to those who watched, it seemed many times over that the last sigh had been breathed with those softly-muttered words, which made them start as a cold shudder ran through their frames. But a warning glance from the doctor, as he still kept on at intervals of every few minutes moistening her lips, told that there was still life, and they waited on.

More than once Mrs Elstree's head had turned, full of expectancy, towards the door, for she thought that Sir Murray would return; but he came not; and at last, feeling it to be an act of duty to send for him, she turned to speak to Jane, who, it seemed to her, had been but a few minutes before sobbing silently in a further corner of the room. It excited no surprise though, then, when she saw that the corner was vacant, for, dulled by long familiarity with the grief before her, other matters seemed to make no impression on her mind.

It was the same with the Rector, for as Mrs Elstree rose to leave the room, he did not remove his gaze from his daughter's face, but still sat watching silently and sadly for the change.

Mrs Elstree sought Sir Murray in his room; but he was not there, and then, as, candle in hand—unnecessary then, for a cold, pale light seemed to creep through the sky light over the grand staircase, to give to everything a chilly, forlorn, and strange look—she descended the stairs, she encountered a servant who, with a scared face, told her that Sir Murray was in the library, and then stood watching her descent.

She reached the library door and knocked, to receive no answer, and her repeated summonses were without effect, when, with a sigh, she turned to retrace her steps.

"He will not come," she said. Then, to the maid, who had been watching her anxiously: "Have you seen Jane?"

"Went out, ma'am, with one of the gardeners, ever so long ago, ma'am."

"Do you know where?"

"No, ma'am. She never said a word to me about it;" and the girl, and another who had joined her, turned to gaze uneasily at the closed library door.

Mrs Elstree slowly retraced her steps—slowly, though shivering the while with anxiety—and returned to the bedroom, to find the scene there unchanged. But she had hardly retaken her place by the bedside when there was a rustling at the door, and she turned her head, thinking that it might be Sir Murray, but, to her surprise, Ada Norton, closely followed by Jane, entered the room.

Ada spoke no word, but, gliding to the bedside, stood, pale and anxious, gazing down upon her cousin's shrunken face. Then, stooping softly, she pressed a long kiss upon her white lips, the doctor making no sign of rebuke.

"Where is her child?" said Ada then, in an anxious tone, for, as she had bent down, Lady Gernon's eyes had opened, and her lips had parted in a faint whisper.

"May it be fetched?" said Mrs Elstree, softly, to the doctor.

"Yes—yes," he whispered, in tones that seemed to imply, "all is over now."

Jane hurried, sobbing, from the room, for the last moments seemed to have come. There was something awful in the strange light of recognition that had come into Lady Gernon's eyes; but when, softly sleeping, the tiny fragile one was borne in and laid in her arms, its soft, downy cheek resting upon her breast, the faintest dawning of a smile played for an instant upon the mother's lip, her eyes gazed straight upwards for a few moments, and then closed, when, as Dr Challen swiftly pressed forward, to lean with anxious mien over the pillow, Mrs Elstree sank fainting into weeping Jane's arms, while, with a despairing wail, Ada Norton gave utterance to one word, that sounded more like declaration than eager demand, as it thrilled through the strained nerves of all present, and that word was: "Dead?"

Not Yet

Ada Norton's wild appeal was answered by the Doctor's hand being held up to command silence, and, for many hours from that moment, as he tended his patient, he refused to answer all questions. At last, though, with a sigh almost of pleasure, he said:

"I'll lie down now for a few hours. Call me when she wakes."

Only those who have watched by a bedside, expecting moment by moment that the grim shade would claim its prey, can imagine the relief afforded to all by that simple sentence. It told of hope and refreshing slumber; of a return to consciousness; and, bent of head, the old Rector left the chamber, feeling that his prayer had been heard, hopeful too, now, that in all its plenitude the rest of his supplication would be granted.

The change from despair to hopefulness was so sudden that, again and again, Ada bent in doubt over her cousin's pillow, to press a gentle kiss upon her pale face, before she could feel satisfied respecting that faint, regular breathing, culminating now and then in a sigh of satisfaction, so faint that it was like the softest breath of summer. But, relieved in spirit, she at length took her departure, thanking Jane for hurrying over to summon her as she had done.

Mrs Norton found her husband excitedly pacing the walk in front of the house, and he made no scruple about displaying the cause of his anxiety, for, hurrying to his wife's side, he caught her hands in his, exclaiming:

"What of poor Marion?" And then, reading in her countenance that his worst fears were not confirmed, he muttered a sigh of relief, "Thank Heaven!—thank Heaven!"

"I fancy now that there is hope," whispered his wife, who, steadfast and true herself, refused to harbour the slightest suspicion. He was anxious respecting poor Marion Gernon's fate, and why should he not be when all circumstances were taken into consideration? To say that his deep interest in her cousin caused her no pain would be false, for it did, and naturally; but that pain she concealed. In her thoughtful moments, when reviewing the scenes at the Castle, and considering the loss of the jewels in connection with her husband's troubles, his words to Sir Murray Gernon, and sufferance even of his cruel blow, she knew that either her husband was a thief, liar, and consummate villain, or else a man of true nobility and the most refined honour. Was it likely that she should pause for a moment in the verdict, as, clinging daily more fondly to him, she tried, by her endearments, to soothe the perturbation of his spirit. He loved her she was sure, and she would not be mad enough to indulge in reproof or upbraiding.

Satisfied in her own mind that her cousin was out of danger, she would visit her no more. It would be wrong, she felt, until the clouds of suspicion that floated around were driven away. For she thought, with hot and burning cheeks, of those suspicions until she angrily drove them from her as unworthy of her notice. If her husband would but take her more fully into his confidence—talk with her freely, ask her counsel, and keep nothing back, she felt that she would be happy; but she thought that it would be an insult to him to broach such matters, and day after day she waited for the confidence that came not. He said nothing respecting his financial troubles, in spite of her eager desire to know his losses; but, to her great grief, he became day after day more sombre and thoughtful, going out but little, save to make one of his long, strange journeys, at a time, too, when her anxiety was at its greatest height.

All would yet be well, though, she told herself, and still crushing down thoughts inimical to her peace, she met him ever with the same smile, but never to evoke a smile in return, save when their child came gambolling forward, when, with swelling heart, she would offer, mentally, a thanksgiving for that gift, and revel in the sunshine of his brighter looks, until once more the clouds would seem to settle over his soul.

To her he was always gentle, kind, and subdued; and, to a stranger he would have seemed a model husband; but Ada Norton was not content: there was a change—a marked change—in him, and more than once, in the bitterness of her heart, she had wished that the Castle had still remained desolate.

But she had one consolation during the long hours she was alone—her boy; and, lavishing her love upon him, she lived on, hopefully waiting for the sunshine; happy that, in spite of the fierce anger and suspicion of Sir Murray Gernon, the quarrel with her husband had proceeded no further, while, save for an occasional scrap of information gleaned in visits to the Rectory, the doings of the Gernons were to her a sealed book.

This had pained her at first, but her good sense told her that it was best for all concerned; and, striving to forget the past, she saw the time glide by in what was to her a calm and uneventful life till, shock after shock, came tidings and blows that, like the storm beating upon some good ship, threatened to make wreck of all her hopes. Tempest, rock, quicksand, all were fighting, as it were, to make an end of her faith—to destroy her happiness; calling forth fortitude and determination to encounter sufferings more than ordinarily fall to the lot of woman to bear.

Sir Murray's Library

There was a buzz of satisfaction amongst the servants as, half hysterically, Jane Barker announced the tidings of a change for the better; but when she added thereto an order from the Doctor that Sir Murray should be made acquainted with the change, there was a look of intelligence passed from one to the other—a scared, frightened look, which she was not slow to perceive, and in eager tones demanded what was the matter.

"Nothing that I know of," said one, "but—"

"You always were a fool, Thomas!" exclaimed Jane, angrily. "Here, James, go and tell master at once."

But James seemed not to have heard the command, for he suddenly disappeared through a door, against which he had happened to be standing.

"You go, then, Thomas," said Jane; "and make haste, there's a good man. He must be anxious to know."

"Shouldn't think he was," said Thomas, "when Missus Elstree knocked ever so long at the libery and got no answer."

Jane's sharp eyes were again directed from one to the other, and then, without further pause, she set her teeth, nipped her lips together, and hurried across the hall to the library door.

She knocked at first softly, but there was no reply; then more loudly, with the same result; and at last, thoroughly alarmed, she beat fiercely upon the panels, calling loudly upon her masters name.

"Go and fetch Mr Elstree, and call up Dr Challen," said Jane, huskily, for there was a horrible fear at her heart, though she resolutely kept it to herself. "Perhaps master may be in a fit," she whispered.

The Rector was there in a few minutes, and after knocking and calling, he, too, turned pale, as the doctor now appeared upon the scene.

"Locked on the inside," said the latter, after a momentary examination. "The door must be broken open, and at once. Is there a carpenter upon the premises?"

There was no carpenter, but one of the gardeners had some skill in doing odd jobs about the place, and he was known to possess a basket of tools. His name was therefore suggested.

"Fetch him at once!" exclaimed the Doctor, as excited now as any one present; and amidst an awe-stricken silence, the gardener's advent was awaited.

But it took a good quarter of an hour to seek Alexander McCray, and during that period of breathless expectation, not a soul present thought of the possibility of an entrance being effected by the window. Thomas had peered twice through the key-hole, looking round afterwards with a pale, blank face, when seeing that it would probably be a quicker way of obtaining information than questioning, Dr Challen knelt down himself, to peer for some time through the narrow aperture, when he, too, rose, thoughtful and silent, the Rector refraining from questioning him, and no one else daring to do so. What Thomas had seen he at length communicated in whispers, but they did not reach the Rector, who, with a shuddering sensation oppressing him, kept on, in spite of himself, watching—as if his eyes were specially there attracted—the narrow slit beneath the door, as if expecting that some trace might probably there show itself of what had taken place within the room.

"Is this man coming?" exclaimed the Doctor at last; and another messenger was sent, while the women huddled together, whispering, and more than one thinking that that morning's occurrences might result in a general discharge of servants, and a breaking up of the Castle establishment.

At last, though, there was the sound of footsteps, and very slowly and leisurely the Scotch gardener made his appearance, walking with the cumbersome gait of the men of the scythe and spade—slow, as a rule, as the growth of the plants they tend.

"Now, for Heaven's sake, be smart, my good fellow!" exclaimed the Doctor.

"Ye'll be wanting the door open, will ye?" said Alexander, slowly.

"Yes—yes!" exclaimed the Doctor impatiently.

"And have ye got authoughreety of Sir Moorray to force it open?" said Alexander.

"My good man, this is no time for authority. Make haste, and break open the door."

"I'm no cheecan, gentlemen," said Alexander, with the most aggravating coolness; "but I've got a verra good seetuation here, and I should be sore fashed if I had to luse it throw being rash. Sir Moorray might be verra angered with me for breaking the door."

"My good man, I'd take all responsibility," exclaimed the Rector. "Pray, be quick!"

"Weel, then, eef that's the case, gentlemen," said Alexander, refreshing his high-bridged nose with a pinch of snuff—"eef that's the case, I'll just go and fetch my tools."

Alexander McCray nodded his head sagely, as he took his departure; and again there was an anxious lapse of time, certainly only of some minutes, but they seemed then to be hours, and, hurrying into the drawing-room, and seizing a poker, the Doctor was himself about to attack the door, when, chisel and mallet in hand, the gardener returned, his rush tool-basket over his shoulder; and then, strenuously exerting himself, he soon made an entrance, first for a chisel and then for a crowbar, with which he strained and strained hard to force open the strongly-made old oak carved door. For a long while the efforts were vain; but at last, with a loud crash, the door gave way, and so suddenly that the gardener fell back with great violence amongst the lookers-on, when, with an unanimous shriek of dismay, the women-servants turned and fled, to gaze from distant doorways for some scrap of interest connected with the elucidation.

But before Sandy McCray had gathered himself together, the Rector, followed by Dr Challen and Jane, had entered the room, when Mr Elstree's first act was to catch Jane by the arm and press her back, as with his other hand he drew to the door.

"My good woman, you will be better away," he said, earnestly.

"I'm not afraid, sir," said Jane, quietly; "and perhaps I may be of some use."

"Keep that door closed, then," exclaimed the Doctor; and the next moment he was kneeling upon the carpet, where, motionless, stretched upon his face, and with his fingers tightly clutching the long nap of the Turkey carpet, lay the tall, proud form of Sir Murray Gernon.

"No, not that—not that, thank Heaven!" exclaimed the Doctor, after a brief examination, as, looking up, he answered the Rector's inquiring gaze. "I was afraid so at first, but it is nothing of the kind. Not his own act, sir, but a sudden seizure, and no wonder. Tall, portly man—predisposition to apoplexy. Here, quick, Jane—basin and towels. Mr Elstree, open that window, and let's have air; then send away those open-mouthed, staring fools outside. Nothing serious, I hope."

As he spoke, he had loosened the baronet's neckband, and torn the sleeve away from his arm, to lay bare and open a vein, his ministrations being followed before very long by a heavy sigh from the patient, other favourable symptoms soon supervening, and in a short time the baronet was pronounced out of danger.

"I don't know what people would do if it were not for our profession," said Dr Challen, importantly, as he fussed about in the hall, superintending the carrying of Sir Murray to his bed-chamber.

"And a wee bit help from a man as can handle twa or three tules," said Sandy McCray, in a whisper to himself, for he was one of the porters; and then Dr Challen had the further satisfaction of knowing that he had two patients instead of one, both, though, progressing favourably.

The Gentle Passion

Some days had passed, and the Doctor had taken his departure, confining himself now to a couple of calls per diem. Lady Gernon was progressing fast towards recovery, and Sir Murray, very quiet and staid, was again up; but, so far as the servants knew, and did not omit to tattle about, he had had no interview with her ladyship. But the heads of the establishment were not the only ones in that house sore at heart, for Jane Barker, in her times of retirement, shed many a bitter tear. She never asked about him, but there were those amongst the domestics who heard the news, and soon bore it to her, that John Gurdon had left the neighbouring town where he had been staying, and was gone to Liverpool, with the intention of proceeding to Australia: in which announcement there was some little truth and a good deal of fiction, the shade of truth being that John Gurdon was going abroad, though not in the way he had published.

"And never to write and ask me to see him again," sobbed Jane—"never to say 'good-bye.' Oh, what a blessing life would be if there was no courting in it! as is a curse to everybody, as I've seen enough to my cost, without counting my own sufferings."

Jane was bewailing her fate at the open window one night when these thoughts passed through her breast for the hundredth time. Certainly, there was a pleasant coolness in the night air, but it is open to doubt whether poor Jane had not nourished a hope that, wrong as it was on her part, besides being unbecoming, John might by chance have repented and turned back just to say a few words of parting. She confessed once that she wished he would, and then she would wish him God-speed, and if he wanted ten or twenty pounds, she would give notice at the savings' bank, draw it out, and send it to him by letter. But not one word would she say to stop him from going—no, not *one* word. He should go, and no doubt it would do him good, and break him of all his bad habits, and "perhaps," she said, with a sob, "he may come back a good man, and we may be—"

"Tst, Jane!—tst!"

For a few moments she could not move, the sound was so unexpected. She had hoped that he might come back, but for days past she had given it up, when now, making her heart leap with a joy she could not conceal, came the welcome sound from the darkness beneath where she leaned.

She had not heard him come, for the reason that Mr John Gurdon had been there for an hour before she had leaned out, and he had been stayed from announcing his presence sooner by a light in a neighbouring window; but now, that apparently all was still in the place, he gave utterance to the above signal, one which he had to repeat before it was responded to by a whispered ejaculation.

"How could I come, you cruel woman!" said Gurdon—"how can you ask me? Hadn't you driven me by your hard-heartedness to make up my mind to go abroad? but only to find when I'd got to the ship that I couldn't go without saying one long 'good-bye.' Oh, Jane!—Jane!—Jane!"

The remaining words were lost to Jane's ear, but she could make out that he was sobbing and groaning softly, and it seemed to her, from the muffled sounds, that Gurdon had thrown himself down upon his face, and was trying to stifle the agony of his spirit, lest he should be heard, and so get her into trouble.

Poor Jane! her heart yearned with genuine pity towards the erring man, and her hands involuntarily stretched themselves out as if to take him to her breast, which heaved with sobs of an affection as sincere as was ever felt by the most cultivated of her sex.

"Oh, John!" she sobbed, "don't—don't!—please don't do that!"

"How can I help it?" he groaned. "Why am I such a coward that I don't go and make a hole in the lake, and put myself out of my misery?"

"Oh, pray—pray don't, John!" sobbed poor Jane, whose feelings were stirred to their deepest depth, and, believing in her old lovers earnest repentance, she was all the weak woman now. "I'm 'most heart-broken, dear, without more troubles. You don't know what has been happening lately."

"No," groaned Gurdon, "I don't know. My troubles have been enough for me."

"What with my lady nearly dying, and Sir Murray being locked up in the library, and the door being broken open to find him in a fit, the place is dreadful, without you going on as you do."

"Don't, please, be hard on me, dear," groaned Gurdon; "and if they did break open the library door, they mended it again, I suppose, for Sir Murray's got plenty of money, ain't he?"

"No, they didn't stop for no mending," sobbed Jane. "It's enough to do to mend poor people's sorrows here as is all driving us mad. Money's no use where you're miserable."

"And are you miserable, dear?" whispered Gurdon.

"Oh, how can you ask?" sobbed Jane.

"Don't seem like it," said Gurdon, softly, "or you'd come down and say a few words to me before I go away, perhaps for ever; for when once the great seas are rolling between us, Jane, there's, perhaps, no chance of our seeing one another no more."

"Oh, how can you ask me? You know I can't!" exclaimed Jane, angrily.

"I thought as much," whined Gurdon, in a deep, husky voice, and as if speaking only to himself; "but I thought I'd put her to the proof—just give her one more trial."

"You cruel—cruel—cruel fellow! how can you torture me so?" sobbed Jane, who had heard every word. "It's wicked of you, it is, when you know it's more than my place is worth to do it."

"Ah," said Gurdon, huskily, "I did think once, that a place in my heart was all that you wanted, and that I had but to say 'Come and take it, Jenny,' and you'd have come. But I was a different man, then, and hadn't gone wrong, and I'm rightly punished now. Goodbye, Heaven bless you!—bless you! and may you be happy!"

"But stop—stop a moment, John! Oh, pray don't go yet! I've something to tell you."

"I dursen't stop no longer," said John, huskily. "People will be sure to hear us; and bad as I am, Jenny, I wouldn't do you any harm. No—no, I'd suffer anything—die for you, though I've been wrong, and taken a glass too much. Good—goo-oo-ood-bye!"

"But stop a moment, John, pray!" sobbed Jane.

"No—no; it's better not."

"Oh dear, what shall I do—what shall I do?" sobbed Jane.

"Won't you say good-bye?" was whispered from below, and there was a soft rustling amongst the bushes beneath the tree.

"Oh, stop—stop!" cried Jane, hoarsely. "Don't leave me like that. What do you want me to do?"

"Oh, nothing—nothing, only to say goodbye, Jane. I did think that I should have liked to hold you in my arms for a moment, and have one parting kiss. I seemed to fancy it would make me a stronger and a better man, so that I could go and fight my way again in a foreign world, and make myself fit to come back and ask you to be my wife."

"But John, dear John, don't ask me," sobbed Jane. "How can I?"

"No—no," he said, sadly; "you can't. Don't do anything of the sort. I only thought you might have come down and let me in through the billiard-room. But don't do it, Jane; you might get into trouble about it, and one of us is enough to be in that way. Bless you, Jane! Think of me sometimes when I'm far away."

Jane did not answer, but with the sobs tearing one after the other from her breast, she stood, listening and thinking. It was too hard upon her; she felt that she could not bear it. How, with all his faults, he still loved her, and should she—could she turn her back upon him when he was in such trouble? There was a hot burning flush, too, in her cheeks as she leaned, with beating heart, further from the window, determined to risk all for his sake.

"John!—John!" she whispered, "Don't go yet; I'll do what you want."

No answer.

"Oh, John!—John! Pray don't leave me like that. I'll come down just for a few moments to say good-bye."

Still no answer, only a faint rustle amongst the bushes.

Had he then gone?—left her while she was silent for those few minutes, thinking her to be hard, and cruel, and indifferent? or did he hope that she would repent, and had he gone round to the glass door by the billiard-room lobby?

"John!" she whispered again; and then more loudly, "John!"

"Is there anything the matter, my lassie?" said a voice—one which made the heart of Jane Barker to beat, for she recognised in it that of the Scotch gardener, who, it now struck her, had been very attentive to her of late.

"Matter! No," said Jane; "I was only looking out at the stars, Mr McCray," and she closed the window.

"Ye're in luck to-neet, Sandy, laddie," muttered the gardener. "Ye've got your rabbit, and reset your trap without so much as a single spiteful keeper being a bit the wiser; and now, taking a fancy to look at her window, ye've seen the little blossom hersel. But she's a neat little flower, and when she's done greeting after that dirty loon of a butler, she'll come round. He was a bad one—a bad one, and as jealous as a Moor; but he's out of the way now, and Jeanie, my sousie lassie, ye'll be mine one of these days, I think."

Alexander McCray stepped gingerly along amongst the bushes, holding the rabbit he had caught tightly in one pocket of his velveteens, secure in his own mind from interruption, for even if he had now met a keeper he was upon his own domain—the garden; and zeal for the protection of his master's fruit would have been his excuse. So he stepped softly along, pushing the shrubs aside, and turning once to look at Jane's window, and during those few moments, as he stood there, looking very solemn, and relieving his feelings by kissing his hand a few times to the darkened window, Sandy McCray was in imminent danger of having his brains knocked out. If he had gone a foot more to the right, or a yard more to the left, the result would have been a fierce struggle; but as it happened, Sandy did neither, but strode safely, straight along, and made his way to his cottage, where he regaled himself with half-a-dozen pinches of snuff, and then turned in, to dream of the fair face of Jane.

Jane's Lovers—Number 1

But Sandy McCray was no sluggard: the little Dutch clock in his room was only striking five, and the dew was bright upon the grass, as he stepped out, crossed the bit of park between his cottage and the garden, and then, taking a rake in his hand, walked towards the shrubbery where he had stood for a few minutes the night before. For Sandy argued that, with all his care, he might have left some footprints about, and that footprints beneath the window of the lady of his love were things not to be thought of for a moment, since they were not tolerated elsewhere.

"Just as I thought," muttered the Scot; and his rake erased a deep footmark and then another upon the border, when, as he half-smoothed over a third, he stopped short, and, lifting his cap with one hand, he let the rake-handle fall into the hollow of his arm, so that he might indulge in a good scratch at his rough, red head.

The scratching seemed to do no good, so he refreshed his intellect with a pinch of snuff, and then with another, when, his senses being a little sharpened, he proceeded to very carefully fit his boot to the footprint, but as he did so, standing upon one leg, he tottered a little, and coming down upon the mark, quite destroyed it as to possibility of identification, and ended by raking it over smoothly. But Sandy had not yet done, for, picking his way carefully through the shrubs, he stopped at last by two very plainly-marked footsteps, and this time, slipping off one boot, he knelt down beneath the shade of an arbutus, and carefully tried the sole, to find that it was a good three sizes larger than the boot that had made the marks. Again the rake was brought into requisition, and the marks obliterated, Mr McCray looking very fierce the while, for a few more steps brought him where the footprints were plainer, and the test of the boot showed that they were of more than one size. He tried here, and he tried there, and had no difficulty in finding his own traces. But those others?

Sandy McCray's face was a study as he stood peering down, and fitting the boot first in one and then another print, ending by returning it to its proper service; and then it was that, if he had looked upwards instead of down, he would have seen that a pale, eager face was watching his every motion, as it had been for the last few minutes, and continued so to do, while, as if struck by a sudden thought, Sandy McCray laid his finger by the side of his nose, grinned a very fierce and savage grin, and then proceeded to erase the marks of trampling. Five minutes later he did turn his head upwards, and stole a glance at the window; but the pale face was not there, for Jane, who had never undressed, had seated herself upon the floor, and now, trembling and agitated, was having what she would have called "a good cry."

There was not a footprint left when Jane had finished her cry, and stole to the window to peep. Neither was Sandy McCray there; but a little off to the right, upon a scrap of grass sparkling in the morning sun with a heavy burden of dewdrops, and as Jane looked, she saw the gardener sharpening his scythe viciously before he began to shave away at the grass, as if every daisy's head were an enemy's that he was determined to take off.

Jane sighed, as well she might, and once more she said aloud:

"Oh, what a happy world this would be if there were no men!"

That was an anxious day for poor Jane, whose thoughts at times made her shiver. Little as she had noticed them before, she could now recall scores of attentions on the gardener's part, all of which evidently meant love. The warm apples from his pockets; the bunches of grapes; the peaches and nectarines; and the roses on Sundays; besides which, for months past it had been his habit to grin at her very widely, so as to show the whole of his teeth—loving smiles, no doubt, while now that he had seen those footsteps beneath her window, what would he do?

She asked herself another question, without trying to answer the former. What had he been doing there himself?

She told herself at last that he would lay no information against her, but that he would watch carefully, and then there would be perhaps a fight between him and Gurdon, who would be sure to come again, for he must have known that she was about to give way to his appeal.

It was plain enough now why Gurdon and McCray had always been such bad friends, quarrelling fiercely, till McCray would tauntingly ask the butler when he meant to use the flower-beds again, because he—the gardener—never liked pigs to sleep in his beds without straw. Jane had never troubled herself about McCray before, but she felt that she must now—that she was bound to do so, for most likely he would get help, and Gurdon, if he came, would be seized for trespassing. It was no use, she could not help it, she declared, and as soon as she found herself at liberty she determined to seek McCray, and trust to her woman's wit for disarming him, should his designs be inimical.

Then she shrank back from the task, for it would be like putting herself in his power, and for a long time poor Jane's mind was a chaos of conflicting doubts. At last, though, she felt determined, and she set off in the direction of the gardener's cottage, telling herself that come what might Gurdon should get into no further trouble.

There was no one at the cottage, and on making inquiry of another of the gardeners, she learned that McCray had gone with a cart to the town to bring back some shrubs sent from some great nurseryman in London.

"But I'll tell him you've been looking after him, Miss Jenny; and he'll be ready to jump out of his boots for joy."

"Don't talk nonsense, Johnson," said Jane, archly. "Just as if there was anything between us!"

"Of course there isn't—nothing at all," laughed the gardener. "There's nothing at all between you, and you'll come together before long. He's always talking about you, and comparing you to the best flowers we have under glass. But I'll tell him you've been asking."

"No, please don't do anything of the kind," said Jane; and she tripped away, trying to appear quite at her ease. But the poor girl's heart was very sore, and though she tried hard, she had no further opportunity during the day of seeking McCray.

It was with a horrible fear, then, upon her that night, that as soon as she could get away from Lady Gernon's room she hurried to her own, softly opened the window, and looked out upon the darkness. For it was an intensely dark night: the moon would not rise for some hours, and, to make it more obscure, there was a heavy bank of clouds to blot out the stars.

Jane listened eagerly, but the soft sighing of the wind through the trees was all she could hear. There was not the faintest rustle beneath her window, and she leaned out as far as she dared, feeling that her only course now was to listen for his coming, and then to whisper him to hurry round to the lobby, where there would be no fear of his being watched, while she spoke to him for a few minutes. That is, if he were watched at all, for a great deal of her alarm might, after all, be due to her own imagination.

Two hours of blank expectation passed, and not a sound had she heard. The stillness was at times even oppressive, and a shuddering feeling of fear again and again made her inclined to close the window, and try to drive away with sleep the troubles that paled her face. Twice over she had ventured to whisper softly his name—the name of the scoundrel whom she was watching there to protect—but there was no answer; and yet she knew that he would come—something seemed even to warn her that he was at hand; so that, when at last she did hear a faint rustling amidst the twigs, and the hard breathing as of some animal, she was in no way startled, but, whispering softly:

"Round by the lobby," she said—"round by the lobby, quick!"

"All right," was the whispered answer; and then, as Jane listened, there came again the rustling, when, with her heart wildly beating, she glided from the room, to stand outside, listening upon the landing.

A False Step

It was one o'clock; the hall time-piece gave a sharp "ting," to proclaim the hour, as Jane looked down over the balustrade, vainly trying to pierce the darkness below. For all was dark in the house, and as far as she could judge, every one was buried in slumber; but she trembled as she passed softly through the corridors, past door after door, beyond each of which some one was sleeping, and in spite of her utmost efforts her dress seemed to rustle loudly. Now and again, too, a board creaked sharply, with a sound that sent a chill through her whole frame. But there was no help for it now, and gliding at length down the grand staircase, she paused by the damaged library door to listen.

All still, but the wind was getting up and beginning to moan round the house, sighing in a way that in her excited state seemed to reproach her, and she stopped, trembling violently.

Why had she not told him to come to the library window? The door would have yielded to her touch, and she could have reached out to speak to him, while now she had to slip bolts and bars, and to turn a key, one and all of which gave forth sounds that seemed to make her blood run cold. Once more she stopped; but summoning her resolution, she proceeded, and the inner lobby door was passed and closed behind her. She stood upon the floor-cloth, listening and trying to pierce the gloom of the great billiard-room to the right, but she could only make out the table, covered with its loose, white dust-cloth. The coats and hats, though, against the wall, looked ghostly, and it was as much as she could do to summon courage to proceed, till, with many a choking sob, she told herself that it was only for his love that she did it, and that she would give him one kiss, and then they would part till he could come back a better man. For weren't they young even yet? She was only twenty-four, and she could wait, for she loved John, after all, with all his failings.

Yes, she loved John; and that thought carried her to the door, and she placed her hand upon the top bolt just as a faint tap sounded upon the little slip of a glass window at the side, when there came a louder gust of wind, telling of the coming storm, and seeming to her excited fancy like a warning.

She hesitated, and stood trembling like one of the leaves without, whose rustling she could plainly hear.

It was only to say good-bye, though, perhaps for many years, and it would be so cruel to let him go without, and besides, it was not wise to tarry, for there was the faint possibility of McCray being on the watch, though this coming round to the other side of the house would, in such a case, perhaps, throw him off the scent.

Again her hand was on the fastenings, and again she paused, listening to the warning voice within her; but a second faint tap roused her, bolt and lock were thrown back, and, with a loud crack, as if remonstrating at being opened at such unholy hours, the door was thrown wide.

The next instant Jane was in Gurdon's arms; her own, too, flung round his neck, and her lips warmly meeting his kisses, as she sobbed wildly and clung to him, thinking of the parting soon to follow.

"Let me shut the door, though," she whispered, disengaging herself after a few minutes.

"No—no," whispered Gurdon, hoarsely, in reply, as he again folded her tightly in his arms. "Leave that as it is; but, tell me, are they all abed?"

"Oh yes, hours ago," she answered; "but you must not stay a minute longer, for I believe McCray saw your footsteps last night, and perhaps he's watching."

"Confound him—yes, he nearly kicked me as he came by," growled Gurdon. "Lucky for him, though, he didn't. But are you sure you've got down unknown to all the girls?"

"Oh yes—certain," was the whispered answer. "And now, John, you'll try, won't you? You will try to keep away from the drink and get on? and— Please don't hold me so tightly."

"Yes, yes—all right. I'll try," he whispered, excitedly—"but be quiet; don't struggle. I'm not going to hurt you, you little fool. There, be quiet!"

Jane's heart beat more violently than ever, and she panted as his arm grasped her more tightly. There was a strange excitement creeping through her frame, she knew not why; but she felt that something was wrong, though no suspicion of what was impending had yet flashed across her mind.

"Tell me quickly," he said now, "has the new butler come?"

"No," she answered, still panting heavily. "Master's been too ill to see about such matters."

"Does any one sleep in the pantry?"

"No," said Jane; "but why do you ask?"

For response Gurdon gave utterance to a low, sharp cough; when, gazing wonderingly at him, as if for explanation of his coldness, a faint rustle fell upon Jane's ears; there was a step outside, and as she started to close the door the blackened faces of two men appeared. A half-uttered groan passed her lips, and a horrible feeling of despair clutched her heart, as at one glance she saw that she had been betrayed, and that the man she loved was a greater scoundrel than she could have believed. It was all plain enough: she had been deluded into admitting an enemy—into playing false to her master; and these men would plunder the house—perhaps murder somebody before they got off with their booty. She thought not of herself; her whole aim now was to alarm the inmates, and as her lips parted she would have uttered a shriek, but that it was too late, for Gurdon's hand was over her mouth, pressing it tightly—almost to suffocation, and the next instant she was thrown upon the floor.

"Make so much as a sound, and one of these men will make an end of you as soon as look at you!" hissed Gurdon, tearing off her apron and thrusting it into her mouth. "Now, then, you proud jade, I've got the better of you this time, drat you; and as soon as we've done, you shall follow where I like. Here, Joe, stop with her, and if she moves, stun her with your preserver. She's my property now. Come along, Harry, this way."

For a few minutes Jane had struggled fiercely, but in vain; a piece of rope was tied tightly round both arms and ankles, and every effort to recover her freedom only resulted in acute pain. There was only one thing open to her, and that was to get to her feet and contrive to fall against the glass door, when she hoped that the crash might alarm the house, or at least be heard by some one. To appeal to Gurdon was, she knew, useless, and for awhile the despair engendered by the thoughts of her misery crushed down every other feeling, but only for a few short moments. Her whole thought directly after was on duty to those whom she felt that she had betrayed, and, taking advantage of her guard's back being turned, she contrived—how, she knew not—to get upon her feet. Another moment, and she would have been at the glass door, when, with a savage oath, the more horrible for being hissed in a low tone, Gurdon stepped back, caught her by her back hair, and dragged her down, at the same time striking her brutally across the face.

Jane moaned feebly, but it was not from pain, but despair at not being able to help others. The despair, though, was driven away, and her dark eyes flashed a fierce resentment as they looked full in Gurdon's, which shrank from the encounter.

"Watch her this time, will you!" he said, brutally. "Hold a knife over her if you like, while I go to the door!"

"Hadn't you best fasten the other first?" growled a companion.

"What, and shut off a way to bolt!" said the other. "No, thanky. Now, Gurdon, look alive; we're wasting time."

"Hold your tongue, will you, with names," growled Gurdon. "Now then, mind the chairs along this passage. No lights, mind—not even a match."

"Here, stay a moment," whispered the other. "This she-wolf will be loose. Drat you—be quiet, will you!"

In effect, with a terrible effort, Jane had freed one of her hands, and was struggling to tear the gag from her mouth, when, as her guard struck at her savagely, there came a dull, heavy crash, and he rolled over upon his side.

Rescue

"Ye maraudin' villin, take that! And there's for ye too, ye deevil!" exclaimed a low, deep voice, and then another heavy, flapping blow was struck; there was a crash, a scuffle, another blow or two, and then came the sound of a heavy fall, succeeded by another, and the crackle of breaking twigs.

"Heaven save us!" ejaculated the newcomer. "There goes half the pots off the stand, and, by all that's good, one of them's gone right amongst the azaleas!"

Then there was a perfect stillness, unbroken even by the night wind, which had lulled once more, when, after listening at the door for a few moments, Alexander McCray, smiling at his opportune arrival and successful exploit, closed the portal, and slipped one of the bolts. Then, taking a box of matches from his pocket, he lit one, and then applied it to a candle in a sconce over the side-table.

"Why, my puir, daft bairn!" he said, tenderly, as he drew the gag from Jane's teeth, and cut the rope which bound her feet. "It's cruel treatment of such a flower. I'd have been here sooner, only I had to go to the tool-shed for a weepun; and it's lucky I did," he said, showing the spade with which he had dealt his blows.

"Oh, McCray!" sobbed Jane, "I'm ruined for ever, and undone!"

"Not you, my wee blossom," cried McCray, stoutly. "You know now what a villin he is, so I won't be ragging his character, seeing that he's done for for ever. An' I won't blame ye a bit, not a wee bit, my sweet lassie," he continued, as he tenderly chafed her swollen wrists. "Ye made a mistake, and trusted a rascal, and not the first poor daft chiel that did, to her cost. But he won't forget the spade of Alexander McCray, of Galashiels, in a hurry, my lassie; and it's all a gude act of Providence that I—"

Sandy stopped short, for he remembered the rabbit.

"It's all gude luck," he continued, "that I happened to hear ye whisper out of the lattice, and then came this morning to rake out the footsteps. I've been watching sin' ten, that I have, and had no chance of warning ye when

I saw the rogue had two to help him. And even then, my lassie, I thought they were only to take care of him, instead of being midnight robbers. But I sune fun them oot."

"Oh, Mr McCray, it was a blessing you came!" sobbed Jane.

"Weel, yes, lassie, I just think it was. But ye'll no foregather with the villin no more, will ye? Ye'll ne'er speak to him again?"

"No, no—oh, never!" groaned Jane.

"That's weel; and I won't judge you for greeting over it all a bit, lassie. Your puir heart's sair now, but it will heal up again, never fear. And now, I won't say ony mair to ye, only recollect, Miss Jenny, I'm an honest man, and I lo'e ye verra dearly."

Mr McCray had been growing somewhat excited as he spoke, and hence more broad in his language; but he cooled down into the matter-of-fact gardener after delivering himself of the above, and took a pinch of snuff to calm his feelings; for he felt that it would be wrong to press his suit with the poor girl while she was in such trouble, and his Scottish dignity was roused. Here was a damsel in distress—and were not the McCrays honourable men, from the time when they all wore plaid and wielded claymore, down to the present day, when their representative followed the pursuit of his forefather Adam?

"Oh, what is to become of me?" sobbed Jane.

"Just nothing at all but an honest man's wife one of these days," said Sandy.

"What shall I do?" cried Jane.

"Just wipe your bright eyes, and don't talk quite so loud," said Sandy.

"Oh, they'll all be down directly," cried Jane.

"Weel, I don't know that," said Sandy. "If any folk had been coming, they'd have been here sooner; so I think as no one knows anything about it but we twain, my lassie, why, ye'd better put oot the candle, and lock the door, and then go up to bed."

"But do you think no one will know?" sobbed Jane.

"That's just what I do think, my lassie; and if ye'll promise me, like a good girl, never to have word again with Mr Jock Gurdon, I'll be up wi' the dawn, and put the damage reet outside, and then nobody'll be a bit the wiser."

"Oh, Mr McCray, how can I ever thank you?" sobbed Jane, catching one of his great hands in hers. "I do promise you, indeed!" And she tried to kiss it.

"Nay—nay, my puir bairn, that's for me to do." And he drew her towards him, and kissed her forehead gently and reverently.

"I'm a great, awkward-looking chid, Jenny Barker, but I've got a man's heart in me. Ye've been sair deceived, and I don't blame ye a bit for being true and faithful to your jo; but, now that's all over, lassie, try and comfort your heart with the thought that there's another man in the world who, while he loves the ground ye tread on, loves ye, too, sae weel, that he won't say word more till he can see that it winna be distasteful to ye. And now, good night, bairn. Let me get my spade, and I'll be off. Keep yer ain counsel, and I'll keep it too; and ye may depend that Jock Gurdon will never say word about it."

With a pleasant, quiet smile upon his broad, honest face, Sandy McCray took his spade and turned to go, when Jane laid her hand upon his arm to detain him.

"What is it, bairn?" said Sandy.

"I'm afraid—" whispered Jane, earnestly.

"Afraid? and why?" asked Sandy.

"Afraid those bad men may be watching for you," whispered Jane.

"Heaven bless ye for that, lassie!" cried McCray, with the tears of pleasure starting into his eyes, as, catching her in his arms, he kissed her heartily. "Ye'll send me away a happier man than I've been for months, seeing that douce-tongued carl hanging round ye. Go to your bed, lassie— go to your bed, and sleep soundly; and I should like to see the face of either of them come within reach of my spade!"

A minute later, and the gardener was listening to the cautious fastening of the door; and then, boldly stepping out on to the lawn, he looked around. But there was, as he had felt, no danger at hand, and soon after he was seated in his cottage, waiting patiently for the dawn, not trusting himself to sleep; and long before another gardener appeared, the last trace of disturbed flower-stand and bed had been removed, so that not another soul at Merland Castle knew of John Gurdon's treachery.

"But I'll e'en keep my eyes wide," said Alexander to himself; "for it strikes me that the rascal may come again."

"Maybe I ought to tell the laird, and put him on his guard, for the bit of siller in the butler's pantry is a sair temptation to a rogue," muttered McCray, as he pondered about the matter; "but I dinna see how I'm going to tell a bit without telling the whole, and getting the lassie into grief. So I'll just say nae word to a soul, but take a leuke round of a neet, and have a peep at the lassie's window as weel, lest the de'il should hang about to try and tempt the puir daughter of Eve to fresh sin. For though she means reet now, the lassie's weak; and though she don't know't, there may yet be a bit of the auld weed in her heart not yet rooted oot; but wait a wee, and I'll have that sweet heart of hers that clean and reet, that it shall blossom again beautifully, and I'd like to see the weed then as would get in."

Sir Murray's Thoughts

It was now an acknowledged fact that there could be no further intimacy between the residents at Castle and Hall. The Nortons led a more than ever secluded life, Mrs Norton finding it necessary to retrench in every possible way to meet their altered circumstances, for the iron company's affairs were worse and worse, and people loudly blamed Norton for his folly. "Why did he not become bankrupt," they said, "as other people would?" But Norton declined all such relief, his brow grew wrinkled and his hair slightly grizzled at the sides, but he was determined to pay to the last penny he could muster, and wait for the change that he trusted would come, for his faith was perfect in his enterprise.

Mrs Norton never complained, but always welcomed him with a smile when he returned from his long absences. Cruel doubts would come at times, brought up, perhaps, by some silly village tattle, but she cast them out with a shudder, as if they were something too loathsome to be harboured even for an instant; and, after such battles with herself, she would greet her husband with increased tenderness, as she strove to chase away the settled melancholy which oppressed him.

Twice only during many months had he encountered Sir Murray Gernon, to meet with fierce, scowling looks of hatred; but no word was spoken, and Philip Norton never knew the curses that were showered upon his head. It was well for him, too, that he did not know that many a night, Marion Gernon, brokenhearted and despairing, knelt by her solitary pillow to say, almost in the words of the old prophet, "It is enough," and to pray that she might pass away.

It was only at times, though, that such despairing thoughts oppressed her; at others she would bewail her wickedness, and pray for strength, as she looked upon the tiny slumbering face of her infant, and then bathed it with tears.

For Lady Gernon's was now a sad and solitary life; Sir Murray seemed to be plunged in some abstruse study, taking his daily ride or walk, but spending the rest of his hours in his library. To the world, and to that lesser one, their household, they were a model couple, dining together regularly, and appearing a little in society, but not much, on account of Lady Gernon's health—so it was said; but Sir Murray, at heart, looked upon wife and child with a hatred that was almost a loathing, and so Lady Gernon's return to convalescence was very slow.

Once—nay, many times—she had clung to her husband beseechingly, her eyes telling her prayer; but she had soon found that such efforts merely irritated him.

"Where is the cross?" he had asked her peevishly, and, upon her weak protest reaching his ears, he had laughed scornfully.

"Lady Gernon," he once said, "had you spoken to me on his behalf—had you told me of his strait—I would have placed thousands in your hands to relieve him. But you have made my life a curse to me."

"But have you no faith?—my words—my solemn asseverations of innocence," sobbed Lady Gernon.

"None!" he said, furiously—"none! I would not believe you were you dying. You have made me a madman, I believe; you have disgraced me in the eyes of the world; and I would have a divorce, but that I will not have the scandal renewed, and in the lips of every idler in the kingdom, the 'Great Lincolnshire Scandal' for a newspaper heading, and endless leading articles upon the gross immorality of the upper classes. Once for all, let this rest. You have gained your title, and you have *aided*—There, I will say no more; I will not descend to coarseness. I was once a man of refinement, and, I believe, generous. Let the past be dead—dead between us for ever. It should have been dead now, but that you try to nurse it into life with your tears. Now leave me. You know my commands; I will have this subject brought up no more!"

"Murray Gernon," said Marion, sadly, "you are in a dream. Some day you will waken."

He did not reply, and she left the room.

As Lady Gernon's strength returned, she had, by slow degrees, taken to her old pursuit; and often she might be seen, basket in hand, laden with specimens, returning from some field or woodland ramble. But, so far, once, and once only, while alone, it had fallen to her lot to encounter Philip Norton, when he turned slowly out of the path, raised his hat, and was gone.

She stood as if unable to proceed for a few minutes, and then walked slowly on; but before night, Sir Murray Gernon knew of the encounter, and fed with it the smouldering fire of his jealousy.

He had not stooped to the meanness before, but now, telling himself it was his duty, he had her watched, finding in one of the servants a willing tool; but his news was always of the most meagre; and growing daily more morose, Sir Murray now gave way to a fresh belief—he felt sure that his wife corresponded with some one at the Hall. At one time he made up his mind to leave the neighbourhood—to return to Como; but he stubbornly decided to the contrary, thinking that it would turn attention to his family affairs. Then he decided to see "that unhappy woman at the Hall," as he termed her, and to enlighten her upon the state of affaire, while, if possible, he would secure her as his coadjutor. He even went so far, during one of Norton's absences, as to ride over; but he repented, and returned home more and more disposed for solitude and misery; for he had almost grown to love his sense of injury, pitying himself, and feeling that he was a martyr, seeing nothing but the past, believing nothing but the evidence of his own eyes, and resolutely shutting himself out from the happiness that might have been his portion.

Suspicion is a ravenous monster, devouring all before it. Matters the most ill-suited often become its food, as the simplest acts of the suspected are magnified into guilt. The feeling grew stronger and stronger every hour that he was being cleverly tricked; but though he waited day after day for the coming enlightenment, it came not.

It must be, then, by night that some arrangement or correspondence was made; and his brow grew blacker, and his head sank upon his breast, as he muttered the thought.

The months had glided by rapidly, when, one night, after a long, gloomy day, he retired to his bedroom—a different chamber to that he had before used—but not to sleep; for, throwing himself upon a low couch, he lay thinking of his present life, and asking his heart what was to be the end?—whether it was possible that a reconciliation would ever take place, and something, if not of happiness, of quiet esteem and smoothness of life-course return?

He could not conceive it possible; it seemed to him then that death alone could be the termination of such a state of being.

It was a gloomy introduction to his thoughts, that word death, and he frowned more heavily as it oppressed him. Should he die himself? The distance was but short, he knew, between here and eternity. But one step, and all would be over: the wretchedness and misery of his life, his torturing suspicions, the great mistake of the past, all swept away in an instant; but then afterwards?

He paused, shuddering, as standing upon the brink, he peered forward into that deep, dark, mysterious, impenetrable gulf of the unknown, shrinking from it, too, for his was not the bold, reckless, daring spirit for such a step. He knew it, too, and again began to find sympathy for himself, condoling and pitying, and telling himself that no man had ever before experienced such suffering as had fallen to his lot. No, he ought not to die: the world at his age ought to be still bright and fair, and ready to offer some goal for his aimless life. He ought not to die, but—

The horrible thought that flashed across his brain made him get up and pace the room hastily, the cold, dank beads of fear gathering themselves upon his brow. He tried to chase out the thought; but he had brooded so long, had given way to such wild phantasms, that it seemed now as if some potent devil were at his ear, whispering temptation, and driving him to the committal of some horrible deed. So strong grew the feeling to his distempered imagination that he commenced muttering half aloud, as if in answer to dictation from an evil prompter.

No, he would not be the first jealous husband who had taken revenge for his wrongs; he had loved her, and been all that it was his duty to be; but he had been betrayed, tricked, and cheated by the false-hearted woman whom he thought he had won. Such a proceeding would be but an act of justice; but the law said such acts should be done by the law alone—that man, however injured, should not arrogate to himself the right to punish, hence it must be done secretly, by some cunning device that should blind men's eyes to the truth, and while amply bringing down retribution on the heads of the guilty, his honour should be unstained, the family shield untarnished.

But would not such a step be cold, blackhearted, premeditated murder? The question seemed to flash across his brain as if prompted by some better angel.

No: only justice, was whispered again to his ear—only justice, and then he would be at rest. It was not right that he should die, but the destroyer of his happiness; and then his mind would be at ease—there would be peace for him for many years to come.

He smiled now: it was like comfort in a dire hour of need; and when the upbraidings of conscience would have made themselves heard, they were crushed down and stifled; for Sir Murray Gernon had been keeping his house swept and garnished for the reception of the wicked spirits, and they had now fully seized upon the offered abode. He smiled, for he thought that he now saw a way out of his difficulties, and that he had but to design some means for removing his false wife from his path to commence a new life.

How should it be? he thought. Should he contrive a boating party upon the great lake? Boats had before now been upset, and their occupants drowned. Such accidents were not at all uncommon. Or there might be some terrible catastrophe with the spirited horses of the carriage; the part of the Castle where her ladyship slept might catch fire at a time when a hampered lock and fastened window precluded escape; or, better still, there was poison!

The evil spirit must at that time have had full possession of the citadel, for it was with a baleful glare in his eyes that Sir Murray Gernon strode up and down his room, stepping softly, as if fearing to interrupt the current of his thoughts—thoughts that, in his madness, seemed to refresh the thirsty aridity of his soul. After all these months of misery, had at last, then, come the solution of his difficulty? and he laughed—and laughed savagely—as he sat down once more to plan.

Mercy? What had he to do with mercy? What mercy had they had upon his life? Had they not blighted it when he was a calm, trusting, loving man, searing his spirit with something more burning and corroding than the hottest iron—the sharpest acid? Let them seek for mercy elsewhere: his duty was to dispense justice, and he would be just!

Who could gainsay it? Was it not written in the Book that the punishment for the crime was death—that the sinners should be stoned with stones until they died? Not that he would stone them: his should be a quiet, insidious vengeance—one that the world should not suspect, and he would plot it out in time.

But what if she were, after all, innocent?

He tore that thought from his heart, accusing himself of cowardice, and of seeking a way out of what would be the path to a new life. No; there was no innocence there. His would be a crusade against guilt; and he vowed a fearful vow that he would carry out his vengeance to the end.

Should it be by poison?

"Tap! tap! tap!" Three distinct, sharp touches as of a nail upon the window-pane made Sir Murray start, shivering, from his guilty reverie.

What was that? Some ghostly warning for or against his plots?—or was he so distempered by his broodings that this was but the coining of imagination?

"*Tap! tap! tap!*"

There it was again, and for a moment a strange sense of terror pervaded him, and he could not stir. But only for a moment; the next minute a feeling of grim satisfaction prevailed. This, then, was to be a night of enlightenment— here was a new revelation—this, then, was the means of communication? Evidently some mistake of the bearer, and he had but to go to the window, stretch forth his hand, and take a letter; or—the thought sent a thrill through him as he stepped forward—was it the keeping of an assignation? The window was many feet above the ground, and if he dashed back the ladder—

He paused, for there was the slight darkening of the blind as if a shadow were passing over it, and now, half-mad with rage, Sir Murray Gernon felt that all his suspicions were confirmed, as, springing forward, he tore the blind aside, just as again, loudly and distinctly, came the blows upon the glass.

Nocturnal

"Perhaps, after all, it's just as weel that he did not come," mused Alexander McCray, as he stood one morning upon the long wooden bridge which connected, at the narrowest part, the two shores of the fine piece of water lying between the park of Merland Castle and the pleasure-grounds. He was leaning over the rail, and gazing down into the clear depths below, where, screened by the broad leaves of the water-lilies, which here and there bore some sweet white chalice, the huge carp were floating lazily, now and then giving a flip with their broad tails to send themselves a few feet through the limpid medium in which they dwelt.

"Perhaps, after all, it's just as weel that he did not come any more, but if he had, I would have pitched him in here as freely as have looked at him, and he wouldn't have hurt neither—a bad chiel. Them that's born to be hanged will never be drowned, and he'll come to the gallows sure enough, and deserves it, too, for ill-using that poor bairn as he did."

"Weel, this winna do," he said, starting from his reverie, and shouldering the broom with which he had been sweeping the bridge. "I'll just e'en go and do the paths under the bedroom windows; the lassie might happen to give a look out."

The gardener walked on, thoughtfully gazing up at the windows, and thinking the while of the nights when he had watchfully made his way, stealthy as a burglar, from bush to bush, or crouched beneath the shrubs. Few nights had passed without his seeing Jane Barker's light extinguished, but there had been no further visit from John Gurdon.

"He didn't like the flat of my spade," said McCray, with a grin, and this seemed to be the case—the ex-butler never from that night having been heard of. Still, more now from habit than anything, the gardener continued his nocturnal rounds, telling himself that he could not sleep without one peep at the lassie's window before going to bed.

But Alexander McCray seemed to make but little progress in his love affairs. Whenever he met Jane she had always a pleasant smile for him, but he knew in his heart that it was not the smile he wished to see.

"But bide a wee," he said. "Her puir heart's sair. Wait awhile and it will all come reet."

The gardener was favoured that morning, for as he applied his broom lightly here and there to the wandering leaves, the early ones of autumn, he heard a window, above his head, thrown open, and as he looked up, there was Jane leaning out, ready to smile and nod down to him.

"Company coming, lassie?" said McCray, leaning upon his broom.

"Company? No, Mr McCray," said Jane; "why did you think so?"

"Because ye're getting ready the best bedroom," said the gardener.

"Oh dear, no," said Jane; "we shall never have company here again, I think. I'm only having this put ready for Sir Murray himself, because some of the old plaster ceiling of his own room's come down."

"Puir lad! he looks bad," said McCray.

"And serve him right, too," said Jane, defiantly. "I haven't patience with him."

"Nay, lassie, perhaps not," said McCray. "But ye've plenty of patience with them as is waur."

"Please don't talk about that," said Jane, pleadingly.

"Nay, lassie, then I winna," said McCray, sadly; "but be patient mysel', if it's for twenty long years ere ye turn to me."

Jane leaned out, giving the gardener one long earnest gaze, such a one as made his heart beat more freely, but the coming steps of some one along a neighbouring path sent Jane to her work, and McCray's broom rustling over gravel and leaf.

Before many seconds had passed Lady Gernon came by, very pale and thoughtful. She had a basket in her hand, and, evidently bent upon some expedition, she made her way through the ring fence, and away across the park, neither looking to the right nor left.

"Siller and titles are nice things," mused McCray; "but they don't seem to make yon puir creature happy."

McCray swept as he thought, and thought as he swept. Jane did not again appear at the window, and if she had done so, the opening of one in the lower range would have kept him from speaking to her, while, as he swept on and on, hunting out errant leaves from the hiding-places where they were waiting for a bit of fun with the wind, he became conscious of the dark, lowering face of Sir Murray, apparently watching the progress of his lady from the side of the house where he now was.

"He's a puir, miserable sort of chiel," muttered the gardener; "he seems to want a rousing up. It's my belief that a few hours' trenching a day wi' a good broad spade wad do him a world of good. He eats too much, and he drinks too much; but I'm sorry for him, puir lad—I'm sorry for him!"

That night Alexander McCray sat in his little room, thoroughly enjoying himself, for he was so elated with the glance Jane had that morning bestowed upon him, that he had treated himself to a pipe and a small tumbler of whisky and water, over which he sat smiling and happy, for it struck him that he had at last got in the thin edge of the wedge, and that the future would all be plain sailing.

"And she's as good a woman as ever the sun shone on," said Sandy at last, as, after draining the last drop from his tumbler of whisky and water, and trying in vain to ignite the ashes at the bottom of his pipe, he tapped the bowl upon the bar, and then stood up to think.

Should he?—shouldn't he? The night was dark and gusty, and he had sat thinking till it was long past twelve. There was nothing to go for, and the lassie's light might be out, and she fast asleep in bed long enough before; but then he would have the satisfaction of knowing that all was right, and for months past now he had not missed a night. He did not think he would go, though, for it was evident now that Jane was beginning to think a little of his words, and no doubt matters would soon brighten up and be settled. No, he would not go to-night—there was no need; and upon the strength of that resolution he took off his coat, and methodically hung it behind the door. Then out came his snuff-box, when a pinch or two seemed to drive away the happy ease engendered by the whisky and water, clearing his brain, and forcing him to think of the realities of life.

"No," he thought now, "it would not be right to give up what he had taught himself was a duty. How did he know but what, after all, that John Gurdon might come back that very night, and put back in a few moments what it had taken him months to erase?"

"I'll go," said Sandy, "if its only for the name of the thing. I mean to win the lassie if leaving no stone unturned will do it; and now, here's a little wee bit of crag lying in my way, and I'm too idle to touch it. Sandy McCray, take your cap, mon, and go and do your duty. It's the little tiny cracks that open out into big splits, so stop them up when they're small. Keep your trees pruned back, my lad, or they'll grow wild and ragged; and whenever ye feel a weed coming up in your nature, pull him up direct. This bit of wanting to stop away is a weed, lad, so pull it up at once."

Sandy McCray must have taken it out by the very roots, for the next minute he had closed his door, and was stealthily walking over the grass towards the pleasure-grounds.

There was not a step of the way that was not familiar, and on the darkest night he could have avoided every flower-bed, as if by instinct, or even have made his way blindfold; hence he had soon crossed the bridge, and walked softly on towards the great lawn, noting, as he went, that there was not a single light visible in the great mansion.

"I'll just go the length of the place, and then stop for a moment by the lassie's window, and home again," muttered McCray, and then he stopped short, for a hand was laid upon his shoulder, and a voice whispered in his ear:

"Stay here a few minutes, Joe. He's gone to have a look up at the back windows, and I'll go this side. Don't move, because it's so confoundedly dark!"

McCray felt the next minute, rather than saw, that he was alone. His breath came thickly, and his heart beat fast, as, wiping the sweat from his forehead, he bent down and ran softly over the grass to the edge of the lawn, leaped the gravel walk so as to land upon the other side, and then, softly creeping amongst the bushes, he hurried towards where Jane's window looked down, a strange beating at his temples, and an aching void at his heart.

"And only to think," he muttered, "me sitting drinking mysel' drunk, and all the while the spoiler coming after my little ewe lamb."

But Sandy's spirits rose as he cautiously crept up, to find that Jane's window was closed; he could just distinguish that from the faint glimmering of the glass. The robbers would gain no entrance, then, there; upon that point he could feel happy, and, with a weight removed from his mind, he stood thinking of what he should do.

He did not for a moment entertain a doubt but that it was Gurdon and his friends come back at last, perhaps ready to force an entrance, and open to murder as well as to rob. But Sandy's heart was glad within him—his lassie was free of all complicity; and if they got at her now, it should only be over his strong body. But he felt that there was no fear of Jane being again deceived; the last occasion had been too plain an unveiling of John Gurdon's character; so, hastily making up his mind as to his proceedings, he crept from amongst the bushes on his hands and knees, and set himself to try and discover where the nocturnal visitors now were, previously to taking further steps to baffle their plot.

The gardener had not long to seek, for before he had advanced far, a faint whispering told him where the enemy lay, while at the same moment the snap of a fastening and the gliding up of a window told him that an entrance had been effected.

The Burglary

"The de'ils ha been quick about it," muttered Sandy; "and they've gone through the libr'y window, while, if that door I broke open has been mended again, it's a strange thing to me. What shall I do?—ring them all up? No," he said, after a pause; "then perhaps we shouldn't catch them, for before I could get round again from the bell, they'd have slipped out of the window. No, we must catch them, for it strikes me verra strongly that if this is Mr Jock Gurdon, I should like to see him transported to the other side of the watter."

For a few moments Sandy McCray stood thoughtful and puzzling what to do. He could easily have alarmed the burglars, for such they evidently were; but then that was not sufficient—there must be a capture made. But suddenly a bright thought struck him—he would run round to the butler's pantry, and try and rouse whoever slept there. But did any one sleep there? Gurdon's place had never been filled up, and it was most likely that the footman and under-butler still kept their places in the hall.

"I have it," muttered Sandy, at last; and setting off across the lawn at a brisk trot, he made his way to the kitchen-garden, but what he sought was not there, of course not: it was round by the potting shed, he recollected then; and on cautiously proceeding there, he picked up from where it lay beside a wall a twenty-round light garden ladder, and set off with it to the front of the house, where he had spoken to Jane that morning.

"One—two—three—four; that's the window," muttered Sandy, and the next instant, exerting his great strength, he raised the ladder and rested the top against the window sill.

Fortunately, the window entered so quickly by the burglars was on the other side of the house, and the gardener was able to take his steps for giving an alarm unheard by them.

"Gude save us!" he muttered, climbing up. "I hope he winna shute me!"

The next minute he listened attentively, and then gave three sharp taps upon one pane, followed by two other similar signals, ere the blind was dragged back, the window thrown open, and Sir Murray's hands were tightly grasping his throat.

"Hoot awa' Sir Mooray, and tak' awa' ye're hands from a man's weam."

"Hand over the letter, you scoundrel, or I'll hurl you down!" exclaimed Sir Murray, through his teeth.

"The duel's been sleeping in his clothes, and gone half daft," muttered Sandy. And then, in a whisper: "Let me in, Sir Mooray, and look sharp, for there are burglars in the house!"

The gardener's announcement seemed to bring his master to his right senses, and, loosing his hold, Sandy stepped lightly into the chamber.

"You'll just have a pair of pistols, or dirk, or something, Sir Mooray," said the man.

His master stepped to a drawer, and drew out a small double-barrelled pair, examined the nipples to see if they were capped, and then handed one to his servant, but the latter shook his head.

"Na—na," he said; "I might be blowing his brains out with the thing, and I dinna wush that. I'll take the poker, Sir Mooray; and now, if ye're ready, the sooner we're at them the better."

"Ring the alarm-bell!" said Murray.

"Nay, nay, gude sir; let's take them ourselves. Stop the hole up where they come in, and then we can ring if ye like; but while we're ringing bells they'll be off, and only to come again."

Giving up the leadership to his servant, Sir Murray followed him into the corridor, and from thence to the grand staircase, but all was still. Hastily descending to the library, the unrepaired door was found—like the window—wide open, when Sandy's first step was to close both carefully, and then rejoin his master.

"Heard anything, sir?" he whispered.

"Not a sound," said Sir Murray, hoarsely; "but, do you think they are burglars? Stay here an instant, while I ascend to her ladyship's room," he said, hurriedly, as a thought—a base, suspicious thought of a meditated elopement—crossed his mind. "They may have gone that way."

"Hoot, mon, stay where ye are," whispered Sandy. "D'ye hear that? They're packing up the plate, and—hist! look there," he said, in a low tone, as a faint light shone in the distance on their right, making plain the face of a man standing in the second of the suite of drawing-rooms, the doors of which had been set wide open.

Sandy recognised the face at the same instant as Sir Murray, and the same name rose to their lips, McCray muttering fiercely:

"Stop ye here, Sir Mooray, and lay hold of the de'ils taking the plate. They winna face yer pistols. I'll deal with this one."

Thrusting his master aside, McCray stepped lightly over the soft carpets, followed for a few seconds by the baronet's eyes, but the light then faded away, and as Sir Murray stood, now breathing hard and excited, as he felt that it was indeed a burglary in progress, he heard a muttered oath, the crashing over of a set of fire-irons, the heavy sounds of blows, and knocking down of furniture, followed directly after by a rapid rush, and he felt himself dashed to the ground, one pistol exploding as he fell; but he was up again the next moment, to be knocked down with greater violence than before, as a Scotch oath rang in his ear; and then, at the same instant, there was a crash and splintering of glass, and as he rose to his feet, he became aware that those who had knocked him down had gone through the library and leapt boldly through the closed window, the night wind now coming with a loud sigh through the shivered panes.

"The scoundrel has escaped, and the other gone in pursuit," muttered Sir Murray, just as loud shrieks for help were heard from above-stairs, followed by the loud ringing of the alarm-bell.

The next minute lights were held over the balustrade, and timid faces were seen, gazing down; but the lights also revealed to Sir Murray's gaze the crape-veiled features of two men, each bearing a bag, which now, upon finding that they were discovered, they dropped, with a loud, jingling noise, upon the stone floor—a sound which told plainly enough of their contents.

"Stand!" cried Sir Murray, as they turned to flee down the long passage up which they had come—a passage leading to the pantry—"stand, or I fire! I cannot miss you at this distance!"

One of the men uttered an oath, in his rage, for now a light appeared at the other end of the passage, showing a footman, armed with a blunderbuss, which seemed to alarm him as much as it did the burglars.

"It's no go," muttered one of the men. "Stow that, gov'nor, and I'll give up. Come on, Joe."

"Not I," exclaimed the other, making a spring to get by Sir Murray, but in vain: true to his word, the baronet fired, and with a shriek of agony, the man sprang into the air, and then fell heavily upon the stone floor, which was soon stained with his blood.

"Why didn't you give up, then, like a man?" whined his sympathising companion, who was now hastily secured by two of the men-servants. "The gent wouldn't have hurt yer, if yer had only give up when he arst. There, don't pull a cove about like that, and yer needn't tie so tight. I ain't agoin' to run away so as to get shot, I can tell you."

"Lift the other up," said Sir Murray, hoarsely; when the man was found to be bleeding profusely, though evidently not wounded in a vital spot.

"You are not hurt, Murray?" whispered a voice at his ear just then, and the baronet turned to find Lady Gernon anxiously scanning his face.

"No; not dead yet," he said, brutally. "Go to your own room."

Lady Gernon turned away with a weary sigh, and Sir Murray stood guard over his prisoners, when a shudder of terror ran through the party assembled; for, faintly heard, apparently from somewhere in the grounds, came what sounded like a wild appeal for help.

A Rival Embrace

Sir Murray Gernon was right in his surmise, for when McCray, eager to secure the person of his supposed rival, hurried across the drawing-room, and in the darkness made a bound to where he had seen the lighted match fade out, his enemy had made a slight movement, so that he failed to obtain a good hold; and in the brief struggle which ensued close to the fireplace, McCray was thrown heavily upon the floor, and his adversary dashed through the drawing-room out into the hall, striking down Sir Murray in his effort to reach the library. But McCray was after him directly, and had no hesitation in leaving his master where he, too, had knocked him down; while, following the burglars example, he leaped, in his excitement, right through the broken window.

"Oh, my best pelargoniums!" groaned the gardener, as he picked himself up, after coming down crash into a flower-bed beneath the window. "Ye shall pay for this, though, Maister Gurdon, or my name's not Sandy McCray!" And then, favoured by a break in the clouds, he caught sight of Gurdon running rapidly towards the bridge.

"Ye'll not get there first, laddie," muttered the Scot, as, exerting all his powers, he dashed over the lawn, to cut off his quarry's retreat in that direction; and being the lustier man of the two, he soon had the satisfaction of seeing his foe double, and run along the brink of the lake, as if to get round the house; for it was growing each moment lighter, the wind springing up, and sweeping the heavy curtain of clouds from the face of the heavens.

"If ye think I canna rin ye doon, Jock Gurdon," muttered McCray, "ye're making a meestake. I'll have ye, if I rin for a week!"

He pressed on, gaining so fast upon the burglar, that he once more doubled, and dodging round a thick plantation of shrubs, McCray was, for a minute, thrown off the scent; but his shrewd Scottish nature stood him in good stead.

"He'll make again for the bridge," he thought; and with a grim smile of determination upon his face, he ran in that direction; but, to his great disappointment, he seemed to be at fault, for there was no sign anywhere of the fugitive. But, for all that, Sandy's idea was correct, as he found, after harking backwards and forwards two or three times. Gurdon—for it was indeed he who had, with his companions, attempted the burglary—had been making his way for the bridge, when his ear, sharpened by fright, told him that his enemy was coming in the same direction, and he directly crouched amidst a bed of laurels, to wait, panting, for an opportunity to escape. He knew that transportation must be his fate if taken; and that if, in revenge, he said anything respecting the character of Lady Gernon, it would merely be taken as the calumny of a discharged servant. No, he thought, he must not be taken—he could not afford yet to give up his liberty.

His breath came more freely at the end of a minute, for his heart had been labouring heavily. Wasted by drink and debauchery, he was in no training for such violent effort; and he was beginning to hope that an opportunity might yet offer for his reaching the bridge, and escaping through the park— the other way by the village he dared not try—when, with a rush, McCray came right through the thicket where he crouched; and, like a hare roused from its form, away he darted, and the pursuit commenced anew.

There was no hiding now: there was too much light, and pursuer and pursued were too close together. Making almost frantic efforts to get away, after dodging and doubling again and again, to the great injury of McCray's long legs, which, when at speed, carried him again and again past his foe, Gurdon made a feint or two and then dashed fiercely for the bridge once more.

"If I'd only got one of those powdered loons to stop his gait there," muttered McCray; and he made a furious effort, nearly catching his prey, and completely cutting off his retreat, for as the Scot shot by him, Gurdon doubled again, and ran along the lake, but only for a little way. There was a bend there, and the water was on both sides of him as he ran along the tongue of land: he must either face his enemy in another rush for the bridge, or take to the black water, gleaming below him.

But Gurdon had, to his cost, always been a hater of the limpid element, and, turning now like a beast at bay, he dashed, with clenched fists, at the gardener, intending to fell him, and then rush on for liberty. But he did not know his man: as he came down, with a fierce charge, McCray merely leaned a little on one side so as to avoid the blow, and the next instant his arms were wreathed tightly round the ex-butler's body, and the two were struggling furiously upon the turf, rolling over and over, their muttered ejaculations and execrations mingling in a fierce growl as of two savage beasts of prey.

"Ah! would ye?" exclaimed McCray, at last. "Ye murderous-minded villin, would ye use a knife? Take that—and that, and—Save us, we shall be—"

McCray's ejaculation was suddenly brought to an end, for in the fierce struggle made for the possession of the knife Gurdon had managed to draw and open, at a time when the gardener thought him about to succumb, they had, unnoticed, drawn nearer and nearer to the edge of the lake, and, perhaps to the saving then of the Scotchman's life, suddenly plunged together into one of the deepest parts.

Gurdon dropped the knife as he rose to the surface, and, loosing his grasp of his pursuer, he struggled furiously to reach the bank; but McCray's northern blood was up to a heat so fierce, that the water seemed only to make it hiss furiously instead of quenching his ardour, and he held on to his adversary like a bull-dog, when, with the fear of drowning before him, Gurdon uttered the wild appealing cry for help that had been heard at the Castle, and turned once more to struggle with his foe.

Once again only, as his head was above water, did Gurdon shriek, giving utterance to a yell of horror that was hardly human, for the feeling was strong upon him now, as they struggled farther and farther from the shore, that the gardener was trying to drown him. But no such thought was in McCray's breast: his determination was to make a capture, and, unlike his enemy, a capital swimmer, the water had no terrors for him. Every one of Gurdon's efforts was interpreted to mean escape, and, heedless of the peril and suffocation, the struggle was continued, the water being lashed into foam, till, at last, McCray, as they rose to the surface after a long immersion, awoke to the fact that his quarry was nearly exhausted, and that they were in deadly peril; for Gurdon's arms were clutched round him in a deadly grip that there was no undoing. They were far from the bank, and, in the rapid glance he took around, he knew that they were in about twelve feet of water.

"There'll be something for the big pike to go at, if it does come to it," thought McCray, with a grim feeling of despair; "but, anyhow, he'll trouble the puir lassie nae mair."

The water, bubbling round his lips, checked McCray's thoughts for a few moments, or rather gave them a new direction; but rising once more to the surface, with one arm at liberty, he struck out fiercely, to keep himself afloat.

"If I could get to the bridge-piles!" he thought, as through the darkness he could dimly make out the little green, slimy pier, not many yards from him. "Gude help me! I dinna want to die yet!"

He fought on for his life, beating the strangling water from his lips, and tearing furiously to reach the pile, where, perhaps, he might be able to hold on till help came. Once, through the darkness, he heard voices, and caught a glimpse of a light dancing about; but the next moment the water was thundering in his ears, and its blackness seemed to blot out all vision.

Another few moments of strangling horror, and he had once more fought his way to the surface; but he was yards away from the bridge-piles, and a feeling now of despair came upon him, dulling his tired faculties, and seeming to warn him that all was over. There was no help that he could see near at hand, for the servants with Sir Murray Gernon did not seem to know which direction to take. It seemed so hard, too, just as he had begun to feel hopeful about his love, to be dragged down by their common enemy to the depths of the lake; and at last, as he felt the water closing over him, he gave another fierce struggle, forcing himself up an instant, till he had uttered the hoarse, harsh, despairing cry of a dying man—dying in the hour of his full strength—and then there were a few bubbles and rings upon the surface of the water, where, locked still in their deadly embrace, the rivals had gone down.

The Helping Hand

Mrs Norton had gone to her rest that night in tears, for her husband had been absent for some days. His restlessness seemed of late to have been largely on the increase, so that when he was at home she was kept upon a tremble of expectation lest at any time he might be gone. True, he was always quiet and gentle, and proud as ever of his boy; but the proximity of the Gernons was like a cloud over him, and as she determinedly drove away the suspicions that would try to fasten upon her, Ada Norton could not but own to herself that while the Gernons were at the Castle, or they themselves stayed at the Hall, there could be no real happiness for her. She knew well enough how it preyed upon her husband's spirits, when, from time to time, rumours of the state of affairs reached them. She had hoped that a reconciliation would long ere this have taken place—that is to say, between husband and wife; but the fact of their complete estrangement, taken in connection with Sir Murray's character, and Captain Norton's strange, reserved behaviour, always seemed to be the hold by which doubt tried again and again to fasten upon her.

Philip Norton came not that night, and Mrs Norton lay weakly weeping, determined in her own mind that, in spite of their poverty, she would try and persuade him to leave the Hall—to go anywhere, so that they might but keep together. She knew that, on account of his connection with the mines, it would be useless to endeavour to get him to move to a distance; but even a few miles farther away would, she felt, bring them more peace; of that she felt assured, telling herself that her husband's frequent absences now were caused by a desire to be away from the place.

But Ada Norton was wrong when, in despair, she gave herself up that night to tears, for her husband was on his way back—at least, he had determined upon sleeping that night at home. He had reached the town rather late, low-spirited and disheartened at the state of his affairs, and had walked towards the primitive inn, meaning to hire a dog-cart and drive over, for months had elapsed since he had sold his own horses, dismissed his groom, and made other reductions in his little establishment. He hired no dog-cart, however, for the state of his finances struck him; and, sturdily preparing himself for the task, he set off to walk the ten miles between him and Merland Hall.

The lonely road seemed well fitted for contemplation, and the thoughts which passed through his breast were many, but none so serious as those which oppressed him when, tired with his long journey, he approached the palings which skirted the park of Merland Castle, stopping at length, in spite of himself, to look over at the nearest point to the house, and gaze long and earnestly at the windows, when suddenly a wild, appealing cry for help smote his ear.

For a moment he paused. Then the cry rang out again, apparently from the direction of the lake—a cry that there was no mistaking, telling, as it did, of a soul in mortal peril; and, heedless of consequence, of the trespass he was committing, and of the relations existing between Sir Murray and himself, he leaped over the palings, and ran in the direction of the sounds.

Naturally his was too generous a spirit to refuse help in need, while now his senses were disturbed by an undefined state of dread, for in some way it seemed that this cry must be connected with Lady Gernon, and once a fearful idea flashed across his mind.

What and if, in utter despair, she had—

He could not finish the thought, but shudderingly dashed on, in a headlong career, till he reached the lake, when he could just make out the splashing and panting in the water.

All was plain enough now: some one was drowning near to the bridge, but more towards the side next the house, while he was in the park.

He would have dashed in upon the instant, but his good sense told him that his plan should be to run along the brink to the bridge, which he did with all the speed he could command, when, divesting himself of coat, vest, and hat, he threw them on the railing, tearing his sleeve, as he hurriedly dragged it off, his every nerve stirred, as from beneath him arose McCray's wild and despairing cry. The next instant, though, Norton had climbed the railing, heedless that he swept his garments into the lake, and then, standing upon a portion of the woodwork, he gazed down at the black water for a few moments, striving to make out the centre of the fast-fading rings, before, with a plunge, he cut the air, divided the waters, and disappeared.

In a few moments he was again on the surface, swimming round, and preparing to dive again, feeling that he had come too late, and that in the darkness it was impossible to render aid, when, within a yard of where he was swimming, and seen but for an instant, the fingers and a portion of a clutching hand were visible above the surface, and ere they could sink far, Norton had grasped them in his hand. The next minute he had avoided a dangerous embrace, and was striking out for the nearest point, the slippery piles of the bridge, where, if he could swim so far with his burden, he could, perhaps, hold up the drowning man till assistance came.

It was a hard task, but Norton was a bold and strong swimmer, and before long he was grasping at the slimy woodwork, to slip back again and again; but, at last, he managed to get one arm over a cross-piece, and his legs twined round an upright, while with his disengaged arm he did all that he could under the circumstances—held the heads of the men above water.

To his great joy he now heard voices, and saw a light moving about in the grounds, when, shouting loudly, he saw a hurried movement of the light, and two or three more cries brought the seekers in the right direction.

"Quick, men—quick!" he cried, as some one ran up, and held down the light, while others clustered round on the bank.

"Fetch the boat up," cried Sir Murray; and his voice sent a thrill through Norton's frame, as he felt that he would have to face him. But he was too much exhausted by his exertions to think much of the threatened encounter. He knew he could hold out but a few minutes longer, and he once more called to them to hasten.

"Who is it? What have you got there?" cried the man with the light.

"Two drowning men," was the hoarse reply; "and I can hold on but a few minutes longer."

But now came the plash plash of oars, and in a very short time the boat was by the bridge—a small pleasure-boat, into which, with great difficulty, the two men, still tightly locked together, were dragged.

"We can't take you this time very well," said one of the grooms, who was in the boat.

"Yes—yes," said another, "we must manage him somehow."

"I can wait till you return," said Norton quietly, for, relieved of his burden, he was able to stretch first one, and then another, cramped limb, and besides, now that he had a little time for thought, the peculiarity of his position struck him. From the scattered words let fall by the servants, he had learned that an attempt had been made to rob the Castle, and that one, if not both the men he had rescued must be connected with the attempt. But, while setting aside as absurd the idea that he could in any way be connected with the matter, he was troubled about the light in which Sir Murray's distempered mind would view his presence in the park at such an hour, and he watched, with no little anxiety, the putting off of the boat.

The man with the lanthorn still kept to the bank, and the bridge remained deserted; so, after a few moments' thought, Philip Norton took a firm hold of one of the cross-pieces of wood, drew himself safely up from the water, and then, all dripping as he was, he climbed the pier till he could reach the railings, and step over. Then, after a little search, he found his hat, but his coat and vest, which he had left hanging upon the rail, were, as we have seen, floating below, upon the surface of the lake.

Meanwhile, his suspicious nature charged, as it were, with so much inflammable matter, ready to blaze up at the contact of the slightest spark, Sir Murray Gernon stood on the bank, waiting the return of the boat. He had heard plainly enough the voice calling for help, and felt sure that he recognised it. Hence, then, he watched eagerly the return of the little skiff, from out of which were lifted the apparently lifeless bodies of McCray and Gurdon.

"The villain! I half suspected him," exclaimed Sir Murray, as he had the lanthorn held down, and recognised in the first the lineaments of his late butler. "But quick—back, and bring off the other. Who was it, do you know?"

"Couldn't tell, Sir Murray," said the groom in the boat. "Seemed to know the voice, too."

"Back at once, then," said the baronet, his brow knitting as he tried to solve this new riddle; for if it were, as he so strongly suspected, Captain Norton, what was he doing in the park at that time of night? Lady Gernon had made her appearance, dressed, when there was the alarm in the house.

For a few moments the rush of blood to his head seemed to blind him, and his knees shook, for he fancied that he was about to have another seizure. But he recovered himself in a few moments, and again took up the train of thought. John Gurdon—burglarious entry—Norton apparently in league with him, and ready to try and save his life. What did it all mean? Was Norton a greater scoundrel even than he had given him the credit of being, and was this some new plot for aggrandising himself at the weak husband's expense? If so, who were mixed up in it?

He staggered again, as the blood flew to his head, in his vain endeavours to piece together the scraps of the puzzle, so as to make a defined whole. But once more, with an effort, he shook off the weakness, and, stooping down, he scooped up some water in the hollow of his hand, and bathed his face, for he was now alone, the servants who had accompanied him having borne the two insensible men to the house.

The next minute the boat returned, and her prow struck the bank.

"Well?" said Sir Murray, eagerly, for the men were alone.

"He's gone, sir," said the groom, solemnly. "The piles are very slippery, and the poor fellow, whoever he was, could hold on no longer. We've been feeling about with the sculls, but we can't find him."

Again that rushing of blood to the head and the choking sensation, and Sir Murray Gernon gasped for air, as he staggered about like a drunken man.

Could it be possible? Was it Norton, and was he removed from his path?—removed by his own act while engaged in some nefarious scheme?

For a few moments a strange sense of mingled exultation and horror oppressed the baronet, and he stood staring vacantly in the faces of his servants.

Would he like them to go and try again? though, as the water was so deep, there was not much chance of finding the poor fellow till morning.

Yes, he would like them to go; and he would come with them himself; and, entering the boat, Sir Murray made the weary men row on and on, backwards and forwards, through the two openings of the wooden bridge, as, armed himself with the weed-grapnel in the prow, he dragged it over the same ground again and again, expecting at each check it received that it was hooked in the body of the man whom he looked upon as the blight of his existence.

At length, the men being completely worn out, the search was given up till daylight, and Sir Murray returned to the Castle, to find McCray sitting up in bed with a blanket round him, sipping whisky and water, hot and strong.

"Gude sake, Sir Mooray!" he exclaimed, as his master entered. "We won the day. I ken a' aboot it—how ye shot one and took the ither; and Jock Gurdon's coming round—the villin!—and no more dead than I am. But it had got verra close to the end, Sir Mooray."

"My brave fellow!" exclaimed his master—"you did nobly."

"Hoot! just naething at a', Sir Mooray. But winna ye try the whuskee?"

"No, my good fellow. But I don't know how I am to reward you."

"Hoot! then, Sir Mooray, I'll just tell ye," said the Scot, whose eye was even now on the main chance. "Tam Wilkins is a gude servant, but he's auld, and past the gairden. Suppose ye mak' me head-gairdener, and give Jenny Barker a hint that she'd better marry me as soon as we've transported Jock Gurdon."

"My good fellow, I'll stand your friend, depend upon it," said the baronet, smiling in spite of himself. But the next moment he frowned heavily, as he said, in a low voice: "Do you know who it was that saved you?"

"No, Sir Mooray, unless it was one of the lads in the bit skiff. But this is rare whuskee, Sir Mooray!"

Sir Murray frowned more deeply before speaking again.

"Did you see any one with the villain you so nobly captured? Though how you came to suspect the attack I don't know."

"Not a soul; only the two ye've taken, Sir Mooray," said Sandy, reddening, perhaps from the effect of the whisky. "And as to suspecting, I have no suspicion in me; but I jist like to see of a night that naebody's after the grapes or bit of wall-fruit, for Tam Wilkins is getting past minding it."

There was nothing more to be learned here, and, day breaking soon after, Sir Murray summoned two more of his men—a couple who had not been so harassed—and proceeded once more to drag the lake, more assistance and better implements being at the same time sent for.

But first he had himself rowed carefully over the water, peering down as he went, but the dragging had fouled the lake, so that this was soon given up as useless, and Sir Murray was about once more to lower the grapnel, when one of the men pointed out, with scared face, what appeared to be the body of a man floating at a short distance.

To reach the spot took but a few moments, and one of the men reached over to draw in a coat and vest, saturated, so that it was a wonder they could have floated.

"His clothes, Sir Murray," said the man, lifting up the coat, when, from the breast, a packet of letters fell out, the directions blurred with the action of the water; but on two of them plainly enough could still be read:

Captain Norton,
Merland Hall.

Gurdon's Lot

"Let the lake be dragged until the body is found," said Sir Murray Gernon, "and set me ashore."

The men obeyed, and watched their master with wondering eyes as he strode off towards the house, his brow knit, and head bent, for he wanted to be alone and to think.

Here was, he told himself, an awful confirmation of his suspicions; and now, rid of one enemy to his peace, he wanted to consider what should be his next step.

All that day he kept himself shut in his own room, merely giving a few instructions to his servants respecting the course to be taken with the prisoners, who were soon handed over into the custody of the police.

But, as might have been expected, Sir Murray Gernon could not fit together the pieces of the puzzle: he could not in his heart conclude that Norton had been associated with the burglarious party, and he was still brooding over the matter, when a note was placed in his hands—one which made him start as if stung by some venomous beast, and sit staring, with dilated eyes, till rage and disappointment got the better of surprise.

The note was very short, too, and merely to the effect that Captain Norton, while passing the park palings on the previous night, had heard an appeal for help, and had taken the liberty of trespassing that he might render some aid; but in the darkness and haste to get home and change his wet things, he had lost a portion of his clothes, containing letters of importance. Would Sir Murray Gernon kindly give orders that, if found, they might be restored?

Sir Murray Gernon sat for some minutes staring blankly at the paper as he mastered its contents. Here, then, was proof in the man's own handwriting that he had trespassed upon the Castle grounds on the previous night—but for what?

Reason gave the answer at once, but suspicion refused the explanation. There must have been some underhanded motive. Lady Gernon was dressed: she had not been to bed. Could it be that an evasion had been planned and interrupted by the fortuitous visit of the burglars? It must be so; and, feeling that he was now upon the right scent, Sir Murray determined to double his precautions, and acting on that determination, he stooped more and more to the meanness of acting the part of spy.

He would have challenged Norton to meet him again and again, but he told himself, with a grim smile, that he was a poltroon—as great a coward as ever breathed—and he felt more bitter than ever against him. It seemed to Sir Murray that he had been hoaxed—that he had been made the object of a trick that should for a few hours make him believe in Norton's death. He could not see that the acting of such a purposeless part would have been insensate to a degree, and that it was all due to the strength of his own imagination—an imagination now ever running riot in its wild theorising.

Norton might have smiled could he have read Sir Murray's heart, in spite of the anger and pain he would have felt. For his own part, he had, on reaching the footway of the bridge, stood thoughtful for a few moments, and then, hearing Sir Murray's voice, had come to the conclusion that the better plan would be to hurry away, and so avoid an encounter, feeling sure that his acts would be, in some way or other, misconstrued. He trusted that it would be supposed he had made his way to a place of safety; but, at all events, he was determined not to meet the baronet, and therefore proceeded quickly homewards, little thinking of the conclusions that would be arrived at, till towards the evening of the day following, when he recalled the fact that his recognition was certain in consequence of the clothes he had lost, the result being that he sent the note above alluded to. The writing of this note involved a full account to Mrs Norton of the night's adventure, to her great discomfort, for beyond a bare outline given in explanation of the wet clothes, Mrs Norton had known little of the state of affairs. By degrees, though, that day the news of the attempted burglary had reached the Hall, and Norton comprehended the cause of the cry for help to which he had so opportunely responded. At the same time, though, he could not but regret that he had been the instrument called upon to save the men's lives, the uneasiness brought upon him by the incident being excessive—an uneasiness fully shared, though in silence, by his wife.

Events in the life of Mr John Gurdon about this time began to succeed each other with great rapidity. An examination before the county magistrates resulted in his committal, and the assizes coming on within a month, the ex-butler stood his trial. The evidence was too strong against him; he had been, as it were, taken red-handed, and, with his companions, was condemned to cross the seas to a land where there should be fewer temptations for him. The judge, taking all things into consideration, seemed to think that Gurdon's crime was more heinous even than that of his companions, and visited it accordingly; for, while the other two men were sentenced to transportation for fourteen years, John Gurdon's sentence was almost equivalent to condemnation for life, inasmuch as he was to be exiled for twenty years.

"All right, gentlemen—all right," he said, coolly; "but I shall come back again. And as for you, Sir Murray Gernon, I'll bear you in mind till my return; for I've not done with you and yours."

"Remove him at once!" said the judge, and a couple of officers seized the prisoner, and hurried him from the dock.

"And now, don't be too hard on me, lassie," said McCray, the day after the trial—for he had managed to encounter Jane in one of the passages—"don't be hard upon me, lassie, for I only did my duty."

"I know—I know," said Jane, sadly; "but please don't talk to me now."

"Weel, weel, I know that your puir heart's sair yet, lassie, and I won't talk aboot sic things; but talk to ye I must, aboot something."

"You're as bad as a woman, Mr McCray," said Jane, pettishly.

"I only wish I was half as good as one woman I ken," said Sandy, gallantly. "But hoot, lassie, I'm glad to see the Squire's coming round. He brought her leddyship with him into the garden yestreen, and told her he'd make me the head-gairdener, and the puir thing leuked as bright and happy as could be; and, dye ken, lassie, I think we're going to hae bright times again at the Castle, and I'm aboot setting things reet, and I'll be as busy as busy, day after day; but ye'll see me a bit o' nichts?"

"Did Sir Murray speak kindly to her ladyship?" said Jane anxiously.

"Kind! ay," said Sandy; "and she turned to him directly, and laid her hand upon his arm, and they strolled off together behind the bushes, and he passed his arm round her—so, Jenny—and stooped him down, and kissed her—just as I'm showing of ye—there, just on her bonnie cheek, like that; for they didna ken I could see."

As Sandy McCray gave his description with illustrations, Jane started angrily away.

"Nay, lassie, gude save us, she didna do so, for she turned her bonnie face up to his, and looked sae loving and airnest in his e'e, that it was quite a sight. And, Jenny, lassie, ain't ye glad I'm head-gairdener noo. I dinna care myself, but I thought ye'd be glad."

"McCray," exclaimed Jane, earnestly, as she came once more closer to him, "you're a good and true-hearted man, and I'm not worthy of you."

"Hoot—hoot! lassie; haud that clap."

"But," continued Jane, "I've no one else to talk to and confide in. You are thoughtful and wise, and see a great deal, and then say nothing about it. You know how Sir Murray and my lady have been of late, and how he has behaved."

"Yes—yes," said Sandy; "he's been feeling just as I used to feel when—"

"Don't, please—don't say any more about that."

"Not I, lassie," said Sandy, caressingly.

"But this soft way of his, now, I don't like it," said Jane. "My life on it, he's never had any cause for his jealousy. I believe now it was all due to that wicked wretch saying things of my dear lady, and Sir Murray getting to hear of them."

"Hoot, not so fast, lassie. What wicked wretch?"

"Oh, don't ask me," said Jane, with pained face. "You know who I mean."

"So I do, lassie—so I do," said Sandy, smiling, and softly rubbing his hands. "But he'll do nae mair mischief."

"Well," said Jane, eagerly, "I saw Sir Murray only this morning talking gently to my lady, and as soon as he left her, he was looking that evil, and muttering so, that it was horrible. I don't believe in him, and there's something wrong. She has offended him, and he hasn't forgiven her. You know how I love my lady."

"Gude sake, yes, lassie, and I love ye for't."

"And that dear, sweet babe! I don't think she loves it better herself. And only a night or two since she was down on her knees, crying fit to break her heart, by its side; and she said to me, 'Jane—Jane, when something happens to me, be a mother to it; never leave her side, come what may.'"

"And ye promised her?" said Sandy, earnestly.

"Of course," exclaimed Jane, as she wiped her eyes.

"Gude lass—gude lass; and it's not me that will ask ye to. Ye shall watch over the little thing, Jenny, and I'll help ye. But what's she mean aboot when something happens her?"

"Oh, it's her low way, and I think she's afraid of Sir Murray; and now all this change in him isn't natural. I tell you, Alexander—"

"Gude; I like that," muttered the Scot, as, in her earnestness, Jane laid her hand upon his arm.

"I tell you, that if anything happens to my dear lady, I shall think it's his doing."

"Hoot—tut—tut! lassie, ye're giving way to strange thoughts, such as oughtn't to be in a Christian woman's heart. And now, lassie, I winna bother ye, but ye'll always talk to me like this, and come to me for counsel. I'm nae Solomon, Jenny, but I'll always tell ye the most I know. And there, there, little one, ye'll be my ain wife some day, winna ye?"

There must have been something very satisfactory in Jane's reply, for, after a few moment's silence, Alexander McCray went softly away upon the points of his boots, making his way into the garden, where he was soon busy superintending the improvement of flower-beds, and making alterations in spots that had long been an eyesore to him, inasmuch as they had been favourite whims of the now pensioned off, prejudiced old man, who had hitherto ruled the grounds.

"Gude sake, she's a real woman," muttered Sandy, as he raised his cap to Lady Gernon, who, basket in hand, passed him on her way to the gates. "I like to see a woman with a lo'e for flowers, even if they be the wild wee bits o' things she picks. But here comes the laird."

Under Orders

Andy McCray, in spite of his dignity as head "gairdner," was not above working hard himself, and he was busy enough when, slowly and gloomily, Sir Murray made his appearance, looking anxiously about the grounds, as if in search of something he could not see. He went first in one direction, then in another, and at last he returned to where Sandy was busy.

"Has her ladyship passed this way, gardener?" he said.

"Yes, Sir Mooray, a quarter of an hour syne. She took the path for the north gate."

Sir Murray Gernon bent his head by way of thanks, and walked slowly down the path till he had passed round the house, when he started off walking swiftly, making for the north gate, through which he passed, and then walked hurriedly on.

There was the wife of one of the under-gardeners at the lodge ready to drop him a courtesy, and from her he could, no doubt, have learned in a moment which direction her ladyship had taken, but he refrained from asking; and, evidently with an idea that he knew the place to which she would resort, he took a narrow path leading off towards a wood, one of the few old forests yet left in England; but, after walking quite half an hour, always anxiously peering to right or left, he seemed to be at fault, and turned sharply back to go in another direction, this time almost at a run.

That he was much agitated was plain enough, for though his face, and even his lips, were white, the veins in his forehead stood out in a perfect network, his pulses, too, throbbing fiercely. Twice over a heavy bead of perspiration trickled down his face, but he heeded it not, but, evidently now settled upon the point he sought, he passed rapidly along a by-path which led into one of the inner recesses of the wood.

Sir Murray had not left the garden ten minutes when, rising from his work for an instant, McCray became aware of the flutter of a dress in the distance, and the next instant made out that the wearer was Jane Barker, who now signalled him to come to her.

"And me so busy, too," muttered the gardener. "I did say that all my bit of courting should be done of an evening; and here's a temptation, coming in the middle of the day. But there, gude save us, I must go when she calls, if I lose my place."

"And there ye are, then," he said, as he reached the place where Jane was anxiously awaiting him, "the brightest flower in the garden, lassie."

"Oh, Alexander!" ejaculated Jane.

"Bless ye for that, my bairn! Ye've taken, then, to ca' me by my name at last."

"Pray—pray make haste and help me. What shall I do?"

"Do, lassie," exclaimed the downright Scot. "Why, tell me what's the matter."

"Yes, yes," cried the agitated girl. "You know my lady went out a little while since."

"Ay, I saw her go."

"And then Sir Murray came down."

"To be sure, and he askit me the which way she'd gone."

"Yes, yes," cried Jane, "and I went up on to the top of the house on the leads, and I've been watching him, and he's followed her."

"To be sure, lassie; and wadna I ha'e done the same if ye'd gone the same gait?"

"Oh yes—no,—I don't know," said Jane; "but I don't like it, and I want you to follow them."

"Me? Follow? What, go after Sir Mooray and my lady?" exclaimed McCray. "Hoot, lassie, and have ye gone daft?"

"Daft! no!" cried Jane, angrily. "You must—indeed, you must go after them. He came to me quite angry when he found that her ladyship had gone out, and asked me where I thought she'd be; and I told him, like the fool that I was; and I don't like things—I don't, indeed; and I'm afraid there's mischief on the way."

"My dear bairn," said the thoughtful Scot, "I'm afraid ye've been letting your fancy run away with ye full galop. Once you women get an idea into your poor little heads ye go racing after it full tear. Now, let me ask ye what is there strange in my lady going out to pick specimens, as she's done hundreds o' times before? and, now that they're making it up, for Sir Mooray to go after her?"

"Nothing—nothing," said Jane, earnestly, "if it were all genuine; but, Alexander—dear Alexander, there's Judas kisses as well as true ones, and I know he did not mean what you saw. I'm troubled about it all, and I come to you for help: don't fail me, please, now this first time."

"Nay, nay," cried the Scot, eagerly. "I'll not fail thee, lassie. But what am I to do? Where am I to go?"

"Follow them and watch them, never leaving them for an instant, and always being ready to give help."

"Yes, yes; I'll do it, lassie."

"I knew you would," cried Jane, pressing his great hand between both of hers; "and now run—run all the way, for he went to his room after he left me, and came out pushing a pistol into his pocket. And, oh! Alexander, if you love me, make haste, for I'm sure that there's something wrong!"

What Sandy did not See

"Gude save us!" muttered McCray, as he set off round the house at a sharp trot—"Gude save us and ha'e maircy! Here's a pretty pickle for an upper gairdner. Only just got my promotion, and I shall be brought down again as sure as my name's Sandy McCray. Trust the lassies for getting ye into a mess. Only foregather with one of the pretty things, and ye'll be in a mess before long. Gude save us! what shall I do? He'll be savage with me as a dog-otter. Nay, I ken what I'll do."

A bright thought had evidently crossed Sandy's mind, for, turning suddenly, he dodged into the kitchen-garden, and round by the tool-house, heralding his coming, a minute after, by a loud rattle, as he appeared, trundling a wheel-barrow, in which he had hastily thrown a basket and a three-pronged fork.

"I'm after ferns for the new rockery, to be sure!" he said, with a grin; and then away he spun at a tremendous rate, dashing along to the north gate, and bringing the woman out to see whether he had gone mad.

"Don't go that way, Mr McCray!" cried the woman after him, as she saw him turn down the path which led to the wood. "Sir Murray and my lady have gone that way."

"Gude save us, that's the right news!" muttered Sandy; and the barrow rattled more loudly than ever, as he dashed along till he came to an alley, down which, a good quarter of a mile from where he stood, he could see Sir Murray and Lady Gernon.

"There they are, then," he muttered; and running the barrow aside, he took out basket and fork, and began to thread his way amongst the trees, so as to approach unseen close to where his master and Lady Gernon were walking.

But Sandy McCray was a cautious man, and before he had gone many yards he had stooped to dig up half-a-dozen hart's-tongue ferns, which he placed, with a fair quantity of leaf-mould, in his basket.

"There's my answer to whatever they speer," he muttered; and then, creeping cautiously forward, he made his way to where, by holding aside the hazel boughs, he could peer out into the alley, where in a few minutes he saw the couple he watched pass by within a couple of yards of where he stood, silently and without hardly a rustle of the leaves amongst which they passed.

But just as they had gone by they stopped short, Lady Gernon holding tightly by Sir Murray's arm, as she gazed, with a wild, eager stare in his face.

"We had better make haste back, Lady Gernon," he said, quietly, and with a peculiar smile; and then they walked on.

"There, now! What could be better than that?" said McCray, as soon as he was alone. "She looks pale, but they were quiet enow. But what did he mean by showing his teeth to her when he smilt?"

Sandy McCray shook his head, and then, in obedience to his instructions, he followed slowly, contriving from time to time to keep the couple in sight, but ever and anon shaking his head as if something troubled him. At last he said, half aloud:

"The lassie is richt, after a'. There's your gude, sweet kiss, and your Judas kiss, and I think perhaps she did richt in sending me; but it's a sail job to leave one's work i' the daytime, and after a' there was not much to come for."

Had Sandy McCray been there five—nay, four—minutes sooner, he would have been of a different opinion, for Sir Murray Gernon, led, perhaps, by some tricksy sprite of the woods—some Puck of modern times—had hurried on and on, each moment growing more and more angry and excited at having missed the object of his search. For days past she had never left the Castle unwatched, but this time she had gone out suddenly, and at an hour when he had believed her to be in her bedroom. That there was some definite object for her walk he felt convinced, and when, after hurrying up and down several alleys of the wood, he at length caught sight of Lady Gernon, he felt no surprise—there was no great feeling of mad anger in his breast, but something like a bitter sense of satisfaction, such as might be that of any one who, after a long and arduous search, comes upon the object of his quest.

He uttered no exclamation, made no excited movement; but, with such a smile as McCray had described, he stood gazing down a woodland arcade, to where, some fifty yards in advance—framed, as it were, in the autumn-tinted leaves—stood Lady Gernon and the man to whom she had first given her love.

They were, perhaps, a yard apart—Lady Gernon, with her head bent, resting with one hand against a tree-trunk; Philip Norton—his hands upon the stick he held—gazing at her, it seemed, sadly and earnestly; but, as far as Sir Murray could tell, no word was spoken.

The next moment, quietly, and still smiling, Sir Murray slowly advanced down the arcade, half of which he had traversed before he was perceived; but even then there was no start—no guilty confusion—only Lady Gernon turned deadly pale, and a shade of trouble crossed Captain Norton's face.

Sir Murray, with the same strange smile, advanced to where they stood, raising his hat in answer to Norton's salute; and then, with the most courteous air, he said:

"Lady Gernon, you look pale."

"I believe, Sir Murray," said Norton, "Lady Gernon was startled and troubled at our sudden encounter."

"Exactly," said Sir Murray, quietly.

"You misunderstand me," said Norton, gravely, the shadow deepening upon his face. "I alluded to her encounter with me. Five minutes since, I met her by accident."

"Most accurate," said Sir Murray, smiling.

"And after the past—after the misunderstanding between our families, Sir Murray," continued Norton, not heeding the taunt.

"Exactly?" said Sir Murray.

"I was sorry that the meeting should have taken place. Lady Gernon," he said, turning to her, as he raised his hat, "I will deliver your message. It is, I know, both pain and sorrow to dear Ada that you should be apart. Still, I think it is for the best. Rest assured, though, that the love you sent her is yours in return. Heaven bless you! Good-bye, Sir Murray Gernon!" he said, turning to the smiling baronet—who stood with one hand buried in his breast-pocket—"I am sorry for the past; but it is irrevocable, and I still repeat that I am sorry for this encounter. Lady Gernon seems pale and ill. Good day."

He held out his hand quietly and frankly to the baronet, though he had forborne to do so to his lady, and there was an air of calm innocence in his aspect, that should have carried with it conviction; but Sir Murray never stirred; his hand was still buried in his breast, as, with a mocking smile, he said:

"Captain Norton, the army was never your vocation, any more than the losing office of mine-director."

"I do not understand you, Sir Murray," was the calm, sad reply, as for a moment Norton's eyes met Marion Gernon's imploring glance.

"Indeed," said the baronet, who had not lost the speaking look interchanged. "I meant that fortune awaited you upon the stage; you should have been an actor."

The colour seemed to fade from Norton's face at these galling words, and the great blue scar stood out more prominently than ever; but the next moment turning his gaze from Sir Murray, he fixed his eyes upon Marion with a soft, earnest, speaking look, that meant volumes; for, changing in an instant from a mocking smile to a look of rage and hate, Sir Murray Gernon drew a pistol from his pocket, and at a couple of paces' distance presented it full at Norton. His finger was upon the trigger—the weapon was fully cocked—and even the slightest contraction of the angry man's muscles would have sent the contents through Philip Norton's breast. But he did not wince—not a muscle moved; the man who had before now stood deadly fire, stood firm, till, with an oath, Sir Murray hurled the pistol into the thicket, and led his wife away.

But before they had gone a dozen yards the smile had come back upon his lip, and he turned to gaze at Lady Gernon, to see on her countenance the same old stony, despairing look that had been there on the wedding morn.

Jane's Suspicions

It is quite possible that in his heart of hearts Sir Murray Gernon had doubts as to who had been the spoiler of his family jewels, but he would admit nothing to his breast but such thoughts as were disparaging to Norton.

At the Castle nods and smiles were prevalent, and the servants gossiped respecting the happy change that had taken place, arguing all sorts of gaieties once more; for—so they said—the old house had been like a dungeon lately, and almost unbearable.

But there were doubts still in the minds of both Jane Barker and her lover, the former watching Sir Murray as narrowly as ever he watched his lady. There was a feeling of uneasiness in Jane's heart that grew stronger every day, a feeling not based upon any confidences of Lady Gernon's—for, though invariably kind and gentle, Marion was not one to make a friend and counsellor of her servant—but upon Jane's own observation. The scraps she gathered she pieced together, and, when alone, tried to form some definite course of action—a trial resulting in a rigid determination which she followed out.

What took place in private was never known, but the pallor upon Lady Gernon's cheeks grew daily of a more sickly hue. A physician was sent for from the county town with great ostentation by Sir Murray, and shortly after, another from London, resulting in prescriptions and medicine, which her ladyship took daily, such medicine being always administered by Jane, who made a point, for some reason or another, of leaving the bottles always upon the table in her ladyship's dressing-room; and this went on for quite a couple of months, the sickness increasing, though not sufficiently to confine Lady Gernon to her room. The walks, though, were pretty well given up, and it was only at very rare intervals that Lady Gernon strayed beyond the boundaries of the park.

The servants said that no one could be more attentive than Sir Murray now was, and that it was quite pleasant to see the alteration. But Jane said nothing, she merely tightened her lips, making no confidant; for once—twice, four different times—she had encountered Sir Murray coming from her mistress's dressing-room; and once, after such a visit, when she went to give Lady Gernon her daily medicine, the poor girl fainted away upon learning that her duty had been forestalled by Sir Murray himself.

Whatever might have been Jane Barkers suspicions, she felt that this could not go on for ever; and worn out, and sick at heart, she one day put on her bonnet, ordered McCray to act as her escort, and made her way to Merland Hall.

Mrs Norton welcomed her heartily, but almost in dread, not knowing what interpretation might be placed upon the visit, should it come to Sir Murray's ears. But, to her great astonishment, Jane's first act was to close the window, and then, crossing the room, she turned the key in the lock; when, coming back close to the astonished occupant of the room, she threw herself down upon her knees, sobbing wildly; and catching hold of Ada's hand, she kissed it fiercely again and again.

"Is anything wrong?" exclaimed Ada Norton, with a horrified look, for a dreadful fear had flashed across her mind.

"No, Miss Ada—I mean Mrs Norton—*not yet*—*not yet*! but unless some one interferes there soon will be! Oh, 'm! I didn't care to go to the Rectory, for I knew that they wouldn't believe me there! but I'm afraid something dreadful will happen to my poor dear lady! I have come to you because you are her cousin, and I know you loved her, though things have gone so crooked since. But what shall we do, 'm? for since that last time when my lady met Mr Norton in the wood, and Sir Murray caught them—" Jane ceased, for Ada Norton leaped to her feet as if some galvanic shock had passed through her frame.

"Oh, what am I saying, ma'am? I didn't think that you'd take it in that way, nor yet that you wouldn't know of it. It was nothing, ma'am; only Sir Murray was telling my lady of it; and she said that they met by accident, and that almost all her words to him were to send her love to you, ma'am."

"It was, then, upon that occasion?" said Ada Norton, in agitated tones.

"Yes, 'm; and I was in the dressing-room, and heard all. Not that Sir Murray spoke angrily, but in a curious, sneering tone that frightens my lady; and ever since then she's been ill, and taking medicine; and—oh, 'm!—you would not get me into trouble for trying to do what's right by my lady?"

"No—no," said Ada, who was trying to recall her husband's words when he had told her of his last meeting with Lady Gernon, for he had said nothing respecting the coming of Sir Murray.

"Well, ma'am," sobbed Jane, "since then"—she sank her voice into a whisper, and sent a thrill of horror through Ada Norton as she spoke—"since then, ma'am, I'm sure Sir Murray has been trying to poison her!"

"Poison my cousin, Lady Gernon?" exclaimed Ada. "Nonsense! Absurd! Jane, you are mad!"

"I hope I am, ma'am, about that—indeed I do!" cried Jane, earnestly.

"But what have you seen? What do you know?" exclaimed Mrs Norton.

"I haven't seen anything, ma'am, except Sir Murray coming sometimes out of the dressing-room, where the medicine's kept; and I don't know anything except that my lady's medicine always tastes different, and looks different, when it's been in the dressing-room a day or two; and every week it turns a darker colour, and tastes stronger than it did the week before. And besides all that, though Sir Murray smiles, and pretends to talk pleasant to the poor dear, suffering angel, than whom a better woman never lived, he hates her dreadfully, and more and more every day."

"And how long has this been going on?" said Mrs Norton, with a faint smile.

"Weeks now, ma'am," said Jane. "But I see you don't believe me."

"I believe you to be a good, affectionate girl, Jane," said Mrs Norton, "and that you love your mistress; but this seems to me to be a fearful and perfectly unfounded suspicion—one that I am glad, for every one's sake, that you have hinted to no one else. Think of the absurdity of the thing. This has, you say, been going on for weeks; and yet, you see, your mistress is not poisoned yet."

"No, ma'am, not yet," said Jane, meaningly.

"Well, then, my good girl, how do you account for that?"

"Because, ma'am," said Jane, in a whisper, "she's never taken any of the medicine but once."

"How? What do you mean?" exclaimed Mrs Norton.

"I've managed to get the stuff made up at two places, ma'am," whispered Jane. "One lot's fetched by the footman from one chemist's, at Marshton, and I get the gardener to go to another chemist's for the other. I only had to send the doctor's paper, and the medicine comes just like what Sir Murray knows is sent for."

"Well," exclaimed Ada, impatiently.

"Well, 'm," whispered Jane, "that which her ladyship takes I keep locked up, and that which stands on the dressing-table gets poured out of the window, a little at a time, upon the flower-beds."

Ada Norton sat silently gazing at Jane for a few minutes before she spoke.

"Jane," she said, "this is a fearful charge!" and she shuddered. "I must think about it, and before many hours I will come over to the Castle, and see either Sir Murray or Lady Gernon. Do not be afraid; I will not implicate you in any way. I must see Mr Elstree, and I will try to make some plan— to arrange something definite; but your words have confused me—almost taken away my breath. The thing seems so monstrous, and even now I cannot believe it true! But I should not feel that I had done my duty if, after what you have said, I did not take some steps; so rest assured that I will do something, and at once."

Jane rose to go, and, trembling and excited, Ada Norton sat for some hours, pondering whether she should ask her husband's advice, ending by putting it off till the next day, when it happened that it was out of her power.

Not at Home

"Did you see the laird?" said McCray, coming slowly forth from behind some bushes, after Jane had been standing some few minutes in the lane where she had left him to wait.

"The laird!" said Jane, starting. "Why, who do you mean?"

"Mean? Why, Sir Mooray himself. I saw him turn round to have a good look at ye, as ye came across the home close from the Hall. And ye didna see him?"

"No—no—no!" sobbed Jane. "Oh dear—oh dear! I'm undone!"

"Nay—nay, ye're not, lassie; for I'll a'ways stand by ye. Dinna greet aboot that. Ye didna tell me why ye came, but I know it's for some good, and that ye'll tell me all in good time."

"That I will, indeed!" sobbed Jane; "but don't ask me now!"

"Nay, then, I'm not speering to know," said Sandy, contentedly. "He was riding the grey horse, ye ken, and he seemed to catch sight o' ye all at aince; when, thinking it wasna warth while for twa to be in trouble, I hid myself in the bushes till he'd gone by."

The next day, one anxiously looked forward to by more than one of the characters in this story, came in due course; and, towards evening, Lady Gernon slowly passed through the hall door, basket in hand, and making her way across the lawn, disappeared from the sight of Sandy McCray behind some bushes at the edge of the park.

The hours sped on, and Ada Norton drove up in one of Chunt's flys from the village public-house, after waiting some time at the Rectory, in a vain endeavour to see Mr Elstree, who was from home. She had, after many hours' thought, but a vague idea of the best plan to pursue, and even now questioned the wisdom of her course. In fact, more than once the check-string had been in her hand to arrest the driver, and order him to return to the Hall; but, from sheer shame at her vacillation, she let it fall again, and gazed slowly out from the fly-window at the glorious sweep of the noble domain through which she was being driven, and sighed again and again as she thought of the misery of its owners. She half shrank from meeting Lady Gernon, for she felt that, in spite of all her assurances to the contrary, her cousin must feel something of repugnance to the woman who had, as it were, taken her place. Not that she had robbed Lady Gernon of her happiness; she had been ready to resign all hope, and had given up, stifling her own feelings, when duty told her that she was called upon so to act. But could Marion feel the same?

She asked herself that question as the fly drove up to the noble front of the great mansion; and then, rousing herself for the task in hand, she prepared to meet her cousin.

"Not at home," was the answer given by the footman to the driver; when Ada beckoned the man to the fly door—a slow-speaking, insolent menial, who had, before now, performed Sir Murray's liest in acting the part of spy.

"I think," said Ada, "that my cousin would see me, even if she is confined to her room."

"Sir Murray give orders, mum, that they were not at home to visitors from the Hall; and, besides, my lady ain't in."

Ada Norton felt that it was cowardly, but it was with a sense of relief that she sank back against the cushions, and began to turn over in her mind what course she ought to pursue. She dreaded the exciting effect it might have upon her husband, if she revealed to him the words she had heard from Jane; and, trembling with an anxiety she could not drive away, she returned to the Hall, to find that Captain Norton had gone out.

"Packed a carpet bag, ma'am," said the servant, "and then wrote a note for you, after sending for Master Brace, and kissing him."

The note was on the table, and snatching it up, Ada Norton read as follows:—

"Dearest Ada,

"Do not think hardly of me. I could not help myself; but I know you will not judge me harshly. More when I write again; but *give no information of my movements to a soul.* I shall be away some time, but I have made full arrangements with Garland and Son about you. Philip."

Abrupt, enigmatical, and strange; but it was like him. There was a vein of affection, though, running through it all. He had made arrangements for her; but the tears dimmed Ada Norton's eyes as she stood with the letter in her hands. What could it all mean? she thought. Had it anything to do with the mining transaction? Should she drive over to Marshton the next day, and ask Messrs Garland and Son, her husband's solicitors? No, she would not do that; it would be like prying into his affairs. She had always had faith in him, so far, and that faith should continue to the end.

She dashed away the tears heroically, little thinking how soon and how sorely she was to be tried. It was nothing new for Norton to absent himself, and she could wait patiently for his return. "Like a good wife," she said, smilingly; and then, sitting down, she took her work, but only for it to fall into her lap, as she tried to divine what would be her best plan to adopt in connection with the strange information which had the day before been imparted to her.

A Storm at Merland

Sir Murray Gernon had, during the past few weeks, made a good deal of use of his horses—another sign, the stablemen observed, of a returning good state of things, for they were growing quite tired of doing nothing but taking the horses out for exercise. But Sir Murray's rides were only round and about his own estate: he never went far, though he was out for hours at a time; and the day before there was again a fierce look upon his face, as he caught sight of Jane Barker hurriedly leaving Merland Hall.

"Of course!" he said; he might have known that before. Time proved all things, and here, at length, was before his eyes the arrangement by which letters and messages had been conveyed.

But he was, if anything, more than usually courteous to my lady that evening at dinner. Sir Murray hadn't been in such a good temper for long enough past, said one of the footmen; only my lady looked so ill and sad, and shivered so. It was almost a pity she should have come down to dinner.

Sir Murray had been out again, riding up and down forest paths, and by copse edges, along by field and meadow; and always with his head bent, and a watchful look in his eye.

About an hour after Ada Norton's visit to the Castle, Sir Murray slowly walked his horse up to the door, and the footman ran down the steps, and laid his hand on the animals neck.

"Stand aside a few minutes, William," said Sir Murray; and the groom, who had also run up to take the saddle-horse, touched his hat and fell back. "Well, what now?" he exclaimed hastily, for something in the footman's face told of tidings.

"I thought I'd better tell you, Sir Murray," said the man, "her ladyship—"

"Not—?" ejaculated Sir Murray, starting, and turning livid, as he checked himself. "Has the doctor been sent for?"

"No, Sir Murray," said the man; "her ladyship ain't worse, only she went out this afternoon."

"Well?" said the baronet. "That's all, Sir Murray," said the man, timidly. "I was called away, and didn't see her go. I didn't know it till just now, when one of the gardeners said he saw her go out, and he thought the pony-carriage ought to be sent for her, as a storm was coming on."

"She has not come back, then?" exclaimed Sir Murray; and then, clapping spurs to his horse, he made it dash forward; but only to check it the next instant, rein back, and descend, beckoning up the groom, and then slowly mounting the steps.

"You have not said a word of all this?" said the baronet, in a low tone.

"Not a word, Sir Murray!" exclaimed the man, with an injured air. "You can trust me, sir."

Sir Murray Gernon smiled bitterly, as he threw his hat and gloves to the man, and entered his library, leaving the door open, and watching for Lady Gernon's return.

An hour elapsed, and then he rang.

"No, Sir Murray; her ladyship has not returned."

Another hour passed, and the storm prophesied of by Alexander McCray was at hand. First came a deep gloom; then the sighing of the wind in faint puffs, as it swept round the house; then there was a flash or two of lightning, and the muttering of thunder; then flash after flash lighting up the heavens, succeeded by a darkness as of the blackest night. A few minutes seemed to elapse, as if Nature was preparing herself for a grand effort; and then, with a mighty, rushing crash, down came the main body of the storm, of which the previous mutterings had been but the *avant-garde*. The rain seemed to fall in one vast sheet, through which the blue lightning cut and flickered; while, with a deafening roar, peal after peal of thunder seemed to burst over the mansion, threatening it with destruction.

"Should the pony-carriage be brought round, sir?" asked the footman, shouting to make himself heard.

"Yes," said Sir Murray, "and my horse. Send McCray, the gardener, here, too."

McCray, who had been trying to console Jane, who was greatly agitated, soon made his appearance before Sir Murray.

"McCray, take one of the horses, and go round from cottage to cottage till you find where her ladyship has taken refuge. Williams, you go south with the pony-carriage, and I shall ride east."

The gardener saluted, and ten minutes after, heedless of the storm— though he had hard work with his frightened beast—he was mounted, amidst the sneers of the grooms, who looked upon such missions as within their province, and resented the coming of the interloper accordingly.

"The puir weak body! But I'll soon find her," muttered McCray, as he cantered on out at the park gates; and then going from cottage to cottage, and at last entering the forest, and riding between the dripping trees, and along the slippery clay paths to the different keepers' houses, but without avail; so that, at last, thoroughly soaked and disheartened, he turned back, feeling sure that, before that time, her ladyship must have returned.

"Not come back," whispered one of the grooms to him, as he entered the yard. "Williams got back an hour agone, and Sir Murray has been in and gone out again."

Just at that moment, with his horse in a foam, Sir Murray galloped up.

"Well?" he said, eagerly.

"No one has even seen her leddyship, Sir Mooray," said the gardener, curtly.

"The same answer everywhere!" exclaimed the baronet. "Let every man mount and set off. Tell the keepers to search the wood. You, McCray, come with me, unless Williams has returned."

"Williams is so wet, sir, he's gone to bed," said a man.

"Quick, then, McCray!" exclaimed Sir Murray; "and keep that tongue of yours silent afterwards!"

"Ye may trust me, Sir Mooray," said McCray, gruffly; and setting off at a smart canter, they were soon nearing the village street.

The storm had by this time passed over, and the stars were blinking out here and there; but from every tree and leaf the great drops fell pattering down, while ditch and channel ran furiously with their unwonted muddy currents.

"Go into that public-house, and ask what conveyances have gone out from there to-day—this afternoon?" said Sir Murray.

McCray returned in five minutes, followed by the inquisitive Chunt.

"Good evening, Sir Murray," he said, hat in hand, and not seeing the frown upon the baronet's countenance. "I've been telling your man, Sir Murray, nothing's gone but the dog-cart as Cap'en Norton came and had out. Carried his bag over, sir, and wouldn't wait for a man to bring the car back; said he'd drive himself, and leave it at 'The Chequers,' at Marshton, Sir Murray."

The mud from the horse's hoofs was splashed in Chunt's face as he finished, for Sir Murray stuck in the spurs so, that the poor brute plunged furiously; and it was all that McCray—not the best of horsemen—could do to overtake him, as he galloped along the main road to Marshton, where they arrived about ten, with their horses blown, and covered with foam, Sir Murray, who had not spoken, leading the way into the inn-yard.

"Chunt's dog-car, sir? Brought in here about five, sir, by a boy as a gent gave sixpence to bring it in, sir. Tall gent, with a mark across his face, sir," the boy said.

So spake "The Chequers" hostler, in reply to questions put by Sir Murray Gernon, who had drawn his hat down over his eyes, and turned up the collar of his coat, as though to prevent his being recognised.

"What boy, sir? Can't say, sir. Looked like lad returning from harvest work. Quite a stranger to these parts, sir."

Without another word, Sir Murray Gernon turned his horse's head, and rode out of the yard, followed by McCray, who clung to him as if he had been his shadow; but the horses were now tired, unused as they were to much exertion, and it was getting close upon midnight when the baronet and his servant rode into the stable-yard at Merland Castle.

Sir Murray asked no questions. It was plain enough, from the silence, that there was no news; so throwing his bridle to a groom, his act was closely imitated by McCray, who followed him into the library.

"I'm sorry for the puir body, wherever she is," muttered McCray; "but, perhaps, after all, there's naething the matter. Onyhow, such a ride, and such a wetting, desarves a drappie of toddy, and perhaps Sir Mooray may ask me to take it. I'll follow him, anyhow, for how do I know whether he's done wi' me?"

Jane Declares

McCray stood watching his master with attentive eye, as, apparently ignorant of his presence, the baronet—drenched as he was with rain and perspiration—threw himself into a chair, and covered his face with his hands.

The gardener stood on one leg, then on the other, then leaned on a chair-back, putting himself into every posture that would give him a little ease, for he was well-nigh exhausted. But no notice took Sir Murray. He was apparently buried in himself; and, at last, unable to draw his attention by coughing and shuffling about, Sandy McCray prepared to speak.

"He's greeting aboot her, puir laddie," he muttered to himself; "but, a' the same, he might ha' brought out the whuskee. We're mair free with the wee drappie up north." Then, aloud: "Hoot, then, Sir Mooray, it's a bad habit to sit in wet clouts. Hadna ye better tak' just a wet o' some kind o' sperrits? I think a little whuskee wad do ye nae hairm."

"You here still?" exclaimed Sir Murray; and then, angrily, as a hand was laid upon the handle of the door: "Who's that? I am engaged."

But the door opened, and, to Sandy McCray's astonishment, Jane crept in, white as a sheet, as if from some great horror; but, all the same, carrying tenderly, as she hushed it to sleep, the little child that, after five years, had been born to Sir Murray.

"Hoot, lassie! and what do ye do here?"

"What do I do?" exclaimed Jane, fiercely, her half-frightened aspect giving place to a look of rage. "I have come to ask that man what he has done with my dear lady!"

"Hoot, lassie! do ye ken it's the laird?" exclaimed the alarmed gardener; and then, stooping over her, he put his face close to hers, and muttered to himself: "There isna a smell of the stuff on her mooth, or I'd say she'd been at the whuskee."

"Stand aside, McCray!" she said hoarsely. "I want to ask him, I tell you, what he has done with my dear lady."

After the manner of a woman of her class, she raised her voice as she spoke; when, in alarm, the Scot darted to and closed the door, turning the little inside bolt, and then hurrying back to his betrothed's side; for there was something threatening in the baronet's looks, as he rose from his chair, glaring the while at his wife's maid.

"Stand back, McCray!" cried Jane, hoarsely, as he laid his hand upon her arm. "I've been silent all these months, but I'll speak now. Let him strike me if he dares, but he dare not! See here!" she cried, "I've brought your little one down to you, to see if it will do anything towards melting your hard, proud, cruel heart, and making you tell the truth! Tell me now, and at once, what you have done with my dear lady!"

"Take her away, and this instant!" hissed Sir Murray. "The woman's mad!"

"Mad! No, I am not mad! Keep back, McCray; I won't go! Touch me again, and I'll scream so as to alarm the house; and then all the servants shall hear what I mean to say to you alone. I'm not afraid, I tell you, and I will be answered. But, oh, Sir Murray!" she cried, softening for a moment, "tell me where the poor thing is! What have you done with her?"

"You Scotch wolf!" exclaimed Sir Murray, in a rage, to the gardener, "why do you not take the mad fool from my sight?"

McCray placed his arm round Jane, and tried to lead her off; but she struggled from him, and uttered a wild, piercing scream that made him start aside, as if the shrill sound had pierced him like a sword.

"I will not go!" cried the girl, stamping with fury. "I will know first! Do you think I am to be cheated and blinded by all this pretended hunting to find my poor darling, ill-used lady? Why did you come, with your pride and your money, to her happy home, and take her away to be your miserable wife? Why did you ever come near the poor, sweet innocent? And then, after all her suffering, to insult her with your cruel, base suspicions, so unmanly—so false!"

"Curse the woman! Am I to strike her in the mouth?" raged Sir Murray, in a hoarse whisper; for there were voices to be heard outside—evidently those of the servants, alarmed by the wild shriek, and once the door was softly tried.

"Na—na, Sir Mooray!" said McCray; "nae blows to a woman. The puir thing's daft wi' grief and passion, and greeting after her lady; but she'll be better therectly. Whush, then, Jenny, let's gang our gait, and leave the laird to himsel'."

"If you touch me again, McCray, I'll alarm the house!" cried Jane; and the great Scot fell back once more, as going closer to Sir Murray Gernon, she continued, hoarsely:

"You've been making your plans for long enough, and this is a part of them! It will blind some people, but it won't me. I've been watching, as well as you; for my heart bled to see the poor, ill-used, neglected, tortured thing pining away, day after day! But Heaven will judge you for this, and bring down punishment upon you! She knew it was coming: she shuddered, and talked of dying, and begged of me to be a mother to her poor little one, and I swore I would; and I will, poor humble servant as I am! But right makes me strong, while wrong makes you weak and a coward, so that you are afraid, and obliged to listen to me. I'm not afraid of your fierce looks, for it shall all out, if I go to the magistrates myself. Hunting round, looking for her, you false, cruel traitor! Do you think you could deceive me? You listened for some purpose to the cruel lies of that wretch Gurdon, who ought to have had his tongue cut out; and now that you have planned and plotted, you think we are all cheated, but you are wrong. I don't care who hears me, I will speak, and I say it now. Look at him, McCray: you are a bold, honest man, before whom he cowers—this great baronet, with his title—like a beaten hound! I tell you that for weeks past he has been trying to poison—"

With an exclamation of rage Sir Murray rushed at her; but she never flinched.

"To poison my dear lady!" exclaimed Jane.

"Hush—hush! for Heaven's sake, hush, woman!" cried Sir Murray; and in an instant he had placed his hand over her mouth.

But it was only for an instant; McCray had dragged him from her, as, reeling as she spoke, Jane gasped:

"Keep him from me; his hands are yet red! I tell you, as I will tell the world, if I live, my lady is not lost, but murdered!"

Sir Murray Declares

"Send those people away from the door! Make her be silent; the woman's mad!" exclaimed Sir Murray excitedly, as, shrinking back, he stood, trembling and haggard, before McCray. "It's all nonsense—folly— that she has said. No; keep her here till those people have gone."

"Ye'll be quiet noo, lassie, winna ye?" said McCray soothingly, as he held Jane in his arms, and then placed her in a chair, when the mad excitement that had kept her up so far seemed to desert her; and bowing down over the frightened child, she kissed and hushed it to sleep, sobbing over it hysterically, and every now and then breaking into a wail of misery. She took no further notice of her master, who gazed at her with an aspect of alarm, fearing, apparently, to speak, lest he might bring forth another such outbreak as the last. But he had no cause for fear; Jane was now tractable as a child, as McCray soon found; and going close to Sir Murray, he whispered:

"That's an ower thick door, Sir Mooray, as I fun oot when I brak' it open. They didna hear what was said by the puir thing, half daft with grief; and gin ye'll trust me, I'll see that she doesna talk ony more sic stuff."

Sir Murray did not answer,—he merely bowed his head; for there was a battle going on in his breast—a strife between dread and mortification at having to humble himself before his own servants. It was hard work to arrest the groan that struggled for exit, and when the door closed on Sandy McCray and Jane, he sank back in his chair as if stunned.

McCray felt that Sir Murray's silence gave consent, and that he was trusted. The trust, too, was not misplaced; for the Scot had obtained sufficient influence over Jane to reason her, in her calmer moments, into silence.

"Supposing, even, that you're right, lassie, ye ken that the puir bodie we've lost wadna have wished ye to bring Sir Mooray to the gallows. But dinna ye fash yourself aboot it; it will all reet itself in time. Ye're sure o' naething, and ye've got your trust in hand; sae mind it weel, and leave the rest to me."

Jane responded to this advice by weeping bitterly over the child, pressing it convulsively to her breast; and in that condition, the next morning, McCray left her, and sought the baronet, to find that he had never left the library.

"The puir lassie was half daft last neet, Sir Mooray; but it's a' owre noo, and she's tending the bairn."

"I wanted you, McCray!" exclaimed Sir Murray, the coming of the staunch servitor seeming to rouse him into life. "I am going to search in one direction: you arrange the men in parties, and leave no place unscoured. Give orders, too, that the great nets be brought out, and let the lake be dragged."

He shuddered as he spoke these last words, and the gardener turned to go.

"What time is it now?" inquired Sir Murray.

"Just seven of the clock, Sir Mooray," was the reply; and then McCray took his departure, heedless of the supercilious looks bestowed upon him by one of the footmen, who could not understand what Sir Murray could be thinking about to have that great coarse gardener in the house, and treat him as an equal.

But Sir Murray had placed matters in the right hands. Before half an hour had elapsed parties were organised, consisting of the servants and labourers from the farm close at hand; and a regular search was instituted, the land being methodically gone over—field and forest, bush and ditch. The lake was dragged in every direction, and hour after hour spent, but always with the same result—failure.

There were not wanting those who asserted that my lady must have wandered right away, and the bounds of the search were extended, but still in vain; and at mid-day the parties rested for refreshment, and to determine upon some new plan of action.

Meanwhile, a horse had been brought to the door; and mounting, Sir Murray rode hastily over to the Hall, where, for form's sake, he asked to see Captain Norton, and upon being told of his absence, requested to be shown in to Mrs Norton.

She met him without rising, but sat trembling visibly, as she drew her boy closer to her; for a sense of dread seemed to rob her of the power to move. But a few hours since, and it had been declared to her that this man had tried to poison her cousin, and now he was here. She could not speak, but motioned him to a chair, trying to overcome her weakness, and to meet with fortitude the new misfortune she felt certain was impending.

Sir Murray saw her motion, but he remained standing; and for full five minutes he watched her, with a look mingled of curiosity and compassion.

"Mrs Norton," he said at last, "I have come to inflict pain, but I cannot help it. You must judge me leniently when I am gone."

Ada bowed, and gazed at him with starting eyes.

"One of the Castle servants was here the day before yesterday. Did you see her?"

"I did," said Ada, huskily.

"She brought a note, did she not, from Lady Gernon?"

"No, Sir Murray."

"A message?"

"No."

"She saw Captain Norton?"

"My husband was from home, Sir Murray Gernon."

"She left a message for him?"

"No."

"Are you sure?"

"Quite. Your servant came to see me, as your wife's old friend and relative; and, saving the housemaid who admitted her, I alone saw her."

"Have you any objection to tell me the object of her visit?"

Ada was silent.

"Did she come at the wish of Lady Gernon?"

"No," said Ada, for she hardly knew what to reply.

"Then you will tell me why she came?"

Ada was still silent.

"Then I will tell you," said Sir Murray, in a calm voice. "She came to tell you of some absurd suspicions that she had nursed—to try and convince you that Lady Gernon's life was in danger; for, like the rest of us, she had been blinded by the treason of a false woman. I see that the news has not yet reached your ears. Mrs Norton, your cousin has fled!"

"Fled!" exclaimed Ada, starting to her feet.

"Yes, fled," he continued, in measured tones, as if he were forcing each word from his lips. "She left the Castle during my absence, yesterday afternoon, and she has not returned. Captain Norton engaged a conveyance yesterday afternoon, and drove away; Captain Norton has not returned."

Ada Norton stood, pale as a statue, gazing at him with lips apart, as she realised his words, and thought of her husband's absence, his note, his strange behaviour, and Jane Barker's words respecting the last meeting in the wood. Her brain reeled, as the thoughts flashed rapidly through, and for a moment she felt that she was ready to fall; but she recovered herself, to hear that her visitor was still speaking.

"I had a last hope that she might be here—that, overtaken by the storm, this might have been her refuge; but my hope was faint. Mrs Norton, I might, perhaps, have kept the truth from you for a few hours; but you must have known it, sooner or later. You have judged me, I believe, very harshly, so far; now, perhaps, I shall command your pity, as I pity you."

"Judge you harshly! Pity you! You pity me!" exclaimed Ada, flashing into a rage, which lit up her whole countenance, as, with one hand she clutched her boy more tightly to her, and held out the other threateningly at Sir Murray. "You cold-blooded, cowardly miscreant—you destroyer of the hope and happiness, perhaps the life, of that sweet, suffering woman! how dare you confront me with your base, clumsily built-up reasoning, as if every woman upon earth possessed your vile, suspicious nature! You dare to come here with your base subterfuges—your dastardly insinuations—to try and make me believe that Lady Gernon, my pure-hearted cousin, and confidante from a child, has fled with my noble, true, and faithful husband! You lie, you false-hearted dastard—you insidious, courtly, smooth villain— you lie, and you know it! Heaven forgive me my passion, but it is enough to madden me! Go! leave here this instant; for you pollute the place, and you tempt me to believe that you have murdered her! Yes, you may start! But my husband! as true-hearted and honourable a man as ever breathed! How dare you?"

"Woman, where is your husband?" cried Sir Murray, fiercely.

"I do not know. He is from home. How dare you question me?"

"Poor, weak, self-deceiving creature!" he said, contemptuously, "I do not question you! I have noticed—Nay, stay here!" he exclaimed, catching her by the wrist. "You shall hear me! They have been planning long enough now! It was a cursed day when I returned to the Castle; and I soon found that out, though you blinded yourself to the truth. But sooner than have any scandal—than have my name dragged through the Divorce Court, and sneered at by every contemptible fool—I have borne all in silence— suffered, as man never before suffered; and, rejoicing in my weakness, they have corresponded and met! Fool that I was, when I found them last in the wood, and covered the villain—the serpent, the robber of my jewels and of my honour—when I covered him with my pistol, that I did not shoot him down as one would a common thief and burglar! But, no; I would not have a scandal afloat, even though I was becoming the laughingstock and by-word of my servants! But, there, go! I pity and admire you; for I can feel—you teach me to feel—that, there may be yet women worthy of faith!"

As he spoke he threw her hand roughly from him just as the door opened, and Mr and Mrs Elstree entered the room.

"You are here, then!" exclaimed the Rector, in agonised tones. "We have been to the Castle. In Heaven's name, Murray—Ada—what does all this mean? We hear that Marion is missing! Can you form no idea where she is?"

"Yes!" said Sir Murray, bitterly; "abroad by this time!"

"What, in Heaven's name, does it all mean?" exclaimed Mrs Elstree, pitifully.

"Mean, madam!" exclaimed Sir Murray, as he strode to the door, and turned to gaze fiercely at all present—"mean? That I married a harlot!"

Changes at Hand

Everything that could be done in the way of searching was energetically carried out. The lake, every pond, and even many of the water-holes upon the moor were dragged; but no tidings—no trace of Lady Gernon was obtained. McCray had seen her walk across the lawn and disappear behind some shrubs, as he was at work, and that seemed to be the last trace. No one could be found who had seen her pass in any direction; and the topic of conversation in Merland village and the neighbourhood began to change its tone, as people learned how Sir Murray had, for a short time, made inquiries respecting the route taken by Captain Norton, pursuing him, too, for some distance, until he seemed to have disappeared, the information he obtained being of a very vague nature.

But it was very plain to those who took an interest in the affair that Sir Murray Gernon's endeavours to trace his lady were made in a half-hearted manner. The search in the neighbourhood of the Castle was strenuous enough, but that was due to the exertions of McCray; and when, at the end of a week, people learned that Sir Murray had shut himself up, after discharging half the servants with liberal wages, they raised their eyebrows, and shook their heads, and wondered whether Captain Norton would ever show himself again at the Hall.

As for Jane, she was nearly having a rupture with McCray, upon his giving in his adhesion to the popular feeling; but the matter blew over, and whatever might be her thoughts, she said no more, waiting in expectation of the battle that she felt to be in store for her when, rousing himself once more, Sir Murray should recall her words, and wish to discharge her.

But the day she dreaded did not come; while, to the great disgust of the servants, McCray seemed to be more and more in the confidence of Sir Murray.

"Why don't he keep to his 'gairden,' as he calls it?" said the footman, indignantly; for he felt himself much ill-used, since he had to wear his livery, eat his food, and do nothing at all in return, for the baronet's simple meals were taken into his room by McCray. Williams, the other footman— Sir Murray's spy, as Jane indignantly called him—had been amongst the servants first discharged.

"The poor gairden's going to rack and ruin, lassie," said McCray; "and just as I was going to make such improvements and alterations! But Sir Mooray says I'm not to let either of the ither sairvants go to him; and I believe he frightened that loon in the breeches, because he would take in the letters."

"But he sha'n't frighten me," said Jane, firmly. "I'll never leave the child, come what may."

"Dinna fash yersel', darling," said McCray, tenderly. "I've got the wages and orders of six more that are to be sent away at once, but ye're nae one of them. Sir Mooray winna discharge ye till he packs me off."

"Indeed!" said Jane. "And how do you know?"

"Why, we've been talking aboot ye, lassie; and Sir Mooray said he had made up his mind to go abroad again, and asked me if I'd gang wi' him; and though it cut me to the heart to leave my fruit and flowers, lassie, I thocht I'd see new sorts in the far countree, and I said I'd gang."

"It didn't fret you, then, to think of leaving me?" said Jane, bitterly.

"Hoot, lassie! and who's aboot to gang and leave ye?" exclaimed McCray. "Sir Mooray said I was to see and get a good nurse to tak' charge of the bairn—one as would go abroad; and I told him he couldna do better than keep ye, when I thocht he was going to fly at me. But I told him, quite still like, that we'd promised to marry, and that if he didna tak' ye, lassie, he wadna tak' me; and that seemed to make him mad for a bit, till I told him that ye lo'ed weel the bairn, and that ye were a gude girl at heart. But he wadna listen."

"Was it to be a good place, Alexander?" said Jane.

"Ay, lassie; I was to have a fair bit o' siller."

"Then you mustn't give it up for me."

"I didna mean to, lassie," said McCray, coolly.

Jane was piqued, and said nothing.

"There, lassie, I winna beat aboot the bush any more. It was settled at last that we twain are to gang thegither; and I agreed for both, and Sir Mooray starts next week for the Lake Como."

"And like you!" said Jane, with asperity. "How could you know that I'd go?"

"Why, didn't I ken that ye'd gang for my sake?" said McCray.

"No, indeed!" exclaimed Jane.

"That's just what I thocht," said McCray, with a twinkle in his eye; "but I was quite sure ye would on account of the bairn."

Jane smiled, in spite of herself, as McCray's arm was passed round her: but her eyes filled with tears directly after, as she placed the child upon a chair, and then went down upon her knees before it, kissing it again and again.

"It was good, and kind, and thoughtful of you, Alexander," she said, turning to the gardener; "and I know you've been having a hard battle for me."

"Weel, lassie, he did want a deal o' pruning, certainly," said McCray.

"But I'm very—very grateful!" sobbed Jane, "for the poor child seems all one has to live for now!"

"All, lassie?" said McCray, dryly.

"Well, no; not all," said Jane. "But I'm not worthy of you, and I never ought to have made you the promise I did, for I can't love you as much as you ought to be loved."

"Hoot, lassie!" cried McCray, kneeling by her side, and drawing her to him, "gin ye try like that, I'm quite satisfied, for what more need a man wush for, than for his couthie wee bodie to try and love him with all her heart?"

Mr Chunt's Toast

Mr Chunt presided over a good many discussions in his parlour, where farmer and tradesman met to talk over the course of events during the first few weeks. The subject of Lady Gernon's disappearance was tabooed by general consent. It was not the first event of the kind that had happened through badly-assorted marriages, and wouldn't be the last, said the baker, sententiously; and then it was acknowledged by general consent that money didn't make happiness, and that there was a deal of wickedness in this world.

Upon another night Mr Chunt took to bewailing in public the injury done to his trade, by the shutting up of the Castle.

"Looks a reg'lar devastation, gentlemen," he said; "things all in holland, shutters closed, stables locked up, and all just as if it didn't belong to nobody."

"Oh, Sir Murray will be back one of these days," said a small farmer, cheerfully, "and then trade will brighten up again; meanwhile, you must be contented with our custom, Chunt. He'll tire of foreign parts, you'll see."

"Don't hear any likelihood of Mrs Norton going, I suppose?" said one.

"Not she, poor little woman; she even looks quite cheerful, and is always out with that little boy of hers. Noble little chap he grows!"

"Ah!" said another, "he played his cards well, the Captain did. He hadn't been gone long before there was two couples down to arrest him—two parties, one after the other. Stopped here, they did. Post-chaises: come down in style. Didn't they, Chunt?" The landlord nodded in confirmation. "Just got away in time. Pity, though. He'd have been a bonny man if it hadn't been for his disappointment, and those iron shares. It was on account of his being director, and answerable for a good deal, I suppose, that the bailiffs wanted him."

A week passed, and then Chunt, who had been waiting to have a good full audience, brought out a large auctioneer's posting bill, and laid it before his customers as a surprise.

"What d'yer think of that, gentlemen, eh?" he said. "Merland will be another place soon. There's poor old Gurdon and poor old Barker both dead within the last four-and-twenty hours, and now that's been sent to me to stick up in the bar. Read it out, Mr Mouncey."

The baker put on his spectacles, and read aloud the list of the "elegant and superior household furniture and effects, to be sold by auction, without reserve, at Merland Rectory, by direction of the Reverend Henry Elstree, who was leaving the place."

"Chunt's about right," said Huttoft, the saddler: "the place won't be the same, soon. The old people at the Rectory ain't looked the same, since I saw them coming back that day from the Hall—the day after Lady Gernon elop—disappeared."

"Well, gentlemen," said the landlord, "I believe I'm as sorry as any one present; but it's no use to fret for other folks' troubles. I propose that we have glasses round of brandy hot, gentlemen, for I feel quite sinking."

"Do you pay, Chunt?" said Mouncey, jocosely.

"There ain't a man present as would be more free, gentlemen," said the landlord, "if I could; but, I put it to the company, with the present fall off in my trade, am I able?"

"No—no!" was chorused; and, the glasses being filled, Jonathan Chunt proposed a toast which was drunk with acclamation, and the landlord's toast was:

"Gentlemen, here's to happier times!"

After Twenty Years

"You dog! you confounded lubber! Drive on, or you'll have them out of sight!" shouted a frank, opened-faced young fellow of some three or four and twenty, as he leaned out of the front window of a post-chaise, and urged his post-boy to increase of speed.

"An' how can I get another mile an hour out on such bastes, yer honner?" said the post-boy in answer. "The crayture I'm riding takes no more heed of the spur than the grate baste the levvyathan of Howly Scripture; and as to the blind mare there, the more I larrup her the more she hangs back out ov the collar."

"Gammon!—nonsense!" cried the young man: "you can catch them if you like."

"Shure, sor, I'd catch 'em if it was me. The spirit of me's been close alongside this last quarter of an hour; but the bastes here 'ave got skins like a rhinosros."

"Half a guinea if you catch them and go by in the next two miles," shouted the traveller.

"An why didn't ye spake sooner, sor? It's meself's the boy to get it out of the bastes if it's to be done at all;" and the effect of the golden spur was soon visible in the way in which the mire of the cross-country road flew up from the whirling wheels.

For a couple of hours now, with the present and the preceding post-boy, had this chase been carried on,—now one chaise, now the other, being to the fore; the explanation of this being of the simplest character.

Lieutenant Brace Norton, of H.M.S. "Icarus," had just arrived in port, and was, as he put it, homeward bound after his first voyage with the rank of lieutenant. In fact, he took so much pride in his epaulette, won after no end of midshipman's adventures, that, until better sense prevailed, he had had some thought of wearing it home. He had travelled as far as the county town by rail, and now, having a rather large idea of his own importance, was finishing his journey in one of the post-chaises—scarce things then— left upon the road. At the railway station he had twice encountered a fair young face, small, dark, oval, and with a pair of sad-looking, lustrous eyes, their owner leaning upon the arm of a tall, grey-haired gentleman; and after making his way to the hotel and ordering his conveyance, spending the time consumed in getting it ready by smoking a cigar, he was startled, upon going to the door to lounge about the steps, by seeing the same travellers take their places in a chaise which had been prepared before his own.

"Do you know who that gentleman is?" he had said to the landlord, who had bowed his visitors to the door.

"Can't say, sir, I'm sure," was the reply. "Please excuse me, sir—I'm wanted."

"Here waiter, my chaise; look sharp!" exclaimed the young lieutenant, slipping a shilling into the man's hand, on seeing the direction the first chaise had taken. "Hurry them on, there's a good fellow, and tell them to put in the best pair of horses."

"Best pair's gone, sir, with number one chaise, but I'll get them to look alive."

In spite of his stamping with impatience, and conducting himself in a most unreasonable manner, even to going into the yard himself, and hoisting the sluggish post-boy—a youth of about sixty—into his jacket, a full quarter of an hour elapsed before the chaise began to rattle out of the yard with the traveller in it.

"Here—hi! stop!" shouted a voice, as they turned down the main street.

"What the deuce now?" exclaimed the traveller, as the post-boy pulled up, after nearly running into a flock of sheep, and the waiter came panting up.

"Please, sir, you ain't paid for the cigar, and sherry and biscuit," exclaimed the man, in injured tones.

"Confound it, no!" cried the young man. "And—I say, I haven't got my portmanteau! There, my man, look sharp, whatever you do!"

Five minutes more elapsed, but at length the bill was paid, the portmanteau secured to the front, and the crazy vehicle was once more well under weigh, the young sailor fuming the while with impatience. But as soon as the town was passed, liberal promises sent the shabby cattle scuffling along at a pretty good pace; and when the traveller had about given up all hopes of again seeing the face that had attracted his attention, the first post-chaise became visible, slowly crawling up one of the hills about half-way between Lincoln and Marshton, when again urging on the post-boy, the vehicle was at length overtaken, and whilst passing it the young man's heart leaped as he again caught sight of the fair traveller, leaning forward to see who was passing, but withdrawing instantly upon seeing that she was the object of attention.

Twice did Brace Norton find the opportunities for a short glance at the now averted face: once during the stages, and again when they changed horses at Marshton; but now, to his disgust, it seemed that he had been favoured with worse cattle than before; and in spite of his urging the fresh post-boy—a native of "Sorrey," as he took an opportunity of assuring his employer—it seemed that he was to be left entirely at the rear, to see the face no more.

But the golden spur prevailed; and as the young lieutenant saw that they were gaining rapidly, he threw himself back, muttering, "What a thing it is that there are no women at sea! It only wants their presence to make it perfect. I wonder who those can be, though? On a visit somewhere. Jove! What luck if it's anywhere near us!"

His reverie was interrupted by the broadly-speaking post-boy yoho-ing to the one in front, and the next minute they passed the first chaise in an easy canter; but Brace Norton obtained no view, for, to his great chagrin, the window on this side—the side occupied by the gentleman—had the blind drawn down.

"Didn't I do it in style, yer honner?" cried the post-boy, turning in his saddle to grin.

"Yes—yes; but easy now. Let them pass you." And then to himself the traveller muttered, "I shall be right next time."

"Is that to be included in the half-guinea, yer honner?" cried the post-boy, with a leer; but he obtained no answer, save a fierce gesture not to look back; for now the passing was to be performed by the other chaise, which in a few moments had again left them behind, while this time again the susceptible sailor had been doomed to disappointment, for as the chaise passed, the momentary glance showed him that the lady occupants head was averted, and that she was talking to her companion.

"But what a neck!" muttered the young man; "and what glorious hair! What a cluster of braids! Why, she could sit on it, I'd swear, if it were down. Confound you! will you go on?" he shouted, thrusting his head from the window. "What are you crawling like that for?"

"Did yer honner want me to be always passing them, widout ever letting them get first again?" said the post-boy.

"You blundering idiot!" muttered the young man, laughing in spite of himself. "Drive on, Pat," he said, aloud, "and pass them again."

"Me name's Jeames, yer honner, av ye please," said the post-boy, with dignity, and for a short distance he drove sulkily on at a very moderate pace, till the thought that he had not yet obtained the promised half-guinea prompted him to try and keep his employer in a good temper; and once more he passed the foremost chaise at a canter, slackening again in obedience to orders received soon afterwards.

Now every one who has been much upon the road must be fully aware that there is a feeling existent amply shared by man and horse, which, however strange the comparison may seem, is fully expressed in the old saying, that most people like to play first fiddle. Be driving, and pass the sorriest old jaded brute that was ever verging upon the cat's-meat barrow, and see if the poor beast does not, for a few minutes, prick up his ears, and break into a trot to regain his place. Generally the driver is ready enough to urge him on, and if you slacken pace for a few minutes, ten to one but you are passed in your turn.

It was so here with the post-boy and horses of the other chaise: to be passed here on the road again and again by a rival was not to be borne; and the slackening under Brace Norton's instructions being taken as a signal of defeat, there soon came a shout from behind to the Irish boy to draw aside, one which, being rather sulky at having had a mistake made in his country, the post-boy refused to heed; and just as Brace was hopefully gazing from his window for another glance, there came the crash of wheel against wheel, the swerving aside of the horses, and in less time than it can be written, to Brace Norton's horror, he saw the vehicle of his companions of the road overturned—the off-wheels in the ditch, and one horse kicking and plunging in a way that threatened death to the occupants of the carriage.

The Wreck Ashore

"'E've done it now, sor, an' I hope ye're satisfied!" said James, sitting complacently on his saddle, and looking at the plunging horses, his fellow-servant with one leg entangled in the harness, and the havoc made at each plunge of the uppermost beast.

"You scoundrel!" exclaimed Brace, furiously, as he leaped down. "Why didn't you give more room? Here, come and help!"

"Can't lave me bastes, sor, or they'd take fright, they're so full of sperrit," said the youth, coolly, as, running to the prostrate chaise, Brace contrived to drag open the door, feeling, as he did so, that he was alone to blame for the accident.

"Here, quick! my child! help her first," exclaimed the gentleman, but most needlessly, for the young man had neither look nor thought for him, but was striving to lift the insensible and bleeding form of the wounded girl from the wreck. For at the first crash of the overturning chaise the window had been driven in, and one of the splinters of glass had gashed her temple.

"Good Heavens! what have I done?" muttered Brace, as he succeeded in passing his arms round the senseless form, lifted it by main force from the door, and then bore it to the grass a few yards further on, where, laying it down, he proceeded to press his handkerchief to the wound.

"Let me come, young man," said a harsh voice at his elbow, and, starting with surprise, Brace saw that the gentleman, till now forgotten, had climbed from the chaise, and now made no scruple in thrusting him aside to take his place.

"What can I do? Had I not better gallop off for a doctor?"

"Thank you, no," was the cold reply, as the gentleman, for an instant, looked the tenderer of service full in the face. "This is no scene from a romance, sir. You need trouble yourself no further. My daughter is more frightened than hurt, I dare say."

"A cold-hearted, unfeeling brute," muttered Brace to himself, for he was greatly excited, and felt at that moment as if he would have given the

world to have been allowed to kneel there and support the inanimate form. For a moment he felt ready to make confession that he had been the cause of the accident, but that he felt would be folly; and once more, heedless of the cold reception his offers met with, he proposed that a doctor should be fetched.

"If I required a medical man, sir," said the gentleman, "there is the post-boy, my paid servant, that I could send for one: unless," he said, tauntingly, "you, sir, wish to earn something more than my thanks."

The colour rose to the young man's cheek as he met the cold, glittering eye turned to him for a moment; but he smothered the resentment he could not avoid feeling, and, without a word, turned away to a clear part of the ditch, returning, in a few minutes, with his navy cloth cap half full of water.

The gentleman frowned as he saw this favour forced upon him as he thought, and unwillingly accepting it, he sprinkled the white face, and bathed the forehead, wiping away the ruddy stains, and binding a handkerchief tightly across the wound. But for awhile there were no signs of returning animation, and once more, in spite of the scowl upon the fathers face, Brace Norton hurried away to bring more water.

"There is a faint shade of colour returning now," exclaimed Brace, eagerly.

"Then perhaps you will have the goodness to retire, sir," said the gentleman, haughtily. "My daughter is not accustomed to the society of strangers; and, at such a time, your presence would be a fresh shock."

"But this is a lonely place, sir. You are miles away from any aid. Pray let me endeavour to be of some service. Surely I can help you."

"I thank you, no," was the cold reply.

"But for the lady's sake, sir," exclaimed Brace, almost indignantly. "You will take my chaise, and continue your journey?"

"Young man," was the rude answer, "I am not in the habit of placing myself under obligations to strangers. I shall not require your chaise: I have no doubt, with the help of some of the labourers about, our own vehicle can be set right in a very short time."

"Sure, sor, the short time will be a month," said Brace's post-boy; "the hint wheel's off intirely, and Jerry Stone siz as the harness is all to tatthers, an' he wants to know if aither of ye gentlemen have got a drop of brandy wid ye, for the poor boy feels faint."

In effect, the other post-boy was seated upon a bank beside his now extricated horses—set free by the liberal use of a knife amongst the harness;

and it was evident, from the way in which the poor fellow was rocking himself to and fro, that he was in great pain; while a glance at the wretched chaise showed the impossibility of making use of it for further proceeding upon that day.

But Brace Norton possessed something of the irrepressible in his composition, and, speaking gently, he said, addressing the late speaker: "I am aware, sir, that it is unpleasant to have favours forced upon you by a complete stranger, but let me beg of you not to let the little I offer be looked upon in the light of a favour. For the young lady's sake, pray make use of my chaise, and leave me to take my chance. I dare not presume to offer you advice, but would not a reference to some medical man be advisable? This long-continued swoon—"

Brace Norton said no more, for, glancing from father to daughter as he spoke, he became aware that sensibility had returned, and that a pair of soft, sad, dreamy eyes were fixed upon him, but only for their lids to be lowered, and a faint blush to overspread the pallid cheeks upon her seeing that her gaze was observed.

"Do you feel in pain?" said the gentleman, bending over her, but paying no heed to Brace Norton's remarks.

"No, papa; only a little faint. But you are not hurt?"

"No, no; not at all." Then, in an undertone: "How very unfortunate!" and he frowned at the shattered chaise as he would have done at its driver.

Brace Norton was wise enough in his generation to see that the less he said the less likely he would be to give offence; but a bitter feeling of disappointment came over him as he found how completely his presence was ignored.

"If it were not for that sweet girl he might walk," muttered the young man; but the next moment his heart leaped with pleasure, when, after standing thoughtfully for a few moments, and then glancing from his daughter to the wreck and back again, the gentleman spoke somewhat more courteously.

"Necessity forces me, sir, to accept the offer of your chaise for my—for reasons of my own," he added, hastily. "I will make use of it on condition that you allow me to pay any—"

"Good heavens, sir!" exclaimed Brace, as haughtily now as the stranger, "give me credit for wishing to act as should one gentleman towards another whom he sees with his jibboom—absurd!—whom he encounters in distress—I beg pardon, I mean in—in a strait," exclaimed Brace, desperately, for his nautical imagery did not find much favour. "I am only a simple officer in the navy, and no doubt a sea life makes me somewhat rude, but my offers of service are genuine, not mercenary."

The stranger bowed, and turned to his daughter, who was now standing at his side.

"Take down that portmanteau," exclaimed Brace to the post-boy.

"Yes, sor!" And after a good deal of grunting, unbuckling, and lifting it was placed by the road side.

"If you will allow me," said Brace, "I will see that the damaged chaise is sent back to its owner."

He turned then to hand the lady into the vehicle, but he was motioned back: not, though, without receiving from her a faint smile of thanks.

"My daughter needs no assistance further than I can render," was the stern response to Brace's offer. "Your handkerchief, sir!"

Brace took the handkerchief handed to him, as if the donor were about to strike him down. Then he drew back as father and daughter entered the chaise, so that he did not catch the order given to the post-boy. Then there was a stiff salutation from the gentleman; a slight bow from the lady; and the horses had started, leaving Brace, bareheaded, handsome, and flushed, standing in the road, till, suddenly the front windows were dashed down, the door partly opened, and, evidently suffering from some strong emotion, the face of the gentleman appeared to be turned the next moment towards the post-boy, as he roared, in a voice of thunder: "Stop!"

Another Encounter

"What now?" grumbled the post-boy, as he turned in his saddle, and then, in obedience to the gesticulations directed at him, pulled up very slowly, and not until he had traversed nearly a hundred yards of road. Flinging down the steps, the gentleman alighted, half dragged his daughter from her seat, so rudely, indeed, that she nearly fell. Then drawing her arm tightly through his own, he walked back to the injured post-boy and gave some order, his forehead netted the while with the swelling veins, and his face now pale and flushed by the passion that agitated his breast.

He seemed to quite ignore the presence of Brace, and before the young man could recover from his astonishment, father and daughter were hurriedly walking away.

"Is there anything wrong?—is—that is, can I be of no assistance?" stammered Brace, as he ran after and overtook them—speaking to the father, but gazing the while in the daughter's pale and frightened face, as if his eyes were riveted there; but only to meet with a strange, imploring look, half horror—half dread.

The stranger tried to speak, as he raised one trembling hand, pointing towards the carriage, but no words passed his lips; and motioning the young man fiercely, he hurriedly led his trembling charge away.

"Is he mad?" said Brace to himself. "And to drag that poor girl away like that! What more can I do?" he muttered, as the post-boy drew up alongside of where he stood.

"I've put the portmanty back in the front, sor, as them two ain't agoing."

But Brace Norton did not seem to hear him, as, seeking for some clue to this strange alteration in the old man's behaviour, his eyes fell upon the seat of the chaise the travellers had so lately occupied, where, forgotten for the time, lay his travelling writing-case, with its brass-plate bearing his name and that of his ship.

Well, yes, he had forgotten that, but what was there in his name to make the old man leap from the chaise as if half mad, unless—

There was a faint suspicion in his mind—a dim and confused mingling of fragments of old stories that had never made any impression upon him before; but now he struggled hard to recall in their entirety these shadowy memories of the past. In vain, though; he only grew more mystified than ever. The strangers were already at a turn of the road, and it was in his mind to run after them and ask for some explanation, when his eyes fell upon the handkerchief that the gentleman had placed within his hands—a handkerchief that now for the first time he saw was not the one he had applied to the injured temple, and his heart throbbed as he thought that it was his that she now held; but the next instant a feeling of trouble and pleasure mingled, as it were, came upon him, and he looked eagerly in the corner of the piece of cambric, to find there, in faint but still legible characters, the two words, "Isa Gernon."

An old quarrel—some unpleasantry between the two families—some feeling of bitterness on the part of Sir Murray Gernon, who, with his daughter, had been resident in Italy for some twenty years. That must be it, for he could evoke nothing from the past—nothing tangible. Sir Murray had seen, then, the name of Norton in the chaise, and he refused to accept service from any one bearing that patronymic. It was absurd, too, after all these years; but it would only be an insult to a man of such pride of speech and mien to follow and press upon him what he would look upon as a favour. A little gentle advance or two upon the part of those at the Hall might put all right; for if that was Sir Murray Gernon returned unexpectedly after all these years to dwell at the Castle, there must be no enmity now. And this, then, was his daughter!

So mused Brace Norton as he mentally smoothed away all difficulties ahead, rejoicing, too, he knew not why, at the prospect of possessing such neighbours. He must, he felt, question them at home about the past, and try to adopt means for a reconciliation.

Here he stopped short, roused by the sight of the wrecked chaise, and recalling the position of those from whom he had but now parted. If that were Sir Murray Gernon, he was a good six miles from the Castle, to which place it seemed impossible that he could walk. What could be done, then, to help them without its being known from whence the help arrived? He had at last determined upon being taken back to the town, and informing the hotel-keeper of the state of affairs, when a heavily-laden fly was driven up, the roof and the driver's box being filled with luggage, when, seeing the state of the post-boy and the injured chaise, the fly-man pulled up, and began to make inquiries.

"No bones broke, Tommy," said the post-boy, in reply; "but I shall be precious glad to get back."

"An' was that the chay Sir Mooray Jairnon was in?" exclaimed a voice; and a massive-looking grizzled head was thrust out of the fly-window.

"Was it your master," said the post-boy: "grey gent with a young lady?"

"Yes—yes! Where are they?" exclaimed an eager female voice. "Pray get out, McCray, and see."

"Dinna fash yersel', lassie," said the first speaker. "There's naebodie hurt, I ken. But where's Sir Mooray, my lad?"

"Walked on," said the post-boy.

"You are, then, that gentleman's servant?" exclaimed Brace Norton, now eagerly joining in the conversation.

"And wha may ye be that ask sic a question?"

"Only a traveller on the road," said Brace, smiling, as he glanced at the comely, pleasant-faced female who had just stepped out of the fly; "but your master and the young lady have just walked on. You have arrived in capital time, for I fear that she is much shaken. It was a very rude fall."

"Gudeness save us, Jenny! jump in again, and let's drive on. I'm verra grateful for your information, sir, and I thank ye."

"Pray make haste, McCray!" cried the pleasant-faced dame, smoothing back the grey-streaked bands of hair from her forehead.

And the next minute, with the satisfaction of knowing that he had sent help where it was needed, Brace Norton was standing alone in the road.

He was very thoughtful and serious as he stood there, once more trying to bring back something of the old history from the past days of his parents' life; but he soon gave it up as an impossible task, and one most unsuited for his present place of study. So, assisting the injured post-boy to mount, upon his reiterated assurance that he could easily reach home alone, Brace once more stepped up to his own conveyance, and, very thoughtful and dreamy, slowly continued his journey.

Four miles further on, having purposely kept the post-boy at a slow rate, Brace overtook the late occupants of the fly, arm-in-arm, and sturdily trudging on towards Merland, when, rightly concluding that their places had been taken by Sir Murray and his daughter, Brace stopped the post-boy, and invited the old Scot and his companion to share the conveyance.

"Na, na, sir; ye're verra kind, but I'd raither not, and the gudewife here is of the same opinion. I wish ye a gude day, sir—a gude day. Ye'll excuse our hurrying on."

There was a something in the man's manner that whispered of exclusiveness, and a desire to avoid strangers, which checked Brace Norton in his desire to press his offers of service. He had the good sense to feel, too, that, with the master so determinedly distant, any advances toward the servant might be looked upon as an insult. So, reluctantly giving the order to proceed, the wheels of the chaise spun round, and the next moment, at a turn of the road, Brace caught a glimpse of the couple trudging along; when, throwing himself back in the vehicle, the young man began to ponder upon what was the cause, his thoughts, too, often being occupied by the faces of his mother and Isa Gernon.

Dread

Twenty winters had not come and passed away without leaving traces of their frosty rime upon the heads of Captain Norton and his wife; but as they stood in the Hall dining-room, hand clasping hand, and gazing into each others face, it was evident that, whatever might have been the past, there was peace, content, and happiness there.

"Yes," said Mrs Norton, now grown into a pleasant matronly dame, "he has come back. The whole village rings with the news. So unexpected, too."

"Poor fellow!" said Captain Norton, after a few minutes' quiet thought. "Heaven grant that he may be more happy! I am sorry, though, Ada—very sorry; for his coming seems to open old wounds. But come—come, darling!" he exclaimed, as he drew her towards his breast. "Don't wear that troubled face. Surely, after all these years—"

"Pray forgive me!" said Mrs Norton, nestling closer to him; and she smiled happily in reply to his caresses. "As you say, Philip, Heaven help him, and clear up the dark mystery of his life! I do not see why we should trouble ourselves about his coming back."

"Well—no," said Captain Norton, uneasily; "but one cannot help recalling how events shaped themselves after his last return. But there, let us dismiss it all, for I cannot trust myself even now to dwell upon all these old matters. I would make up my mind to leave, and at once, in spite of the inconvenience, only that it would be like a tacit acknowledgment that I was afraid to meet him; and you know how charitable people can be."

"Oh no; we could not think of leaving," said Mrs Norton, hastily; "but I think—nay, I feel sure that with him the past will be buried entirely; for, Philip," she added, solemnly, "may Heaven forgive me if I am uncharitable, but I believe that the man who could so cruelly malign my husband must have had his own ends to serve. I could not refrain from saying this, as the subject was brought up; but whatever evil—whatever wrong-doing was connected with poor Marion's disappearance, must some day or other be brought out into the light of day. Twenty years—twenty long years—has the matter slumbered, and it may slumber twenty more; and, in spite now of my utter indifference to public opinion, I cannot help longing for the mystery to be cleared up in our day. But, whether or no, promise me this, dearest, that it shall not be allowed to trouble you—that you will not brood over it; and that, come what may, you will avoid all encounter with that bad, proud man, whose coming seems like a cloud sent over dear old Merland. I almost feel thankful that poor Mr and Mrs Elstree are now far away from trouble and care. There was that dread suspicion, though, in both their hearts; I feel sure, however, they struggled to the last to keep it back. But there: let us dismiss it all; and you promise me, do you not?"

Captain Norton's calm, quiet smile was enough to reassure his wife; and as he took his seat at a side-table, covered with correspondence, she stood behind him, leaning her hands upon his shoulder.

"We are going on at a famous rate, Ada," he said, after a busy pause, in short, sharp, decisive tones, that smacked of the man of business—"returns increasing every month. Some of the prophetic old wiseacres would give their ears now for shares in our rusty old iron company. By the way, though, Brace has not written for any money lately. Is it not time we heard from him?"

"Yes," said Mrs Norton, with anxiety in her tones; "and—"

"Now, don't be an old fidget," said the Captain, laughingly, as once more he drew her towards him. "That poor old head of yours is as full of shipwrecks and disasters at sea as one of the wreck-charts or Lloyd's ledgers. What a pity it is that we did not have half-a-dozen boys for you to share that weak old heart of yours amongst, so that you need not have had to worry yourself to death about one!"

"But surely we ought to have had a letter a month since."

"Certainly, my love, if the poor boy had had a post-office close at hand into which he could pop it. Don't be so unreasonable. You don't know how even an adverse wind will keep a vessel away from port for weeks together. You must study statistics, so as to ease that heart of yours, by learning how seldom a mishap befalls a ship. We shall be hearing from him before long, and—There, bless my soul, I must keep a clerk; I've forgotten to answer Harrison and Son's letter."

"What was that about?" said Mrs Norton, as, pleased to see how happy her husband was in his business pursuits—upon which, in spite of adversity at the outset, fortune had of late smiled in full sunshine—she tried to enter into each matter, knowing full well how his busy life had been the cure for a mind diseased.

"What was it about?" said Captain Norton, dreamily. "Oh, about the marsh—the warping, you know. I am to have two thousand acres."

"But I don't know," said Mrs Norton, smiling; "you promised to explain."

"To be sure; so I did!" he exclaimed, eagerly reaching down a rolled-up plan, and spreading it upon the table. "Now look here, Ada; this will be an expensive affair, and we shall reap no benefit from it ourselves, for it is a matter of years and years; but that young dog will have an estate which will make him hold up his head as high as he likes. Now, see here—this is my side. I've bought these two thousand acres of worthless marshland—worthless save for peat-digging and wild-duck shooting. This is the piece, Ada, love," he said, solemnly, as he laid a finger upon the plan. "I chose this so that I might preserve the pine-wood untouched."

He stopped to gaze up in his wife's face, and as she recalled the past, she bent over him until her cheek touched his forehead.

"Well, love," he said, raising himself and speaking cheerfully, "we—that is to say, the other purchasers and myself—dig a large drain, or canal, through our marsh pieces right to the Trent, and fit our drain with sluice-gates, so that at every high tide we flood our low tract of marsh with the thick, muddy waters loaded with the alluvial soil of Yorkshire and our own county, brought down by many a river and stream, which, after the fashion of the hill floods, by slow and almost imperceptible degrees, is deposited upon our peat and rushes, in a heavy, unctuous, wondrously rich mud, or warp, till, in the course of time, we have it two, three, and in places even four feet deep. Then comes the change: we cease flooding, and give all our attention to thoroughly draining our warp land, which now becomes, in place of marsh, fit only to grow water-plants, a rich and fertile soil. Nature has converted it for us; and twenty years hence, instead of marsh, Master Brace will have a couple of thousand acres of the best soil in England. That is all I can do for him, and after all I don't think that it will be such a very mean heritage. Now, love, what do you say to that?"

Mrs Norton's answer was a cry of joy: for at that moment, free of step, bright and happy, in came Brace Norton, to be strained again and again to his mother's breast.

There was a grim smile of pride and pleasure upon Captain Norton's scarred face, as, after hastily rolling up his plans, he caught at his son's disengaged hand.

"My dear Brace, how well and hearty you look!" he exclaimed, as he scanned the broad chest and muscular limbs of his son.

"I Well? Ay! father, never better," was the reply. "And I don't know that I ever saw you look better."

"Oh! I'm well enough," said Captain Norton. "But, my dear boy, what a pity it is that you did not join our service! With that build of yours, you would have drilled as upright as a dart."

"And broken my heart over the pipe-clay, eh, father?" laughed the young man. "I'm right enough—make a tolerable sailor, perhaps, but I should have been a poor soldier. But, I say," said Brace, after half-an-hour's questioning and answering, "I have had quite an adventure coming over: came across a fine, fierce, grey old fellow, with—oh! mamma, the most lovely girl you ever saw in your life!"

"Pooh!" laughed the Captain, "the sailor's Poll. What asses you boys do make of yourselves!"

"All right, father; only let me bray in peace."

"Fell in love at first sight, and would have eloped, only the fierce, grey old fellow was watchful as a dragon, eh, Brace?" said Captain Norton, smiling.

"Belay, there, will you!" cried Brace. "How can I go on with my story? Not quite so fast as that. But there, sir, we can spare you for the present. I'm talking to some one here who can sympathise. Really, you know," he continued, passing his arm round his mother's waist, as she gazed at him fondly, and drawing her to the window, "she was about the sweetest girl I ever set eyes on. Quite an adventure: chaises passing; theirs overset; sweet girl's temple cut; insensible; offering aid; received very haughtily by the old gentleman—quite a Spanish grandee!"

Ada Norton started, as those words seemed to carry her back five-and-twenty years, and the smile upon her lips slowly faded away.

"Well," continued Brace, lightly, "I spoiled my cap by fetching water in it from a pool, like a true knight-errant would have done with his casque, and bound up the bleeding temple with my handkerchief. Then, after a great deal of snubbing from the old gentleman, I was rewarded by a sweet smile of thanks from the lady as I prevailed upon the Don to take my chaise and come on. Got them in at last, after a great deal of ceremonious fencing, and they drove off, but only to stop directly. Old gentleman leaps out, drags sweet girl after him, and goes raging off; and all, I suppose, because he had seen my name upon my leather writing-case; while, for explanation, I have the young lady's handkerchief, bearing the sweet name of Isa Gernon. But, good heavens, my dear mother, how pale you look! Father, what is the matter?"

Captain Norton had risen from his seat and advanced to his wife, who, pale as death, stood gazing at him with a terrified expression upon her countenance.

"My dear father, what does all this mean?" exclaimed Brace, with real anxiety in his tones. "What mystery is there here? Of course I concluded that the elderly gentleman was Sir Murray Gernon; and I have some misty recollections of an old family quarrel, and Lady Gernon running away. There, I have arrived at my cable's end. What is it all? I trust nothing wrong."

"Speak to him, Ada!" cried Captain Norton, hoarsely. "There must be no more of this!"

And without another word he hurried from the room; while, perfectly astounded, Brace turned to his mother for some explanation of what was to him a profound mystery.

On the Bygone

"And where had my father been at the time?" said Brace Norton, after sitting with knitted brows listening to his mother's narrative of the past.

"France—abroad—to avoid arrest; for his affairs in connection with the mine were then in a sad state. It was his absence which made matters wear so suspicious an aspect."

"Suspicious? Yes," said Brace, angrily, "suspicious enough to base minds! How long was he away?"

"Five, nearly six, months," said Mrs Norton.

"But you never believed this charge, mother? You never thought my father guilty?"

"Guilty? No!" exclaimed Mrs Norton, proudly. "Your father, Brace, is the soul of honour, and above suspicion; but matters shaped themselves most cruelly against him."

"That Gurdon must have had the cross," said Brace, after a thoughtful pause; "and you say that he obtained his deserts—transported?"

Mrs Norton nodded her head.

"But Lady Gernon's disappearance—what could have become of her? Was it possible that she was deluded away out of revenge—perhaps with the cross for a bait—by some one or other of Gurdon's associates, so that she fell into some trap?"

"My son—my dear boy, pray do not talk of it any more," said Mrs Norton, sadly. "It is a rock upon which our happiness was nearly wrecked; but avoid it now. It was right that you should know all after the strange meeting of to-day; but you see now the reason for your father's—for my agitation, and for the strong emotion displayed by Sir Murray Gernon. It is quite impossible, as you must see, that the old intimacy should be renewed. Your fathers—my peace of mind depends upon our keeping at a distance—upon the past, Brace, being deeply buried. You see that I am speaking freely—that I am keeping nothing back, in order that you may be upon your guard, and do nothing to endanger the happiness of what, my child, has been these many years a happy home."

"But," exclaimed Brace, impetuously, "if the mystery could be cleared up! I do not like that, even with Sir Murray Gernon, there should be a doubt of my father's honour."

"Brace, my dear boy," said Mrs Norton, laying her hand upon the young man's arm, "let the past rest; it is a subject that has brought white hairs into more than one head. It has been thought upon till left in despair. I pray to be forgiven if I am unjust, but I do not think that Sir Murray Gernon entertains a single suspicion against your father, whatever he may once have felt. Time must have removed old impressions; but for his own black conduct—There, I dare not say what I think, even to you, Brace!"

There was a contraction of the young man's features, as an inkling of the meaning of his mother's hastily-spoken words flashed across his mind. Then, rising, he began to pace the room with impatient strides, for there was a sense of disappointment at his heart which he could not overcome; and in spite of his efforts, there seemed to be continually before him the sweet, timid face and the reclining figure that he had for a few minutes supported; while, as he pondered upon his mothers words, again piecing together her long narrative, it seemed to him that he was every minute being removed further and further from one who had made what in another case he would have called an impression upon a susceptible nature. It was as though each moment a deep, black gulf was opening wider and wider between them—a gulf that it would be impossible for him ever to pass. Then, as Mrs Norton watched him anxiously, he stood gazing from the window, telling himself that it was absurd to treat matters in such a light; that he had seen Isa Gernon but for a few minutes; that he had barely spoken to her; that she might be engaged to another; that she might be in disposition unamiable, and in tastes utterly opposed to his; that, in short, he was making an utter ass of himself. But, all the same, there were those two large, sad eyes ever before him, gazing reproachfully in his face from beyond that great gulf— ever widening more and more, more and more, till, impatiently stamping upon the floor, he made an angry effort to cast the "folly" from him, and went and knelt down by his mother's side.

"I am sorry, Brace," she said, as her hand played, with all a proud mother's tenderness, amongst his fair, crisply-curling hair—"I am grieved that my words should have made so troublous an impression."

"It is not that—it is not that! There, what am I saying?" he exclaimed, with assumed cheerfulness. "I've come home in high spirits, brimful of happiness, and ready to enjoy myself; so, dear mother, don't let us trouble about the past—let it be buried."

"Yes, better so—far better so!" exclaimed Mrs Norton. "For our sakes, Brace, never refer to it before your father in any wise; for those incidents were so many shoals in the way of his happiness; but, Brace, I set myself to try and make his life happy, and sometimes I cannot help thinking that I have succeeded."

"Indeed, no happier home than this could ever have existed, I'm sure," cried Brace, smiling in his mother's pleasant face. "But," he added, as he kissed her, laughing, "it does seem hard that when you have cured a husband of a roving disposition, you should have a son turn out far worse."

Mrs Norton smiled, but a grave, sad expression swept the next moment over her face.

"Save for his business transactions, Brace, that was your father's last long absence from me—for I suffered deeply then. I think that on his return from France, when he had had some arrangements made by which he gained time to pay off every demand, he saw how I had felt his absence, and made a resolve to leave me no more, and he has kept to that determination."

"The mines nearly ruined him, then, in the first place?" said Brace.

"Very nearly; but he had such faith in them that for five years we lived almost in poverty that we might pay off debts; when, as his last creditor was satisfied, your father's faith met with its reward, and ever since the mines have gone on increasing their returns year by year. But let us go to him now. You will be careful, though, Brace; you see now how necessary it is that not even a reference should be made to the bygone?"

"Yes—yes, mother—yes!" said Brace, with a troubled sigh; and they rose to leave the room, when, with the traces of his former emotion quite passed away, Captain Norton entered, looking inquiringly at mother and son, and then entering into conversation upon indifferent topics, as if nothing had happened.

Right Honourable

"Now look here, Josh: it's of no use for you to come bothering me like this. Here have I been back from Italy only a few days, and you're down upon me like a leech—I mean like a hawk!"

"If your lordship had condescended to tell me that you were going abroad, and consulted me about the meeting of those little bills when they fell due, it would have been a different thing."

The scene was a heavily-furnished room in a fashionable London hotel, and the speakers were George Viscount Maudlaine, son and heir to the hampered estates and somewhat tarnished title of the Right Honourable Valentine, twentieth Earl of Chiltern; and Joshua Braham, Esq., solicitor, of Drury Chambers, St Alban's Place, Regent Street. The former, as he lounged back in his purple dressing-gown, appeared to be a tall, well-made young man, with a somewhat dreamy or tobacco-contemplative cast of countenance, more remarkable for bone, and the prominence of the well-known Chiltern features, than anything particularly definite; the latter was a gentleman, very smooth, very swarthy, possessing a ruddy and Eastern development of lip, aquiline of—nose, hair short—black—spiky—of a texture, in short, that threatened, should a lock be sent for, to fly off in dangerous blinding showers of capillary stubble.

"You see, I don't recollect these sort of things," said his lordship.

"Only when your lordship requires a fresh supply of money," said Mr Braham, smiling like a shark, and rubbing his hands together so that his rings rattled.

"There, don't make a bother: sit down and have some breakfast, Braham," said the younger man. "These sort of things are so dooced unpleasant."

"Unpleasant? There's nothing further from my thoughts, my lord, than making things unpleasant. I only came, after writing twice to remind your lordship that three bills, which fell due a month since, were all returned, and now lie in my hands, with interest and expenses attached. Unpleasant? Why, I give you my word, that Moss, or Peterson, or Barcohen, would have had your lordship arrested and in Bream's Buildings or Cursitor Street days ago. But I don't do business like that. I only accommodate gentlemen of position, and then, in return, I expect to get the treatment one meets with from gentlemen of position."

"You Israelitish hound!" muttered his lordship, "I'd pitch you out of the window if I dared!"

"Did your lordship speak?" said the visitor, bending his head aside in an attitude of attention.

"Speak? No! Only I've such a confounded headache this morning, I'm not fit for business matters. Richmond last night with some friends."

"Yes; I heard so," said the visitor, softly. "Mad'moiselle Duval was of the party, I think?"

"How the dooce did you know that?" exclaimed his lordship, uneasily.

"Oh! really I hardly know. It is one of the troubles of position, my lord, that every one hears of your movements."

"I'll lay twenty to one that you've had some hook-beaked, unshaven dog watching me ever since I've been back!" exclaimed his lordship, impetuously.

"He, he, he!" laughed the Jew. "Your lordship may have a headache, but you are really most keen and business-like this morning."

His lordship growled.

"*You* are," he said, after a pause.

"Exactly so," said the money-lender. "And now, perhaps, your lordship will give your attention to the matter in hand?"

"Well, I am attending!" grumbled his lordship.

"Then, perhaps, your lordship will give me a cheque on your banker for the total of the bills, interest and expenses. Let me see," continued the visitor, drawing a large bill-case from his pocket.

"There, keep that confounded thing out of my sight! My head aches quite badly enough without having that thrown in my teeth. Now, look here: I haven't fifty pounds at the banker's, and what there is I want for present expenses."

"Then what does your lordship propose doing?"

"Nothing at all," said his lordship sulkily.

"Does your lordship wish me to ask payment of the Earl, your father?"

"If you like," said his lordship, with a grin; "but while he has this fit of the gout on, I should not advise you to get within his reach. He holds to the fine old idea of his Norman ancestors, that knocking a Jew on the head was meritorious. But there! he won't pay—he can't, even if he felt ever so disposed. Now, look here, Braham: you must stick some more interest on, and renew the bills."

"Renew, my lord?" exclaimed the money-lender, expressing with eyebrows and hands the greatest of surprise. "Impossible! I've renewed till I'm as sick of it as of your broken faith."

"No, you're not; so don't be a humbug!" said the Viscount. "I'm not very sharp, I know; but I'm keen enough to see through that. You've milked me pretty well, and worked me nicely with all your professional cant. I don't recollect how much I've had in cash—I did put it down on old envelopes, but they're lost—but I know that those pictures and the wines were horrible stuff; and one way and another you've made those bills grow till now they amount to—"

"Four thou—"

"There—there, that'll do; I can't pay it, so what's the good of bothering one about how much it is? I've got it down somewhere, I tell you, and perhaps I can find it when I want to know, and I don't now. Well, as I was going to say, you've made the bills grow to that size, now make them grow a little bigger."

His lordship yawned, stretched himself, and then poured some pale brandy into a coffee-cup, before filling it with the rich fluid in the biggin.

"Totally impossible, my lord," said the money-lender, rising. "I'm very sorry, my lord, but I must set the law to work. I have, as you well know, always been most desirous of aiding you during pressing necessities; and when unable to help you myself, I have always introduced you to some one who would. But, to speak plainly, this trip of yours to Italy, without a word to me first—"

"Why, confound it all! was I to come and ask you if I might go abroad?" exclaimed his lordship, furiously.

"Oh, dear me, no! Of course not, my lord; but as I was saying, this trip to Italy looks so much like trying to bilk me, that I must, for my own sake—"

"And that of the gentleman in the City," sneered his lordship.

"No, my lord, I don't do business with men in the City," said the Jew, in injured tones; "and for my own sake alone I must take strenuous measures for the recovery of the debt."

"'Tisn't a debt: it's only a money-lending affair," growled his lordship.

"Well—well, we won't argue upon that point, my lord. The Sheriff of Middlesex has his ideas upon these matters—ideas in which I have implicit confidence."

"Here, Braham; I say; come, no nonsense. Don't be a fool, you know. Don't be hard on a fellow because he's bilious and put out!" exclaimed his lordship, who, with the immediate prospect of a sponging-house before him, displayed an unwonted degree of perturbation. "But, I say, you can't— you know you can't do any thing yet;" and his lordship's face brightened.

The Jew laughed.

"Your lordship forgets. Hyman has a little affair out against you, which will just work in well with mine. I shouldn't be surprised if some one is already waiting for you!"

"Oh! come, I say—you know; I can't stand this. You mustn't do anything, Braham; and you must stop Hyman, because I've come home—come over— come on purpose—that is, I have something good on my book."

The money-lender watched him narrowly.

"Have indeed—matter of great importance—case of thousands, in fact—clear me of all my little unpleasantries."

"Pooh!" ejaculated the money-lender, dropping the servile now that his client began to implore. "Something on the Heath, or the Derby, or Oaks. I never knew one of your family yet with *nous* enough to do anything but lose. Now, look here, my lord: are you prepared to pay me four thousand three hun—"

"No; not a penny!" exclaimed his lordship, earnestly; "but, look here, Braham," he cried, catching his visitor by the button; "I've got something in hand—I have indeed: not betting. Something safe and paying; but you must give me time, and let me have a few hundreds to carry on with."

"Bah!" exclaimed the Jew fiercely, "I'm not going to be shilly-shallied with any more. Now, look here, my lord; I've given you time, and I've been patient. You've had documents served upon you; but even to the last I wouldn't be hard. I said to myself, I'll give him every chance; and I've done it; but you only turn round upon me like all the rest, friend as I've been to you. And now it has come to this—I've asked you to pay me, and you won't."

"I can't, I tell you—'pon my word I can't," exclaimed his lordship, following his visitor to the door, and pressing it back, as the other tried to get it open.

"Very well. Then I must have my pound of flesh!" said the Jew, with a bitter grin. "Only, you see, my lord, we are wiser than our old ancestor, Shylock: we do not bargain for exact weight, and, to avoid the punishment awarded to the shedder of blood, we take the whole body. Your lordship weighs twelve stone, I should think?"

"Fourteen stone," said the Viscount, complacently.

"Plenty of weight, and to spare, then," said the Jew, laughing.

"But you don't mean what you say, Braham?" said his lordship, anxiously.

"I never joke on money matters, my lord; I've a couple of sheriff's officers and a cab across the road, my lord. If you will take the trouble to walk across to the window you can see them."

Lord Maudlaine took a step across towards the window; but he was back in an instant.

"But I say, Braham," he exclaimed, "this is getting serious—it is, indeed—and you mustn't, you know; 'pon my word, you mustn't. Think of the scandal and the expense; and you won't do yourself any good, besides ruining me."

"What do you mean by ruining you?" said the Jew, for the young nobleman's earnestness was such as no dread of a spunging-house, pure and simple, would have evoked—"what's in the wind?—what do you mean?"

"Well, I tell you, don't I? I've got something in hand—something good, you know."

"What is it?"

There was a few minutes' silence as, driven to bay by his necessities, the scion of the not very noble house stood frowning and biting his lips.

"Just as you like," said the Jew, coolly. "I don't want you to tell me." And he again tried to leave, but his lordship stayed him.

"Now, look here," said the Jew again. "I've always been a friend to you, Lord Maudlaine, and I'll give you one more chance. What did you go to Italy for?"

There was no answer; and as his lordship stood with his back to the door, the visitor walked across to the window, as if to signal to one of the men waiting with the cab.

"Well, there," exclaimed his lordship, "to get out of your way."

The Jew smiled.

"I expected as much. And now, why did you come back?"

"To—because—Well, there; it's connected with the—with the—the good thing I told you of."

"Now, look here, young man," said Abraham, without the "A," "are we to be friends or enemies?"

"Friends, of course," said the young nobleman, scowling.

"Then, look here: I must have perfect openness. Just show me that this is something genuine—something worth waiting for, and I'll wait—of course, for a consideration."

He waited for some response to his words, but none was forthcoming.

"I'm not going to be treated like this!" exclaimed the visitor, with mock anger. "I'll soon—"

"There, there—stop, and I'll tell you all about it. It is worth waiting for."

His lordship stopped short again, and his by no means intellectual countenance displayed strongly the shame and humiliation he felt.

"Well?" said the Jew.

"It's about a marriage—a matrimonial affair."

The Jew looked at him as if he would read his every thought.

"Plenty of money?" he said, at last.

"One of the richest heiresses in England."

"Are you sure of that?" said Braham; "or has some foreign countess got hold of you again?"

"Sure? Yes!" cried Maudlaine, excitedly. "The father has been living out of England for years past at the rate of a couple of thousand a year, and his income's at least twenty. All been increasing and piling up ever since."

The Jew again looked piercingly at the young man; but it was plain enough that the ability was not in him to invent this as a fiction upon the spur of the moment.

"Well," said the interlocutor, "go on. Have you any chance?"

"Yes; of course I have," said Maudlaine.

"Father agreeable?"

"Yes!"

"Lady?"

"Well, yes—pretty well; but that's all right, I tell you."

"Meet them abroad?"

"Yes."

"Have they come back to town?"

"To England—not town."

"Humph!" ejaculated the visitor, still narrowly scanning his victim. "And that's why you came back?"

"Of course."

"Now, look here, Maudlaine," said the Jew, fiercely, "I'm not a man to be trifled with. I was your slave once, and you did not forget to show it. You are mine now, and you must not be surprised at my turn, now it has come, being brought strongly before your attention. But I'll be frank with you: I lend money for interest. Well and good: I'd rather wait and let you pay me that money and that interest than have to arrest you. I don't want to get a bad name amongst your class. Now I've not much confidence in you as to promises to pay; but I'll believe your word of honour. Is all this true?"

"On my word of honour, yes!" said Maudlaine, angrily.

"Who is the lady, then?" The Viscount flushed deeply, bit his lips, and was silent; for to answer this question seemed to him too great a humiliation. "Who is the lady?" was asked again. There was no answer. "I suppose you don't want my help, then?" said the Jew. "Just as you like. Prove to me that this is worth my while to wait—say six or twelve months—and I'll lend you a few hundreds to go on with. But, there, I'm not anxious; just as you like. Shall I call up the men?"

"Confound you, no!" exclaimed the young man, angrily. "She is the daughter of a wealthy baronet, of Lincolnshire. Now are you satisfied?"

"No," said the Jew, taking out pencil and pocket-book; "I want his name."

"Good old family," said the Viscount, hastily. "Only child. I am invited down there, and the baronet is quite willing. Will that do?"

"Name—name—name!" exclaimed the creditor, impatiently.

"Sir Murray Gernon. There, then!" cried the young man, furiously.

"Sir Murray Gernon," said the Jew, quietly, as he tapped his teeth with his large gold pencil-case—"Sir Murray Gernon. Ah! let me see; there was a screw loose there, if I recollect right, years ago. Rich family, though—very. Young lady's mamma bolted, I think; but that don't matter to you. Yes, that will do, Viscount—that will do. I think I'll wait."

"And you will advance me what I require?" said his lordship, eagerly, forgetting all humiliation in his brightened prospects.

"In reason, yes," said the Jew, with a mocking smile once more overspreading his face; "but I shall not do it for nothing, my Lord Viscount Maudlaine—I shall not do it for nothing."

"No," muttered the young man, "I know that."

"It's quite possible that I may go so far as to make my own terms," said the Jew, with a grin. "But I'll leave you, now, to think over the matter; and if you want any little help, of course you'll come to my chambers, where we can renew one of the bills."

"Confound the bills!" cried the young man, angrily; "I must have a cheque for some hard cash to go on with."

"Very good. Come to me, then, my lord," said the Jew, all suavity once more. "Excuse me for hurrying away, but it is for your sake. It is not seemly to have Sheriffs' officers waiting opposite to an hotel. Good morning, my lord!"

"Good morning!" said the Viscount, sulkily.

"You shall fly a little longer, my fine bird—just a little longer!" said Mr Joshua Braham, as he went out; "but it shall be just as long as I like, and with a string tied to your leg—a string, my fine fellow, of which I hold the end?"

In Peril

"It is of no use," said Brace Norton, one day, when he had been home about a month, "I can't fight against fate. I vowed that I'd think no more about her, and I've thought about nothing else ever since. I go out very seldom, but when I do, I always seem to meet her. I've heard a good deal of milk-and-sugar talk about love; and if this is what is called love, all I can say is that it's worse than mast-heading. I can't help it—I can't keep free of it! What in the world did I get looking at her for, as I did, that day coming home? Brace Norton—Brace Norton, I'm afraid that you are a great ass!"

He sat thinking for awhile, trying to be light-hearted, and to sweep his troubles away, but he soon owned to himself that it was no laughing matter.

"Heaven help me!" he groaned, "for a miserable, unhappy wretch—one who seems fated to make those about him suffer! It seems almost as if I were to endure the same torments as my poor father, without the alleviation of some other gentle hand to heal my wounds. Wounds! Pooh! stuff! What romantic twaddle I am talking! It is time I was off back to sea. But, there, I've fought against it, all for their sakes, till it has been enough to drive me mad. I suppose men were meant to be butterflies, and to burn their wings in the light of some particular star; so the sooner I get mine singed off, and get on board ship, the better. There's no romance there. Anything's better than this state of torment. Here am I, making myself disagreeable to the best of fathers and the tenderest of mothers; and because things run in a rut different from that which suits me, I go sulking about like a spoiled child in love with a jam-pot; and after making everybody miserable at home, go sneaking and wandering about after the fashion of a confounded tramp poaching somebody's goslings. I expect I shall be locked up one of these days. Seriously, though, I wish I had not come back," he said, dreamily; "I wish that a reconciliation were possible; I wish I had never seen her; I wish—I wish—There, what is the good of wishing? What a wretched life this is, and how things do contrive to get in a state of tangle! I don't think I ever tried to meet her, and yet how often, day after day, we seem to encounter! Even the thought of the old past sorrows seems to bring her closer and closer. Why, then, should not this be the means of bringing old sorrows to an end, and linking together the two families?"

Brace Norton brought his ponderings to a close, as, bit by bit, he recalled the past; and then he groaned in spirit, as his reason told him how impossible was a reconciliation.

"I must dismiss it all," he at last said, bitterly. "They have had their sufferings; I will not be so cowardly as to shrink from mine. I'll take an interest in the governor's pursuits; and here goes to begin. I'll run over to the Marsh, and see where they are pegging out the drain; but I may as well take a gun, and see if I cannot bag a couple or two of ducks."

Brace Norton's reverie had been in his own room; and with this determination fresh upon him, he walked, cheery of aspect, into the room where Captain and Mrs Norton had been discussing the unsatisfactory turn matters had taken, when the young man's bright look, and apparently buoyant spirits, came upon them like a burst of sunshine.

"Gun? Yes, my dear boy!" exclaimed the Captain, delighted at the change that seemed to have come over his son. "Here you are," he said, opening a case—"everything to your hand. You'll be back to dinner?"

"Ay, ay, sir!" cried Brace, strengthened in his resolve, on seeing the pleasure his high spirits seemed to impart to his elders. "I am going to see where they are marking out the drain."

"To be sure. Quite right, Brace—quite right. I should like, above all things, to go with you."

"Well, why not?" said Brace, heartily.

Captain Norton smiled, and shook his head, as he pointed to his writing-table, covered with correspondence.

"Too much engaged, my boy—too many letters to write. I'll go over with you one day, though, if you will."

"To be sure," said Brace.

And then he saluted his mother, who held his hands tightly, as if unwilling to part from him, as she gazed fondly in his face. Then having secured the gun and ammunition, he started off, with a bold, elastic step, apparently as free from care as if no cloud had crossed his young career.

He had not gone far before again and again came the longing desire to sit down beneath some shady tree, and picture the soft sweet face that his heart whispered him he loved—the face that seemed to be so impressed upon his brain, that, sleeping or waking, asked for or uncalled, it was always there vividly before his gaze; though, beyond a distant salute and its response, since the day of the accident, he had never held the slightest intercourse with Isa Gernon. He might have laughed at another for being so impressionable; but, none the less, he felt himself to be greatly moved, and hour by hour he felt that the task he had imposed upon himself was greater than he could ever expect to master.

But that day Brace would not yield to the sweet temptation, striving manfully and trying hard to tire himself out. He visited the portions of the great marsh where arrangements were being made for forming the drain; he tramped to and fro over the boggy land with his gun, hour after hour; and at last, utterly weary, he entered the pine-wood on the marsh edge, having unwittingly wandered to the spot where, years before, his father had, in his wild despair, so nearly cast away his life.

It was with a sigh of satisfaction that he leaned his gun against a tree, and seated himself upon the fallen trunk of a large fir; for there was something soothing to his feelings in the solemn silence of this vast nature-temple. There was a soft, warm glow cast aslant amidst the tall smooth pillars by the descending sun, and but for the soft sigh of a gentle gale, and the sharply-repeated tap of the woodpecker sounded at intervals, there was nothing to break the stillness, which to another might have seemed oppressive.

And now, with a fierce rush, the dammed-back thoughts made at him. Now was the time for reverie—here in this solitary place. But no—he would not weakly succumb. It was not to be: he had made a resolution, and he would keep it. He boldly set himself to fight with a power stronger than himself, blindly thinking that he might succeed.

How had he succeeded with his gun?

He smiled as he looked at the result of his many hours' tramp—one solitary teal; and then for a few moments he was dwelling musingly upon the great subject that had filled his mind during the past month, but only to dismiss it angrily. He sighed, though, the next moment, and the soft breeze bore away the word "Isa"; and then romance faded as Brace sought solace in the small case he drew from his pocket, from which he selected a very foreign-looking cigar, lit it, and leaning back, began to emit cloud after cloud of thin blue vapour, till the tobacco roll was smoked to the very end, when Brace rose, calm and refreshed, ready to journey homeward.

"A sonnet to his mistress's eyebrow," said Brace, as he moved over the pine-needles. "Not so bad as that, though, after all."

He had not proceeded a dozen yards, though, before he remembered that he had left his gun behind, leaning against a tree; and hurrying back, he was in the act of taking it, when a distant cry came floating through the trees.

"Hullo!" exclaimed Brace, as he caught up his gun. "Curlew? No, it was not a curlew; but I've grown so used to the wail of the sea birds, that I don't know those of my native place. Ha! there it is again."

For once more the cry came ringing faintly by—a long, low, prolonged scream, as of some one in peril; when, roused by the exciting promise of adventure, he ran swiftly in the direction from whence the cry seemed to have come.

In a few minutes he was at the edge of the grove, gazing over the open marsh, to see nothing; when, fancying that he must have come in the wrong direction, he stood listening intently for another cry.

A full minute elapsed—a minute during which he could hear his heart beating heavily—and then once more came the loud wail, plainly enough now, and forming the appealing word that goes home to every heart:

"Help!"

The next moment Brace Norton was dashing over the treacherous bog, leaping from tuft to tuft of the silky cotton rush, avoiding verdant patches of moss, which concealed watery, muddy pools, and finding foothold where the heather grew thickly. Twice he sank in to his knees, but he dashed on to where, at the distance of some three or four hundred yards from the pine-wood, he had made out a figure struggling in one of the profound holes filled with deep amber-coloured water, while, as he rushed on, at times floundering and splashing in the soft peat, it seemed to him that his aid would arrive too late.

A light muslin dress, a portion of which, still undrenched, buoyed up its wearer; a little straw hat, fallen off to float on the dark waters; a pale, upturned, agonised face; long clusters of hair rippling with the troubled element; and two dark, wild, appealing eyes, seeming to ask his aid. Brace Norton saw all this in the few moments ere he reached the side of the pit; but as he recognised the features, a cry of anguish tore from his heart, as, falling heavily, it was some little time before he could regain his feet. Then, with a rush and a plunge, he sent the water foaming in great waves to the green and deceptive sides of the moor-pit, still trembling with the weight that had lately passed over them. Another minute, and with the energy of a stout swimmer he had forced himself through the dozen yards of water that intervened, to reach at and grasp an arm, just as the water was bubbling up above a fair, white forehead, and playing amidst the long tresses floating around. Another instant, and Brace's arm was supporting the drowning girl, as he swam stoutly towards the side.

The distance was short, but unfortunately the side he reached was but a semi-fluid collection of bog vegetation, half floating upon the water, and which broke away from the arm he threw over it again and again.

He swam off after two or three essays, laboriously now, with his burden, to another part of the pool, but that was worse; the moss breaking away at a touch. He looked towards the other side, some forty yards away, but with his precious load he dared not try to swim the distance.

To make matters worse, the sides of the pool were not perpendicular, but the loose vegetation grew out a couple of feet or so over the water, as if, in the course of years, to cover it with the treacherous green carpet, spread in so many other places over deep black pits; and thus any attempt to gain foothold and climb out was vain; while, for aught he could tell, the pool might have been fifty feet deep beneath his feet.

To stay where he was seemed impossible, so, swimming a few yards, he made to where—partly to rest, partly to think upon the best plan of procedure—he could tightly grasp a tuft of rushes with his disengaged hand. But even this was no safeguard, for he could feel that a very slight effort would be required to draw the tuft from its hold. And now, for the first time, he turned to gaze earnestly in the pallid face so close to his, to find the eyes dilate and horror-stricken, while two little hands were tightly clasped round his neck.

"Do not be alarmed, Miss Gernon," he whispered, his heart throbbing almost painfully the while. "Give me a few moments to recover breath, and then I will draw you ashore—or rather," he said, with an encouraging smile, "on to this treacherous moss."

The smile was intended to chase away the dread of there being imminent danger, and it had its effect.

"I am not very—very much frightened," she half sobbed, though, unable to conceal her agitation, she clung to him tightly. "I was picking marsh flowers when the rushes suddenly gave way beneath my feet."

"The place is very dangerous," said Brace; and then, in an earnest voice—"Thank Heaven, though, that I was so near at hand."

He paused for a few moments to gaze in her face, and in that brief space of time danger—the water—all was forgotten as their eyes met, for hers to fall directly before his loving, earnest look. For there, in spite of what he had said, in great peril, but with her heart beating against his, so that he could feel its pulsations, all Brace Norton's resolutions faded away; and for a moment he thought of how sweet it would be to die thus—to loose his hold of the rushes, to clasp his other arm round her, and then, with an end to all the sorrow and heart-burning of this life, with her clinging to him as she might never cling again, to let the water close above their heads, and then—

"What a romantic fool I am," thought Brace. "Here, a month ago, I thought life one of the jolliest things in the world; and now I'm thinking in this love-sick, unhealthy, French, charcoal-and-brimstone style of suicide."

The reaction gave his mind tone; for directly after, Brace Norton was thinking how sweet it would be to live, perhaps earning Isa Gernon's love as well as her gratitude, for saving her sweet life; and with a flush upon his cheek for his weak thoughts, Brace nerved himself for the effort he was about to make.

With his right hand tightly clutching the rush tuft, he tried to thrust his feet into the bank beneath; but in spite of a tremendous and exhausting effort, the sole result was, that the portion of the edge he clung to came away in his hand, and with the plunge, they were the next instant both beneath the water. A few vigorous strokes, though, and Brace was once more at the side with the half-fainting girl well supported, as a bunch of rushes once more supplied him with a hold for his clinging fingers.

"Oh, pray—pray save me!" murmured Isa, faintly, as a cold chill shot through her, and her pale face grew almost ghastly.

"With Heaven's help I will!" exclaimed Brace, thickly, "or I'll die with you!"

The words seemed to be forced from his lips by his strong emotion, and he could perceive that she heard them. He knew, too, that she had recognised him at the first. The words took their impassioned tone, in spite of himself; and he repented, as he saw a faint flush of colour—it might have been from indignation—rise to her cheeks.

But there was no time for dallying with thoughts of such engendering, for he knew that every moment only robbed him of so much power, and he prepared for another effort.

"Hold me tightly," he said. "Don't be afraid; only let me have both hands at liberty, so that I may be able to drag myself out."

She did as he wished, and he struggled hard; but the weight clinging to him frustrated every effort, and after five minutes' vain expenditure of strength, Brace had great difficulty in finding firm hold for his grasp; while his heart sank, as he found that what at first had seemed but a trifling mishap, and an opportunity for displaying his knight-errantry, now began to loom forth in proportions ominous to them both.

He looked in every direction now, where the tall reeds did not shut out the view, for he was beginning to mistrust his own power; but there was not a soul within sight. And now, for the first time, he raised his voice, to cry loudly for help—despairingly, though, for he could not think it possible that aid could be near. He called again and again; but his voice seemed to be lost in the vast space, and sounded faint, adding to the chill of despair creeping to his heart; till, rousing himself, after regaining his breath, he adopted the plan that he should have tried at first.

"Miss Gernon!—Isa! For Heaven's sake, speak!" he cried, earnestly, as he gazed at the half-closed eyes and the drooping head. "Try and rouse yourself for one more effort!"

She heard his words, and her eyes unclosed, and rested upon his for an instant.

"That's right!" he cried, joyfully. "Now, quick! loose your hold of me! Don't cling, but take hold here of these reeds where my hand is, and hold there tightly for a few moments. I can, then, perhaps, get out, and draw you after me: I am quite powerless here. Can you hold on for half a minute?"

Isa's pale lips parted, but no audible words came. She obeyed him, though, and he guided her cold, white hand to the sharp-edged leaves.

"Now, then, be brave! Keep a good heart, for the sake of all who love you!" he whispered; and loosing his hold, he paused for an instant or two, to find that she was striving gallantly to obey him. "Only a few moments!" he cried; and then, summoning all his strength, he left her, and by means of a desperate effort fought and plunged his way through the now clinging— now yielding mass, till—how he could not tell—he forced his way on, to lie panting, at full length, amongst the rushes. The next moment a cry of despair burst from his breast; for, as he drew himself along to where Isa Gernon clung, he saw that the tuft of reeds, disturbed by his frantic efforts, were parting from the edge, and directly after the poor girl's head sank again beneath the black water.

A rush—a plunge—a fierce struggle, and Brace was nearly free of the mosses and water-weeds; but now they seemed to cling round him more than ever, hampering his efforts, and minutes seemed to have elapsed before he had shaken himself clear, and dived down into the depths of the pool, forcing his way lower and lower till half strangled, when, rising to the surface, he drew a long, gasping breath, and then again plunged down.

It was well for Brace Norton that many a time he had swum and dived for sport in far off tropic waters, till he had gained a mastery over the element which now stood him in good stead; for at this second plunge far down into the black depths his hand came in contact with Isa Gernon's long, flowing hair, and the next instant he had risen to the surface and held her at the pool edge, with her lips well above water, he clinging the while to the reeds, as, with all the force he could muster from his panting breast, he once more shouted hoarsely for help.

Rescue

"I've done my part," muttered Brace Norton, as, in spite of the despair of the moment, he yielded to his feelings, kissing fondly again and again the cold pale lips of the insensible girl. "I can do no more. Help must come from elsewhere, or—No, I will not give up, if only for her sake." And once more he hoarsely shouted for the help that he could not think would come.

The loosening of one arm so that the burden might glide from him—a strong effort, and he could once more have been amongst the reeds and mosses; but it would have been like leaving the brighter portion of his life to death; and his eyes glared fiercely as he clutched the fair, slight figure more tightly to his breast. It was like fighting against a cruel temptation, one which whispered to him of the brightness of his young life that he was casting away for the sake of an enemy's daughter—of his home, and his weeping mother.

The temptation was strong, but he could not play the coward's part; and he held Isa to him more and more closely, gloating over the soft, regular features, as, with a pang hard to bear, he told himself the next moment that, even if help came, it would arrive too late.

That same afternoon Sir Murray Gernon strode out into the pleasure-grounds, thoughtfully crossed the lawn, avoiding, as it were, more by instinct than care, the various flower-beds, till he roused himself, with a start, on finding that he was standing at the very edge of the lake, gazing down into its deep waters, as if they possessed for him some horrible fascination.

He stood there for full ten minutes, his brow corrugated, his eyes staring, and his teeth clenched firmly upon his lower lip. Then with an effort he seemed to drag himself, shuddering, away, to walk slowly muttering to himself.

Fifty yards of winding amidst flower-beds and shrubs, and Sir Murray came suddenly upon Lord Maudlaine, his guest, seated upon a garden-chair, a half-smoked cigar in one hand, a newspaper at his feet, his mouth half open, and his aristocratic head resting upon his open palm.

It is quite possible that Sir Murray Gernon might have passed his visitor, who had already been for some days at the Castle, but for the fact that certain strange sounds arrested his attention. Had these sounds proceeded from Alexander McCray, there would have been no difficulty about the matter, and one would have immediately said that the ex-gardener was snoring loudly; but when a nobleman is concerned, a diffidence—an unwillingness is felt to use such a term. However, Lord Maudlaine was loudly trumpeting forth the announcement that he was devoting a spare hour to the service of Morpheus, and Sir Murray Gernon, hearing those sounds, was attracted thereby.

"You here, Maudlaine?" exclaimed Sir Murray.

"Eh? Why, what the deuce—Dear me! I suppose I was dozing," said his lordship, lifting himself up a bit at a time, as he indulged in a most unmistakable yawn.

"Not with Isa?" said Sir Murray. "I thought you went out with her?"

"Ya-as—ya-as! no question of a doubt about it, I did," drawled the Viscount; "and I've just been dreaming that I was boating with her on the lake—not your fish-pond here, but Como—same as we did before we came away."

"But you went out walking with her?" said Sir Murray, anxiously.

"Ya-as. Not a question of a doubt about it! I did go out and walked a little way with her."

"Did she turn back, then?"

"N-n-no!" said the Viscount; "point of fact, she as good as told me she didn't want me, and went on by herself."

"My dear Maudlaine," said Sir Murray, smiling, as he clapped his guest upon the shoulder, "I'm afraid that you are not half a lady's man. It is a fine thing for you that you have no rival in the field."

"Ya-as—just so—no doubt about that," said his lordship laughing. "But a—a I began talking to her on indifferent subjects, and, point of fact, she didn't seem to like indifferent subjects—seemed as if I bothered her, you know, and of course I didn't want to do that; so seeing, as you say, that there was no one else in the field—regular walk over the course, you know—I didn't bother her nor myself either. We're getting on very nicely, though, Sir Murray—very nicely indeed. No question about that."

"I'm glad to hear it," said Sir Murray, dryly.

"Ya-as; beginning to understand one another's idio—what is it?—syncracies, don't you call it? I think Isa likes me."

"Oh! yes, of course—of course!" said Sir Murray. "By the way, Maudlaine," he continued, taking the young man's arm and walking slowly with him down a path, "I hope you will be particular about the place; for I dare say I shall give it up to you young folks. I mean to be pretty stringent, though, I can assure you: I won't have a tree touched—no timber felled; there is none too much now. I should not like the lake drained either: I should particularly object to that. It might be said," continued Sir Murray, hastily, "that it made the place damp; but I don't think it—I don't think it."

"Wouldn't dream of doing anything distasteful, of course," said the Viscount. "Always be glad of your advice, of course, if I had any ideas of improving anything. By the way, though, Gernon, she's mad after botany."

"She? Who is?" said Sir Murray, starting.

"She is—Isa, you know. I shall have to work it up, for she don't seem to like my not being able to enter into the names of weeds with her. Not a weedy man myself, you know, eh? Ha, ha, ha!" And he laughed at what he intended for a joke.

"Was she botanising to-day?" said Sir Murray, huskily.

"Ya-a-as! Said it was her mother's favourite pursuit, though I don't know why she should like it for that reason, eh?"

"Who told her that absurd nonsense?" exclaimed Sir Murray, angrily.

"Well, she did tell me," said the lover; "but, a—a—really, you know, I can't recollect. Don't particularly want to know, I suppose?"

"Oh no—oh no!" exclaimed Sir Murray, impatiently. "But this place, Maudlaine—I should like it kept as it is: the timber, you know; and you would not drain the lake?"

"Oh no! of course not. But, I say, you know, I—a—a—a suppose it will be all right?"

"Right—all right?" said Sir Murray, whose face wore a cadaverous hue. "What do you mean by all right?"

"Well, you know, I mean about Isa. I haven't said anything pointed to her yet, though we two have made it all right. She won't refuse me, eh?"

"Refuse? No: absurd!"

"Well, I don't know so much about that. I get thinking sometimes that she ain't so very far gone with me. Snubs me, you know,—turns huffy, and that sort of thing."

"My dear Maudlaine," said Sir Murray, with a sneering laugh, which there was no need of the other interpreting, "you are too timid—too diffident for a man of your years."

"Well, I don't know," said his lordship, "I don't think I am; but she's a style of woman I'm not used to. Don't seem dazzled, and all that sort of thing, you know. Some women would be ready to jump out of their skins to be a viscountess, and by-and-by an earl's wife; but she don't—not a bit—not that sort of woman; and if I never said a word about it, I don't believe that she would, even if I went on visiting here for years."

"Most likely not," said Sir Murray, dryly; "but you see that it is as I say—you are too timid—too diffident."

"I say, though, you know," said his lordship, "was her mother that style of woman—quiet and fond of weed-hunting—botany, you know?"

"You will oblige me greatly by not referring to the late Lady Gernon," said Sir Murray, stiffly.

"Oh, beg pardon, you know. No offence meant."

"It is granted," said Sir Murray; and then, in a different tone: "There goes the dressing-bell."

The gentlemen strolled up in silence to the entrance, where the major-domo—Mr Alexander McCray—who seemed to rule supreme at Merland, now stood waiting the arrival of his master.

"I'm thinking, Sir Mooray," he said deferentially, "that ye'd like a pony-carriage sent to meet my young lady."

"What—has she not returned?" said Sir Murray, anxiously.

"Nay, Sir Mooray, not yet awhile, and I should hae sent wi'oot saying a word, but that I thocht my laird here would tell us which road she gaed."

"Towards the waste—the snipe ground, you know," said his lordship, on being appealed to.

"Send at once, McCray. No: go yourself," said Sir Murray.

"I'll go with him," said his lordship, who now seemed about wakening to the fact that he had grossly neglected his intended; and five minutes after the old Scot was driving briskly towards the village.

"Ye dinna ought to have left her, my laird," said McCray, sturdily. "She's ower young to be left all alone."

"What? Were you speaking to me?" said his lordship, haughtily.

"Ay, that I was," said McCray. "Ye mauna mind me, my laird, for I'm a'most like her foster-fairther, and nursed her on my knee mony's the time."

His lordship did not condescend to answer, and the lanes were traversed at a good rattling pace; but though McCray pulled up from time to time to make inquiries, the only news he learned was that Miss Gernon had been seen to go towards the marsh, but not to return; while one cottager volunteered the information that young Squire Norton, the sailor, went that way too in the morning time, and that neither of them had been seen to come back.

This news had no effect upon Lord George Maudlaine, but a close observer would have seen that the wrinkles upon Alexander McCray's brow grew a little more deeply marked.

"He's a douce laddie," muttered McCray, as he drove on, "and warth a score sic birkies as this one; but it was ill-luck his meeting as they did that day, and it winna do—it winna do! We shall be having sair wark yet, I'm afraid. They're kittlecattle these womenkind, and I nearly suffered shipwreck with them mysel'."

"There's no one here," said his lordship, now condescending to speak, as they drove to where the road faded away into a faint track, which, in its turn, led to the pine-grove.

"We'll get doon and hopple the ponies, my laird, and walk on to the pine-wood. My young leddie may be in there."

"Confound his barbarous tongue! Why don't he speak English?" muttered the Viscount. "I don't understand one-half he says."

But McCray's acts were plain enough, even if his words were obscure; and, descending, he secured the ponies, and was about to start towards the wood, already looking black and gloomy, when one of Brace Norton's cries for help smote his ear.

"Gude save me! Hearken to that, noo!" cried McCray, excitedly.

"Only a marsh bird," said his lordship, contemptuously.

"Gude save us! Come alang; that's a soul in sair peril, my laird," And starting in the direction of the cry, as fast as the treacherous nature of the ground would allow, McCray soon came in sight of that which made him redouble his pace.

"Here! Help, here!" cried a voice from behind. "I'm sinking!" When, with a glance over his shoulder, McCray saw that his companion was already above his knees in a soft place.

"De'il help ye—ye ill-far'ed, handle-named loon!" muttered McCray, fiercely. "Why couldna ye walk like a Christian, and not get in that way? I've ither work in hand."

Then hastening on, he stepped from tuft to tuft, with an agility not to have been expected in a man of his years, till well within reach of words:

"Haud oup, then," he cried—"haud oup, my bra'e laddie, I'm with ye. There!" he cried, as he threw himself at full length upon the yielding moss, and reached to where, ghastly of face, Brace still clung, and held up his charge—"there! I ha'e yer hand. Loose the rushes, and grip it weel—grip it weel."

"Her first—take her first," sobbed Brace, hoarsely.

"That I will!" cried McCray, working himself forward. "Gude save us, though, it's sair wet work here, and I'm a deal heavier than I thocht. Noo I ha'e her, and she's leet as swansdoon aifter a'. The puir bairn, I ha'e her safe, but she's half dead. Lie there, my pretty, while I pu' out the laddie. Noo, my laddie; that's reet—that's reet; the ither hand. Noo again. Gude—gude! another pu'. Hech! laddie, mind, or I shall be in wi ye. Noo then, anither pu'! That's weel! I ha'e ye noo. Puir lad, ye're cauld indeed, but ye're safe, and reet too, so lie there while I tak' the lassie."

In effect, with the exertion of his great strength, McCray, broad-shouldered and iron muscled, had drawn both Isa and Brace from what had so nearly been a watery grave, but not without clanger to himself. Twice over the moss gave way with the stress placed upon it; but at last he had both lying safe beside him, and not before it was time, for Brace was completely exhausted.

"Let me carry her," said Brace, hoarsely, as he staggered to his feet; but only to sink down again, his numbed limbs refusing their office.

"Ye're a bra'e laddie," said the Scot; "but your sperrit's stronger than your power. I'll carry the lassie to the carriage, and be back for you in a minute."

"Never mind me," groaned Brace. "I'm only cold. For Heaven's sake drive off with her, for she is nearly dead with her long immersion."

But before Brace's words were well uttered, McCray was sturdily trudging over the sinking way with his dripping burden, which he placed in the pony-carriage, covered with a rug, and then returned to help the young man, who was crawling towards him.

"Bra'e laddie, ye air," muttered McCray. "Ye found and savit her, I ken, and noo, half dead yersel', ready to help, while that loon stands stoock there shouting for succour, and afraid to move. Here, hi! my laird, move yersel', man, and, Gude sake, get out of that!"

"Here, give me your hand, my good fellow," cried his lordship: "I'm in a dangerous spot."

McCray growled fiercely as he went first and helped Brace to the chaise. Then turning back, he reached out the asked-for hand to extricate his lordship, but in so rough a manner that he nearly brought him into a horizontal position.

"Why, ye micht ha'e done that yersel', my laird," said McCray, angrily. "And noo I must leave ye, and hurry hame wi' those two puir bairns."

His lordship began to offer expostulations as he began to scuffle out of the bog, but it was to deaf ears, for McCray had run back, and before the noble suitor was on *terra firma* the ponies were unloosed and being made to gallop over the rough roadway.

"They'll be dead wi' cauld before I can get them to the Castle," muttered McCray, as he held Isa in his arm, and rattled the reins with the other, so that the ponies plunged along furiously. "Puir bairns—puir bairns!"

McCray's words were muttered, but Brace caught their meaning.

"Drive to the Hall," he said, hoarsely; "it is quite a couple of miles nearer."

"Gude sake! I might just as weel commit a murder," muttered the Scot. "But I shall commit one if I dinna get house-room for the lassie directly. I'll e'en do as he says, if I dee for it. Get on wi' ye!" he roared to the ponies, already speeding along like the wind, when, being no inexpert Jehu, he kept them at a sharp gallop, till a few minutes after, when he drew them up on their haunches at the door of Merland Hall.

How Doctors Rule

Pale and agitated, Mrs Norton hurried out, followed by the Captain, for Brace's long absence had been causing them great uneasiness; but Mrs Norton's agitation increased to a painful degree as soon as she saw in what company he had: returned. Isa's state was the first consideration; and dismissing every other thought, the insensible girl was borne to a bedroom by Captain Norton, as reverently as if she had been something holy, his lip quivering as he marked in the sweet features the lineaments of the one whom he had so fondly loved. Whilst, with all a mother's care, Mrs Norton tended her, taking the first steps towards insuring the poor girl's recovery—steps but for which the services of Dr Challen, for whom McCray had directly galloped off, would have been in vain.

An hour after, when Isa had begun to show signs of returning animation, her wondering eyes ranging from face to face—letting them rest longest upon the soft, motherly countenance bent over her to kiss her so tenderly—there came the sound of wheels, and Dr Challen hurried up to the bedside, to express his approval of what had been done.

"And noo I must go and tell Sir Mooray," said McCray to Captain Norton. "I thought I'd get the doctor first."

"I sent a groom directly you had gone," said the Captain.

"'Deed and you did weel," said McCray; "but I must stay here and face him, sir, for he'll be over directly with my laird, there, like twa roarin and rampagin' lions."

In effect, five minutes after, there was again the sound of rapid wheels, followed directly after by Sir Murray Gernon's voice in the hall.

"How dared you to bring her here?" he exclaimed, in a hoarse, harsh voice, to his old retainer, who met him boldly on the step.

"'Deed, Sir Mooray, so as to save the dear bairn's life, and not have to face ye wi' a cauld dead bodie. It was a case of seconds, Sir Mooray, and I ken ye wadna ha'e likit for me to bring the puir laddie wha savit her from drownin' to the Castle."

"And who saved her?" exclaimed Sir Murray.

"Hoot! Sir Mooray, naebodie else but the douce sailor laddie ye passed camin' hame, when the chaise was broke up."

A bitter epithet was hissed from Sir Murray Gernon's lips, as he listened to this announcement; for to his excited imagination it seemed as if Fate were struggling against him and striving to bring together two who, could he contrive it, should be through life as far removed, to all intents and purposes, one from the other, as the two poles.

Sir Murray ascended to the bed-room, and then descended to pace impatiently up and down, frowning and angry, till, after seeing his patient sink into a quiet slumber, Dr Challen gave a sigh of satisfaction, and then joined the baronet.

"What?" exclaimed the doctor, after listening to Sir Murray's first remark.

"She must be taken home directly," said Sir Murray.

"Quite out of the question, my dear Sir Murray," said the doctor, pleasantly, as he partook of the glass of wine left upon the sideboard.

"But the carriage is waiting, Challen," said Sir Murray. "I came over in the close carriage on purpose. Surely if she is lifted in and driven slowly it cannot hurt her."

"Now look here, Gernon," said the doctor, sturdily, "I brought that child into the world, and saved her life, sir—saved her life, when not half-a-dozen doctors in England could have done it. I've been your—Capital glass of port, by Jove! Try one. You won't? Very good; I will. Let's see—what was I saying? Ah! I've been your family medical attendant ever since I began to practise, and save and except such times as you chose to go abroad and put yourself into the hands of foreign poisoners, I've had your welfare at heart. Now, I'm a crotchety old fellow—better try a glass of Norton's port: I'll swear it's '20 vintage—crotchety old fellow—over professional matters; and if the Queen herself came meddling in a sick-room where I was engaged, I'd order her out as soon as look at her: ergo, I'm not at all afraid of a baronet."

Sir Murray made a gesture of impatience.

"There, confound you, sir," cried the doctor, testily, "I don't care for your fuming—I'm not going to give way. Now, look here, Gernon: you ought to have more confidence in me, and in what I say. I don't want to boast; but I saved your life; I saved your wife's life; and, as aforesaid, I saved the life of that child up-stairs when it was a tiny spark that a breath would have destroyed. I'm proud of it, you see. Now you want to kill her, because she is here in the house of the people you most dislike in the world—out-and-out good sort of people, and good friends of mine, all the same. Can't help it—I must speak plain. This is a case where plain speaking is necessary, so you need not fling about. You must sink all these family quarrels, and thank Heaven that the poor child was brought here, where there was a clever, sensible woman like Mrs Norton to take the first steps towards warding off fever."

"But, surely, Challen," exclaimed Sir Murray, deprecatingly now, "with plenty of wrapping, and the carriage!"

"My good man," cried the doctor, now thoroughly angry, "if you will be obstinate, and want her to have plenty of wrapping, go and fetch a lead coffin, and if she is to go in a carriage, send old McCray over to Marshton for Downing's hearse. It will be the most sensible thing you can do; for she will be dead before she gets home, or soon after. What the deuce is the use of your talking? Do you think I want her to stay here, or that I take two straws' worth of interest in your confounded affairs and squabbles? That child's life is the first consideration. I won't put up with it, Gernon—I won't indeed. How dare you interfere and want to meddle with things which you don't understand? That child's constitution is not a political matter for you to meddle with. Why, confound you, sir, here we have just got her into as lovely a perspiration as ever I saw upon a human subject! There's the threatened fever evaporating, as it were, from her system, and she sleeping gloriously, when you must come in with your family pride, and want to destroy all that I have done! I tell you what it is—"

"My dear Challen," exclaimed Sir Murray, "I don't want to upset your arrangements. I only thought—"

"Confound you, sir! how dare you to think, here, in a case of life and death? It's a piece of consequential, confounded, titled presumption—that's what it is!"

There was no mistaking, either, that Mr Challen was in a professional passion; for, as he said, "in matters of medicine he would give way to none," while being, certainly, a very clever practitioner, and well knowing that fact, he was somewhat ready to leap upon his own little hill, and to crow loudly. He had just descended, proud and elate with the state in which he had left his patient, when, as he mentally termed it, this impertinent interference on the part of Sir Murray made him erect all his hackles, and give battle most furiously for his rights.

"There, there! Don't be angry, Challen," said the baronet. "I give way—I suppose I must bear it."

"Bear it! Of course you must," said the doctor. "I tell you what it is, Sir Murray Gernon: I was within a point of throwing up the case, and leaving you in the hands of that offensive wholesale killer at Marshton—that new man. I was only restrained by a feeling of respect for the poor child. But I'll give up now, if you wish it."

"My dear Challen," cried Sir Murray, "pray don't be so impetuous. I say no more. Have it all as you wish."

"Say no more! Of course you will not!" grumbled the doctor, whose feathers were gradually subsiding to their natural smoothness.

"Only," continued Sir Murray, "get her well, and let us have her home as soon as possible."

"There you go again!" cried the doctor, bristling up once more. "The old story! I suppose you think I want to keep her ill, so as to swell the bill, with 'One draught at bed-time,' and 'The mixture as before.' Ugh! It's a pity, Sir Murray Gernon, you have not a dozen people about you who are like me— not in the least afraid of you. What are you going to do now?"

"Going back," said Sir Murray, who had just risen.

"Going back, indeed!" said the doctor, impatiently. "Better stay—stay, and see how she is when she wakes. Let's have Norton in and Mrs Norton, and perhaps their son will join: he's none the worse—used to water—salt, fresh, or marshy. A tumbler of punch and a rubber at whist would pass the time away comfortably. There, hang it, man, twenty years ought to be long enough to heal up these old wounds. They'll have to be healed up when you journey to the great abroad. Take my advice—advice I shan't charge you anything for. Norton's boy has saved your girl's life. Let this unlucky accident be the means of bringing you together—good out of evil, you know. Hold out the right hand of fellowship, and—trust me—I know Norton; it will be taken in a hearty grasp. Make friends at once, Gernon; you'll be obliged to do it in heaven. Oh! there, then, I've done. Advice gratis is never valued at its true worth."

"Let me know, Challen, how all goes on when you leave here," said Sir Murray, sternly, as he strode towards the door; and five minutes after the doctor shrugged his shoulders and took another glass of port to console himself for the rejection of his good offices, as he listened to the wheels of the departing carriage.

"I'm afraid," he said aloud, "contact with all sorts of people has robbed me of this refined sensibility—this keen appreciation of injury. I fancy if any one had done me a wrong, that I could forgive it in less than twenty years."

"But there never was any wrong, Doctor," said a low, sweet voice, when, turning, Dr Challen became aware that Mrs Norton had entered unperceived.

Mother and Son

"Mother," said Brace Norton the next morning, as, none the worse for his immersion, he stood by her side, she holding his hand the while and gazing up into his face,—"mother, I went out yesterday with the full intention of dreaming no more of my foolish love; and what was the result? Strange, too," he said, with affected gaiety; "one would have thought that an hour's immersion would have quenched it. But there, you will, perhaps, laugh at me, and think me childish and full of folly; still, I cannot help it—I love her more dearly than ever, and feel no shame in owning it to you. How am I to give her up now, after holding her to my breast as I did for a whole hour yesterday, her arms clasped the while round my neck, and her poor head resting upon my shoulder? Mother, it was a mingling of misery, despair, and bliss; and when, at last, I had given up all hope of being saved—when I had struggled till I could struggle no more—when I had called till my voice failed in my throat—when I felt that my—our last hour was at hand, I broke faith even with myself."

Brace paused for a few moments, for his voice was husky, but recovering himself, he went on:

"I dare say it was wrong; but I was under the impression that all was over. I could have saved my own life, perhaps; but I could not leave her to perish. The sun had sunk, and darkness was fast coming on; the evening breeze was sighing what seemed to my excited fancy a dirge amidst the rustling reeds; and again and again some curlew flew over us giving utterance to a loud wail. At one time it seemed so hard to die just in the spring of life; but the next instant, as I looked down at the poor head resting upon my breast, the sorrow was all for her, and with that sorrow there was a strange—an awful pleasure. It was, I should think, about ten minutes before help came that she raised her head, and her sweet beseeching eyes looked full in mine.

"'Is there no hope?' she whispered; and I feared to tell her the cruel truth.

"'But you could save yourself,' she faltered; 'you struggled too hard before; why should you perish in trying to save me?'

"She spoke so earnestly, and with such a sweet resignation, that the tears came gushing from my eyes—weak, womanly tears, mother; for I am weak, very weak, I know, or I should not tell you all this."

"Is it weak to confide all things to her who gave you birth, Brace?" whispered Mrs Norton.

"No—no!" he replied; and then, as if recalling the scene of the preceding evening, he continued:

"'Try,' she whispered to me—'try once more, and you may bring help.'

"As she spoke she unloosed her arms from my neck, and it was like adding despair to despair.

"'Why do you tempt me?' I said; for it seemed that now the time had come when I might speak. 'Do you think that I could live without you? and do you not know that since the day when we first met my every thought has been of you, and that I have vainly struggled to free myself? You will believe me now—now that we are, perhaps, within a few minutes to stand in the presence of our Maker. Isa, I love you with a pure and holy love—a love that makes me, despairing as I am of ever possessing you in this life, look forward to the prospect of being with you in death,' I whispered, as I held her more tightly. 'You know little of me, but you know, perhaps, the sad misfortunes of our families, and how it seems that by some strange intervention of fate my heart has been led to you.'

"She was silent, but her arms once more rested upon my shoulder, and her sweet innocent, girlish face was close to mine, as there, chilled to the heart with the icy water, I asked her to forgive me my declaration, and kissed her pale lips again and again.

"It was then that—urged once more by the strong desire for life—I tried once more to utter a cry or two for help; and, five minutes after, that help was at hand."

Brace Norton was silent now for a few minutes; and then, as if in answer to his mother's look, he said:

"Must I, then, go?"

"Yes, Brace—yes. Your father leaves in an hour. It will be far better. Only for a few days, till she recovers and is removed."

"But may I not see her first?" he pleaded.

"Brace, my dear boy," said Mrs Norton, proudly, "would it be honourable to take advantage of her position here? Too much has already passed for your peace of mind. Go, now; and leave the house free to Sir Murray Gernon to come and go untouched in his sensitiveness. You must fight still, and bravely, too."

Without another word the young man slowly left the room; and before an hour had elapsed Captain Norton and his son were on their way to Marshton.

A Discovery

Ten days elapsed before Dr Challen gave his consent for Isa to be removed, and during that time she had been carefully tended by Mrs Norton and Jane McCray, who had made her way to the Hall as soon as she heard of the accident. But two days would have been sufficient to have shown to Mrs Norton the character of the gentle, inartificial girl, whose gratitude was extreme for every act of attention she received. Hour after hour would Mrs Norton sit by her bedside watching her sleep; but once, and once only, came a dread suspicion that made her heart leap with agony.

She had driven that thought away, though, the next minute, as something too hateful to be nurtured even for an instant. Then, kneeling down, she prayed long and earnestly that, come what might, rest and happiness should be the lot of her son, as well as that of the gentle spirit whom she had already begun to love as a child of her own. For, irrespective of a sweet disposition and clinging ways to attract her when the poor motherless girl had been thrown, as it were, into her arms for protection, there was the recollection of the past—the old affection for her mother, and pity—shuddering pity—as she thought of her old friend's mysterious fate and the sad position of her child.

Had she required more to interest her in Isa Gernon, Mrs Norton possessed it in the knowledge that Brace loved her, that he had confessed his love, and that Isa knew it. If such a thing could have been possible, how Mrs Norton would have rejoiced in the union! But, with many a sigh, she told herself that it could never be, and to the best of her ability she strove to avoid all reference to her son.

That was a hard task to the loving mother, whose every thought turned to the frank, handsome young fellow who was her pride—who had, year by year, won for her more and more her husband's love, binding him tightly and more tightly to her, as time rolled on, till she owned to herself that, in spite of the stormy past, hers was a life of true happiness—of happiness greater than usually fell to the lot of mortals. For as time had softened the grief and despair in Philip Norton's heart, he had learned to thank Heaven for the blessings that had, after all, fallen to his share, so that his feeling of friendly affection had gradually grown into a firm and lasting love for the woman so full of faith in him—a love that grew stronger as the years glided on.

Weak, and hardly yet recovered, Isa Gernon was, one day, lying sleeping gently. Sir Murray had paid his morning's visit, and, meeting Dr Challen there, received another sharp snubbing for evincing a desire to remove the patient.

"I'll tell you when she may go," said the doctor; "but let me tell you that you ought to go down upon your knees and thank Mrs Norton for her motherly care. Like a mother to you, isn't she, my child?" he said, turning to Isa.

The look of love directed by Isa at Mrs Norton was like gall and wormwood to Sir Murray, whose dark face grew more black; but he was too courteous to display his annoyance in his words; and besides, though he looked upon Mrs Norton as a weak, foolish woman, at heart he retained for her a profound feeling of respect; for he admired her faith and constancy under troubles that might have broken another's heart. In spite of himself, too, he could not help noticing the respect that had been paid to his feelings, for he knew that the departure of Captain Norton and his son must have been on account of this unforeseen train of circumstances. He was glad of this, for he was troubled about Brace, from feeling an instinctive dread that he might presume to assert himself as a suitor for Isa's hand.

Matters had gone very unfortunately; but as soon as he could get Isa home, he determined that Lord Maudlaine should press his suit, and that the wedding should shortly follow.

Sir Murray felt a confidence in Mrs Norton that was not misplaced, for hardly once had Brace's name passed her lips till this morning, when some time after father and doctor had taken their departure, Mrs Norton entered the room to find Isa sleeping.

She stood watching the sleeper for some few minutes, tracing again the lineaments of Marion Elstree, when the likeness was completed by the unclosing of two soft, appealing eyes, which gazed full in hers for a few minutes, as a sweet smile of recognition swept over the countenance; then Mrs Norton bent down and kissed her, Isa's arms being passed round her loving nurse's neck, and there for a few moments she clung.

"So much better!" whispered Isa; and then, as her eyes fell upon a locket-brooch which Mrs Norton was wearing, she asked, in the course of conversation, whose countenance it contained.

"It was my son's twelve years ago," said Mrs Norton, softly, as she covered it, she knew not why, with one hand, watching keenly the face before her as she spoke, and in the change that came over it, she saw something that for the moment gave her she hardly knew which, pleasure or pain; for Isa's pale face became gradually suffused with a deep crimson flush, she shrank away from Mrs Norton as if guilty, her eyes filled with tears, and then, casting her arms round the mother's neck, she nestled there, weeping long and hysterically.

No word was spoken; but the mother's thoughts required no further confirmation. She religiously refrained, though, from speaking, telling herself that a greater will than hers should be done, that her duty was rather to check than encourage, even while she tremblingly hoped that a happier future might be the result.

There was no need for interpretation of Isa Gernon's tears: her heart spoke for itself; and it was not surprising that he, against whom she had been warned by a parent—now loving almost to doting, now fiercely morose— should form the object of her musing thoughts. She had met him frequently during her walks, at a time, too, when distasteful attentions were being paid her, and she felt that her heart was being treated as a piece of merchandise.

There was something winning and frank in Brace Norton that had attracted her in spite of the chiding she gave her wandering thoughts; and young, ardent, unused to the ways of the world, she had allowed herself to dwell upon the face of the young sailor more often than was right for her peace of mind. Then came the ramble by the marsh, the leaning over the black pool-side to pluck a blossom, and her narrow escape from poor Ophelia's fate. Was it, then, strange that when he appeared rushing to her rescue, and after his many vain struggles, told her, as he promised to die by her side, how he loved her—told her what her heart had before whispered— was it, then, strange that this should be the hour which should, in spite of her efforts, sweep away the impression of all warnings and forbidding words, and that she should yield up the heart only partly hers?

Rivalry

Dr Challen's permission at last, and after many formal, courteous thanks, Sir Murray Gernon had come over to the Hall to fetch his child.

"You will often come over and see us," whispered Isa, as she clung to Mrs Norton; and then she trembled as she saw the tear in her hostess's face and the slight shake of her head.

"Come, Isa!" exclaimed Sir Murray, almost harshly; for the sight of the affectionate parting was bitterness to him.

At the same moment Lord Maudlaine, hitherto an unnoticed member of the party, had advanced to hand Isa to the carriage.

"The Castle has been like a dungeon ever since you left us," he whispered; and Mrs Norton noted the parting of his lips. She also observed, too, that Isa did not touch his hand, but stepped unaided into the carriage; and the mother's heart gave a throb of joy. But only for an instant: the gleam of sunshine that had seemed in those trifles to shine forth for her son was shrouded directly after by the clouds of the past, and she re-entered the house, tearful and sad, as the sound of the departing carriage seemed to fade away in the distance.

For the house seemed sad now and desolate. It was as though a sweet spirit that had pervaded the place had passed away; and it was only by an effort that she composed herself so as to write to Captain Norton, and inform him that there was no longer need for his absence.

There were no long conversations between Mr and Mrs Norton on the former's return to Merland Hall; but they read each others thoughts, and avoided all reference to their son's acts. At times Captain Norton was for expostulating with Brace, but he always came to the conclusion that matters must take their course, and that he would leave all speaking to his wife, trusting to her to point out to Brace the folly of his hopes, and then looking forward to the time for his return to sea, when, long before the cruise had come to an end, Isa Gernon would, without doubt, have become Lady Maudlaine.

Brace, upon his return, was restless and excitable; his father ready to plunge into business to drown his thoughts; while the mother anxiously watched the actions of her son, longing, in her indulgent love, to whisper hope, but feeling all the while that it was a thing she dared not attempt.

The second day after his return home, Brace's heart sank, as, turning into a lane, he came suddenly upon Isa, side by side with Lord Maudlaine. They were mounted, and a groom rode at a short distance behind. He already knew by rumour that Isa was supposed to be engaged to the Viscount, and, bitter and angry, his hand was raised to his hat, in order to pass with a cold salute; but Brace's resentment was in an instant disarmed, for Isa reined in her horse, and with a quiet, earnest smile, held out her hand, which he took in his for a moment, and then, with her companion, she was gone.

A couple of days of mingled hope and fear passed before he encountered her again, when Brace Norton's brow flushed and his pulses beat rapidly, for Isa was alone, save that a groom followed at a distance, with difficulty restraining his highly-bred steed, while his mistress's little jennet gently ambled along.

It was to both like a dream, that meeting; as, walking slowly beside her horse, his hand resting upon the saddle, Brace listened to Isa's faltered thanks, turning from time to time to gaze in the sweet, gentle face bent towards him—a face whose eyes met his with a soft, trusting look, that made his heart swell within his breast, till a rapid step from behind told of an intruder, and Lord Maudlaine made his appearance; when, with a sigh of regret, Isa held out her hand to be taken by Brace, who retained it within his own, while he unflinchingly encountered the fierce, haughty look of contempt and pride cast upon him by the Viscount.

The next minute Isa had withdrawn her hand, and, attended by Lord Maudlaine, gone towards the park, leaving Brace, as he strolled slowly home, to recall a score of things which he wished to have said.

Another meeting, and once more Brace was walking with her side by side, the hand which held her little whip not being withdrawn when he laid upon it his own, to stand at last gazing up in her face, and peering into her soft, sad eyes.

He tried to speak twice, but the words did not come; but he felt that time was passing, and with an effort he broke the silence.

"Isa," he said, in deep, earnest tones, "I am going to be very bold. I have a question to ask—one whose answer shall make me happy, or send me wretched away. That gentleman—Lord Maudlaine—you know what rumour says: is the rumour true?"

She returned his gaze for a few moments by one as earnest, and in that brief space she saw once more the scene in the marsh—felt, too, the icy water, and the chill as of coming death stealing over her, even while those brave arms held her so tightly; and, as she thought on, it seemed to her that the life he had won from the black pit should by right be his; and her look, as she gazed on unflinchingly in his face, was even, though abstracted, loving, trusting enough to have sent him away at peace. It was an answer to his question; but not yet content, he whispered, softly: "Isa—dear Isa, may I, then, hope?" "Miss Gernon, Sir Murray has requested me to see you back in safety," said a harsh voice at their side; and, on turning, Brace became aware of the presence of Lord Maudlaine, who must have approached upon the grass by which the lane was bordered for his coming to have been unperceived. "Sir Murray understands," continued the Viscount, "that you are often encountered during your rides, and thinks it better that you should not be alone."

"And, pray, who was his informant?" exclaimed Brace, fiercely.

"I was," said his lordship, in cold, meaning tones. "If you have any more to say you know my address."

Brace Norton felt that he had, indeed, much more to say, but a glance at Isa Gernon's troubled face restrained him, and in silence he allowed them to pass away; but not without his seeing that Lord Maudlaine was talking earnestly to what seemed unwilling ears.

The next day, after a sleepless night, Brace Norton rode over to the Castle, sent in his card, and asked to see Sir Murray Gernon.

In five minutes the answer came back that Sir Murray Gernon was engaged.

Feeling the slight deeply, but all the same nothing daunted, Brace called again and again, nerved by his strong, honest love, and determined to avow boldly that love, so as not to be accused of clandestine acts. Had he gained an interview, he would have earnestly pleaded his cause with the father, and have asked his sanction; but it was evident to Brace from the very first that Sir Murray would not see him, so he wrote a long appealing letter, the blood burning in his cheeks as he indited each line, asking favour towards his suit, but not with shame—his love was too honest for that.

Restless and impatient, Brace Norton awaited the reply, till he seemed almost in a state of fever. Both Captain and Mrs Norton knew the cause, but they were silent from the impression that it would be better for their son to find out for himself the hopelessness of his suit. Now Brace thought that the letter had miscarried, and wrote another, but paused before sending it, as he recalled the short space of time that had elapsed since the first was written.

But at last came Sir Murray's answer, written in a cool, formal, gentlemanly spirit, exceedingly courteous, but with every sentence bearing a cold, despairing feeling to Brace Norton's heart as it requested that he, as an officer and a gentleman, would refrain from seeking further intimacy with Sir Murray Gernon's family. Intercourse even of the most formal nature was quite out of the question. In conclusion, Sir Murray thanked Mr Norton for the services he had rendered to his family, and left it to Mr Brace Norton's good sense to see that no further advances could be countenanced. Did Mr Brace Norton wish to know more—always supposing him ignorant, as his behaviour led Sir Murray Gernon to imagine—Mrs Norton would doubtless supply certain links, such as would show to her son the truth of Sir Murray's assertion—that intercourse between the families was out of the question.

Every word of that letter was so much molten misery, so much bitterness, that Brace Norton felt himself forced to drain to the dregs. He had no occasion to refer to his mother for confirmation of Sir Murray's words; and yet why could not reconciliation come? Despair was his answer, and he hurried out to walk for hours, seeking the spots where he had encountered her, when at last he saw her riding slowly along a lane, followed at some little distance by Lord Maudlaine.

For a few moments Brace stood irresolute. What should he do? Resign himself to his fate, and, waiting what time would bring forth, be patient? Had Isa been alone, perhaps he might have so acted; but there was the suitor favoured by the father dodging her like a shadow, and he smiled as he thought of the madness of waiting, when, as to what time would bring forth, there was the answer in the shape of the Viscount. It was of no avail: the heart, he told himself, was ungovernable; and, forgetting Sir Murray's letter and all else in his love, he strode forward, and the next minute was at Isa's side.

"One-Two!"

It is said that money has little to do with love. Be that as it may, the more often Lord Maudlaine's thoughts reverted to his friend Mr Braham, the more he increased his attentions to Isa Gernon. At first he attributed her indifference and coolness to the innate shyness of a young girl who had passed the greater part of her life in absolute retirement; thinking, too, that as Sir Murray had all along shown himself in favour of the connection, all he had to do was to go on quietly for a few months, when the day would be fixed, the wedding take place, and he, possessed of the handsome dowry brought by his wife in exchange for an empty title, would be free from the unpleasant visits and reminders of his money-lending acquaintances.

But of late matters had assumed an aspect that troubled him. This appearance of, to him, an entirely new character upon the stage, was a something for which he had not bargained. At first it was too ridiculous; the idea was preposterous that a young naval lieutenant should compete with him—should come between his nobility and the object upon which he had set his choice: he—Lord Maudlaine—son of an Earl, with the said Earl's coronet looming for him in no very distant part of the future's horizon.

But there was the mishap in the marsh. Deuced unfortunate thing, you know. It wouldn't have mattered if it had been himself, and he had dived in after her; but for this impertinent fellow to be on the marsh, and run and jump in after Miss Gernon, it was too bad, you know—a deal too bad—and he couldn't stand much more of it.

"Horsewhip him!" said Sir Murray, with a fierce snarl, when, after a good deal of circumlocution, his lordship complained of the coolness of his intended, and her frequent encounters with Brace Norton.

"But—a—a don't you think—wouldn't it be better if you spoke to her upon the subject—forbade her, you know, to see him any more?" said his lordship.

"Horsewhip him, I tell you!" snarled Sir Murray. "Or, would your lordship like to wake up some morning to the fact that she had disgraced us by a foolish escapade—gone off, for instance, with this vagabond?" said Sir Murray, fiercely.

"No! By Jove, no!" exclaimed the Viscount, turning pale at the very thought, and suffering from incipient symptoms of Braham on the brain.

"Because," said Sir Murray, giving an involuntary shudder, as he thought of the past—"because any anger on my part, any undue influence, would militate against your prospects—drive her, as it were, into the scoundrel's arms!"

"Don't put it in that light, please," said his lordship, faintly.

"You are young, strong, and active," continued Sir Murray. "Pay more attention to her; and, as for this man, if he will not take notice of the letter I have sent him, horsewhip him—shoot him, if needs be; for he is a cowardly hound, the son of a coward father!"

Sir Murray Gernon's eyes flashed, and his dark face grew darker, as he angrily hissed the latter words, before turning with clenched teeth, and walking up and down hastily.

"Think he is?" said the Viscount, in a low voice.

"Think!" echoed the baronet, with a world of scorn in his utterance of that one word.

"I won't stand any more of his nonsense, then!" exclaimed his lordship, nodding very fiercely. "It's quite time it was stopped, and I'll stop it!"

Sir Murray gave him a short, sharp look—half assent, half contempt—and then turned upon his heel, leaving his proposed son-in-law alone.

"What a savage bear he grows!" muttered his lordship, as soon as he was alone; but the next instant his harsh opinion was softened down by the recollection of Sir Murray's wealth; and he stood gazing for an instant from the open window over the lake at the line stretch of park land, with its noble timber, and recalled the last quiet conversation he had had with the baronet, when he was requested—in words which told most plainly of the owners intentions—not to cut down any of the timber, nor yet to drain the lake.

Five minutes after, his lordship walked into the drawing-rooms, and went through the whole suite, expecting every moment to see Isa reading on some lounge; but she was not there. He then walked into the breakfast and dining-rooms, the conservatory, and Lady Gernon's boudoir, ending by taking a turn in the garden; but Isa was still invisible.

"Seen Miss Gernon?" he said at last to the major-domo, whom he encountered in the hall.

"Me young lady went oot for her morning ride a gude half-hoor ago, my lord," said McCray; when, taking a hunting-crop from a stand close by, his lordship walked hurriedly away.

"Jenny, my gude lassie," said the old Scot, as he entered the housekeeper's room some five minutes after, when returning from watching his lordship across the lawn—"Jenny, my gude lassie, here's the auld coorse of true love rinning rougher than iver, and our wee pet bairn, I fear, going to be made unhappy. The ways of the world are very crooked, and I canna help thinking it wondrous strange that young Norton should be thrown in our darling's way as he is. I'm pitying him, too, lassie, for he's a bra'e lad, and my heart wairmed to him for the way he saved the child; and he puts me in mind, too, of ane Alexander McCray twenty year agane, whose heart was sair as this laddie's is, I ken. But it all came reet for mine, Jenny. Will it come reet for the Nortons' boy?"

The housekeeper shook her head.

"What's to be done, lassie?"

"Nothing," said Jane his wife, quietly, but with a sad look; "these things are beyond us, McCray, and must take their course."

"I'll put a stop to it, that I will!" muttered Lord Maudlaine, as he strode off across the lawn, and disappeared from McCray's sight. "Only let me see him hanging after her again!"

If his lordship's wish to see Brace Norton with Isa Gernon again were genuine, his gratification was quick in coming; for, at the end of half an hour's sharp walk, he caught sight of Isa and Brace almost at the same moment—just; in fact, as the latter hurried up, so as to reach the young girl before his favoured rival.

"Shall I horsewhip him before her, or shall I wait till he comes away?" muttered his lordship. "He didn't take any notice of what I said last time, though I half thought that I should have heard from him."

His lordship stood irresolute for a few moments, but the way in which Brace was received forced him into action, and he strode past the groom, who stood at a respectful distance, and up to the pair.

"Look here, you!" he exclaimed to Brace, coarsely. "This sort of thing won't do! You've been told that you're not to follow Miss Gernon about. Do you hear?"

"Isa," said Brace, in a whisper to the trembling girl, "will you ride on?"

"No," she answered, in the same tone, as she bent down towards him. "Please—my first request—for my sake, Mr Norton, do not let there be any quarrel."

"I will do my best to avoid it," said Brace, with a quiet, re-assuring smile; when, apparently enraged by the understanding which appeared to exist, but really nerved thereto by the words let fall that morning by Sir Murray, Lord Maudlaine strode fiercely in front of Brace, who, however, stood coolly and unflinchingly before him.

"Look here!" exclaimed his lordship. "Once more I say this sort of thing won't do! Are you listening to what I say?"

"Yes," said Brace, quietly. "I am listening."

"Then, look here: you've been warned times enough, and I shall put up with no more of it! Now go; and I warn you that if ever again you dare to speak to Miss Gernon, or to intrude upon her with your insolent attentions, I'll—I'll—I'll horsewhip you!"

These last words seemed to be forced from him by an effort; when, pale with anger at being so addressed in the presence of Isa, Brace took a step towards the Viscount, with his fists clenched, and his teeth set upon his upper lip. But at that instant, when a collision seemed imminent, an ejaculation of fear took Brace again to Isa's side.

"Do not be afraid," he whispered, with the anger fading out of his countenance. "Forgive me for my thoughtless passion." He laid his hand upon hers, pressing it upon the pommel of the saddle, as he gazed up in her face. "This is rather hard to bear; but I will try."

"Confound you! are words of no use whatever?" exclaimed his lordship angrily. And at the same moment the hunting-crop was raised, whistled through the air, and descended heavily upon Brace Norton's shoulders, causing him to start as if stung by some venomous reptile.

That which followed seemed to take place in an instant, for as Lord Maudlaine's hand was raised to repeat the blow, something darted through the air, striking him full upon the cheek, and he rolled over in the dusty road, felled by a blow that would have shaken the equanimity of a bullock.

"You dog—you cowardly miscreant!" hissed Brace between his teeth, as, beside himself with passion, he stood with clenched fists over his fallen adversary, till, recalling his promise, he once more hurried to the side of the trembling girl.

"I forgot myself," he exclaimed, hastily; "I thought that I had more self-control." Then seeing the working features and agitation the fracas had caused, he added, hastily: "Dear Isa, I know I deserve your anger—your contempt; but I have only one excuse to offer: it was something new to me, and evoked passion of whose existence I was in ignorance."

Isa could not speak; but as she listened to his pleading words, poor girl!—perhaps she was very weak and foolish—she thought that she had never seen Brace Norton look so brave and handsome before, and her eyes betokened more love than anger as they returned the young man's gaze.

Meanwhile, foaming with rage, and covered with the chalky dust in which he had involuntarily rolled, Lord Maudlaine stood, looking anything but a hero, as the dismounted groom grinned to himself and dusted his master's guest, rubbing him down with a gorgeous orange-and-white silk handkerchief, all hot from out of his livery; but polishing away, and accompanying the task with the hissing noise generally accorded to horses.

His lordship did not speak, but turned his back upon the group; and but for sundry recollections of his embarrassments which at the present moment intruded themselves painfully upon him, it is most probable that my lord the Viscount and prospective Earl and peer of the realm, would have hurriedly taken his departure from the neighbourhood of Merland. As it was, he submitted to the cleansing process so liberally bestowed upon him by the groom. Then, holding his handkerchief to his cheek, he turned to face Norton, to find that he was already a hundred yards off, walking by the side of Isa's mare; and soon after they disappeared at a turn of the road.

"Curse him!" exclaimed his lordship, with a fierce and bitter imprecation.

"Ketched yer unaweers, my lord, didn't he?" said the groom, who, with his bridle over his arm, still kept up his hissing and rubbing process. "If you'd ha' throwed up your left arm sharp, my lord, and then let go with your right, I don't know but what you might ha stopped him, and planted one for yourself. But per'aps, arter all, it was very doubtful, for that was as sharp a cutter as ever I did see."

His lordship did not seem to heed the friendly counsel, for, turning upon his heel, he strode hastily away in the opposite direction to that taken by Isa Gernon, muttering angrily, and evidently smarting with pain.

"I'm blest if I don't think," muttered Peter, the groom, as he slowly inducted a foot to its stirrup, and then lazily threw a leg over the horse's back, and began to put on his gloves—"I'm blest if I don't think as the higher yer gets up in serciety, the shabbier yer grows. Now, if that 'ere had been, say, a working man, or a lab'rer, and I'd set him upon his pins, and rubbed him down, he'd per'aps not ha' said, 'Here's the price of a pint, mate,' but he'd ha' stood a pint, safe; and if it had been a plain gent, such as that young

Squire Norton, he'd ha' give a shilling, per'aps 'arf a crown, or one o' them duffing two-bob bits; but as for my fine lord here, he don't so much as say thanky, let alone show you the colour of his money; while, getting up higher still, if it had been a Juke, blow me if I don't think he'd ha' kicked me for what I did. Well, just as they like, and it's all one a hundred years to come. All I can say, though, is, as it served his grand lordship jolly well right, and it was as neat and prettily-planted a blow as ever I did see put in. One—two! one—two! one—two! that was about it," he continued; as, tucking his whip under his saddle-flap, and laying the reins upon the pommel, he began to square with his fists in imitation of the blow he had seen delivered. "He's learned the noble art of self-defence, safe. One—two! one—two! one—two! Hold up, will yer!" he shouted, for in his excitement he had rammed one spur against his horse's side, and the poor animal had plunged sharply so as to nearly unseat his rider, who now gathered up his reins, and cantered after his mistress.

He had not ridden far before he came upon Brace Norton, apparently watching for him, in the middle of the road, and ready to slip a crown-piece into his hand.

"I think, my man," said Brace, quietly, "that it would be as well if the little unpleasantly you saw between Lord Maudlaine and me were not talked about up there at the Castle."

"Dumb as a jockey, sir," said the groom, striking himself over the mouth as he spoke; "but—you won't be affronted, sir?"

"Affronted!—no. What is it?" said Brace, smiling.

"If you'd—if you'd take that crown back, sir—" hesitated the man.

"Take it back? Nonsense! Keep it, my lad."

"And just show me how to give that blow, sir. 'Pon my word, sir, I'd rather know that than have half-a-dozen crowns. I never did see such a settler!"

Brace laughed, and strode on hurriedly, shaking his head.

"Ride on, my man," he said. "Your mistress is a long way ahead."

"That's true enough," said the groom to himself, as he looked after the retiring figure; "but he put him down just like a sack o' chaff, that he did; and my lord didn't like it, neither. I'm blest!" he exclaimed, slapping his thigh, and checking his horse suddenly. "Don't say nothing up at the Castle, which I won't; but if there don't come coffee and pistols out of this job, I'm a Dutchman!"

Magnanimity

"Lord Maudlaine presents his compliments to Lieutenant Norton, and begs to say, that although Lieutenant Norton's behaviour has been such that the meeting in such cases necessitated by wounded honour may seem absolutely imperative, yet, feeling compassion for his youth and inexperience, Lord Maudlaine is willing to forego the customary arrangement on one condition—namely, that Lieutenant Norton immediately quit Merland, and in no way, previous to his departure, trespass against the wishes of Sir Murray Gernon."

"He will understand that," said his lordship, who, after many hours of sheer hard work, contrived the above magnanimous epistle, and despatched it by a special messenger to Merland Hall, where it was read by Brace, with a quiet, scornful smile.

"When a man's fate leads him in one direction," he muttered, "it takes something stronger than such a letter as that to turn him out of the way."

The result was that Brace tore up the letter with an impatient "pish!" and cast the fragments away, Lord Maudlaine the while nervously looking for the reply that did not come, even when two days had elapsed, during which time both Sir Murray and he learned that Isa had been seen twice with Brace Norton, and the former angrily asked him how much longer he intended "that boy" to stand in his way.

"I should have thought," said his lordship, sulkily, "that I might have counted upon your help, and that you would, at least, have ordered Miss Gernon to confine herself to the house."

"Did I not give you my reasons," said Sir Murray, angrily. "Any coercion on my part would be snatched at by this Norton as an occasion for persuading the silly child to fly with him. I had more faith in you, Maudlaine; I thought that you would have striven harder to undermine his influence, instead of which, you turned tail in her presence—he struck you! I saw it all!"

"I struck him first," said his lordship, sulkily.

"Look here, Maudlaine," said Sir Murray, haughtily, "when I was a young man such an insult would have been followed by something more than words. You will stand and have her stolen from you."

"Perhaps this will go further yet," exclaimed the Viscount, firing up; for the thought of losing the prize he had looked upon as gained stung him to the quick, and without another word he hurried from the room, leaving Sir Murray thoughtful and frowning as he recalled the past. At times, though, his face softened, as the remembrance of Isa's gentle features crossed his imagination, and he dwelt for awhile upon her resemblance to her mother; but soon morose and bitter feelings prevailed, and for no reason, save that it seemed an eligible match, with a title, to which the name of Gernon would be allied, he cast aside all thoughts of affection as childish, and determined to take some steps himself for assisting his proposed son-in-law in his pretensions.

McCray Scents Mischief

On leaving Sir Murray Gernon, the energy which Lord Maudlaine had displayed seemed to disappear, and he entered his own room, pale and drawn of countenance. His hand, too, trembled, as, taking up a small silver flask which lay upon a side-table, he drained it to the last drop.

The brandy seemed to supply him with the nerve he required; and with a renewed energy, that wore something of the air of desperation, he opened a drawer in the bottom of his dressing-case, and took from it a pair of small, handsomely-mounted pistols. But his hands trembled as he turned them over and over, and the hue of his countenance became more and more sallow, while dark lines showed themselves beneath his eyes.

For strange thoughts were intruding themselves upon his mind, and it seemed to him that unless Brace Norton were out of his way he might just as well apply one of those pistols to his own forehead, and draw the trigger. This was not Italy, where he had first made the acquaintance of the Gernons, or how easily he might have been rid of his rival. But rid of him he must be, or ruin stared him in the face. Gambling and betting had taken his last shilling, and now, supplied with cash for the prosecution of his matrimonial project by one of the money-lending fraternity, he knew what his fate must be should he fail. Confound this Norton!—he was always starting up in his path; and he knew in his heart that he was afraid of him; and, but for the recollection of the fierce blow dealt him—a blow whose smart he still seemed to feel—the Viscount dared not have prosecuted the intent for which he was now preparing.

The age of duelling was long past, and he gave Brace Norton the credit for sending a note of challenge to the police, the result probably being a summons before the bench of magistrates at Marshton, and his being bound over to keep the peace towards Brace Norton and all her Majesty's liege servants. So, in accordance with the plan he had laid down, he proceeded to carefully load both pistols: powder and bullet, cap, and one was ready; powder, wad, cap, and another was ready; and then—perhaps by accident— his lordship took up a pen, dipped it in the silver inkstand close by, and let it fall, so that one pistol-butt was slightly marked with the black fluid. Then he sat, pen in hand, thoughtful and silent for some time, but he did not write; and at last, still very pale and anxious of mien, he took up the pistols, sounded the barrels one by one with the ramrods, and then placed one in each pocket of his coat, and slowly left the room, encountering, as he did so, the quiet, thoughtful countenance of shrewd old Sandy McCray, who watched him out into the pleasure-grounds, and then, having seen that his lordship's valet was in the housekeeper's room, walked swiftly up-stairs, and into the bed-room the Viscount had just vacated.

"He's been writing, seemingly," said the old Scot; "but he looked woondrous bad. But what ha'e we here, spillit a' ower the table-cover? Gude presairve us! if it isn't poother; and whaat would he be wanting with poother?"

Sandy McCray's pondering was arrested by the sight of the dressing-case drawer partly opened; and pulling it out, and gazing within it for a few moments, he hurriedly closed it again, and hastened down-stairs, and out into the stable yard, where he was not long before he found Peter, his young lady's groom. Peter had coat and vest off, his braces tied round his waist, and his shirt sleeves rolled-up to the elbows, squaring away at a corn-sack stuffed full of hay, and stood up on a bin in the large stable.

"One, two—one, two!" he kept on repeating; and, after a slight feint each time, he delivered a most tremendous blow, at the height of a man's face, right in the tightly-stuffed sack. "One, two, thud—one, two, thud!" went the blows, as the active little fellow sparred away, perspiring profusely the while, till he became aware of the old major-domo's presence, when he stopped short, abashed.

"So ye're practising boxing, my lad, air ye? Gude-sake! gi'e up that, and lairne to wrastle and throw the caber and put the stane. But leuke here, my laddie: does it ever happen that my young leddy meets Mr Norton when she's oot? There—there, I dinna wush ye to betray ony one, laddie; but ye lo'e her weel, like we all do, and I hae a soospeeshun that a' isn't reet. Noo, I've been a gude friend to ye always, Peter, and eef there's iver been anything wrang, I've been like Sir Murray himsel' to all ye sairvants, and paid yer wage, and seen ye raised, and that no ane put upon ye; so now tell me, like a gude laddie, has there been any clishmaclaver with Maister Norton and my laird here?"

Peter nodded shortly.

"Gude lad; it's for the gude of all I ask ye, sae tell me all. Did they come to blows?"

"Lordship hit Mr Norton with his whip," said Peter.

"Weel, laddie?" said McCray, for the groom paused.

"Mr Norton turns round like a shot; and 'one, two'—that's the blow; and my lord goes over just like that sack—that's the cut, sir!"

As he spoke, the groom rushed at the sack, and with one of his vigorous blows struck it right from the corn-bin to the ground.

"Gude, lad—gude, lad, and weel planted!" said McCray. "But noo, keep yer ain counsel, and put on yer duds, and come wi' me." Then, slowly making his way from the stable, McCray muttered: "And that accoonts for the poother."

The Meeting

When, pale and thoughtful, Lord Maudlaine strode across the lawn, his mind was agitated strangely by the feelings that oppressed him. He felt that matters had arrived at a pitch when, if he did not make some vigorous effort, he would lose even the partisanship of Sir Murray Gernon. The baronet's language, and his dislike for the Norton family, were sufficient to insure his protection and favour, let what might befall; and with something of his old gamblers feelings, when about to make some grand *coup*, or when he was backing largely some horse in a desperate venture, he pressed on.

But his heart told him that never had he attempted so great a stroke as he meditated now.

He was in no wise surprised when, half an hour after, he met Isa returning from a ride, ready to answer his bow with a slight inclination of her head; but he was not weak enough to imagine that, when he turned and saw her looking back, it was for any other reason than to see the direction he would take.

Old experience told him what to do, if he wished to encounter Brace Norton; and taking a short cut, he found, as he expected, that the young man was sauntering along the lane in front; so that the Viscount had but to leap a gate, and wait a few minutes for his rival to come, slowly and thoughtfully, up to where he stood; when Brace gave quite a start, and then stopped short.

Lord Maudlaine said nothing, but stood, for a moment, deadly pale, and hesitating. On one side there were ruin, exile, and bodily safety; on the other, wealth, position, and a beautiful wife. But there were also risk and treachery. He paused for awhile, and then nerved himself for the desperate plunge.

Laying his hand upon his cheek, still slightly discoloured, he then touched his pockets in a meaning way; one well understood by Brace, who followed him without a word, until they had crossed a couple of fields, and leaping a ditch, entered a copse, where—an open glade, suitable to their purpose, being reached—the Viscount stopped. Then, for the first time, Brace spoke:

"I have followed you, my lord, lest you should think I fear you; but, let me ask, have you well considered the step you are about to take? Of course, those are pistols you have with you; but without seconds—without a medical man present, people will be ungenerous enough to say that the survivor is a murderer. I am willing to meet you, if such an encounter must take place; but I must say it ought to be deferred."

"He *is* afraid!" thought his lordship; and, speaking hoarsely, he said: "I give you still the option of withdrawal on the terms I named."

Brace laughed scornfully.

"Then take your weapon," said the Viscount, whose pallor was now fearful. "They are both loaded, and we can easily pace the ground."

Brace frowned as he advanced and took the pistol nearest to him, glancing down at it for a moment to see that it was capped, then drawing out the ramrod, he thrust it into the barrel to feel for the bullet.

"My lord," he said, "let me once more appeal to you—to your manly feeling—to ask whether this is necessary. Surely you must be aware that your pretensions are vain, and that even if you disable, or slay me, your presence will be more than ever distasteful. I am cool now, and, forgiving you the blow you struck me, I ask pardon for my passionate haste. Let us put aside these deadly weapons, and in her name let me ask you to be generous, to have pity on us both, for it lies in your power!"

Brace ceased, for there was a sneer upon his rival's face that was almost devilish. He had watched Brace's actions, and seen him probe the pistol-barrel, when, apparently satisfied, the young man had let the weapon fall to his side.

"Dog! coward! scoundrel!" exclaimed the Viscount, now half-beside himself with a passion that seemed fiendish. "Once more I give you a chance; give her up for ever, and write what I will dictate, or take your place."

For answer, Brace Norton's lips moved as he slowly took his place opposite to his adversary, when, with a malignant look of hatred, that could hardly have been expected from a man of his character, Lord Maudlaine smiled triumphantly, as he too examined the cap of his pistol, and then drew the ramrod, to thrust it down the barrel. Then, as if stricken by paralysis, the look of hate and triumph faded from his face, to leave it of a sickly green hue, his jaw fell, his hand trembled visibly, and his knees shook beneath him; for, in spite of his management, Lord Maudlaine was at his opponent's mercy: he had carefully charged one pistol only with ball, and, in his agitation, he had let that weapon pass into his rival's hand, while his own contained but a blank charge.

The Viscount's aspect was truly pitiable, and for a moment it was in his heart to beg for mercy; but, as if mechanically, he faced his rival, and with the dread upon him that his treachery would be discovered, he prepared to fire.

Guilt requires no accusers: he could not think then to say that his pistol was not fully charged—he could not see that he had a generous enemy to deal with. He measured his adversary by himself; and, feeling that his last hour had come, he prepared to fire.

"Will your lordship give the signal—the dropping of a handkerchief?" said Brace. "We have no seconds to take the duty."

"No! You!" gasped the Viscount; and Brace gazed wonderingly at the pitiable fear evinced by his opponent, who had nerved himself into standing upright, and now retained his position in almost a cataleptic state.

Brace drew forth a white handkerchief, and then with his pistol covered his adversary—the man whom his heart told him a careful aim would remove from his path for ever.

"At the word *three*," said Brace, calmly; and then, after a pause, "One—two—three!"

One pistol only exploded, there was a faint puff of smoke, and Lord Maudlaine fell back in the woodland path; while with scorn, contempt, almost pity for the coward before him struggling for the mastery, Brace Norton, with his undischarged pistol in his hand, slowly walked up to where, pale, and with his face bathed in perspiration, Lord Maudlaine, who had fallen, half fainting with fear, gazed up at him with the most horrified aspect conceivable.

"Would you murder me?" he gasped at last, as Brace, pistol in hand, stood over him.

"Murder you!" said Brace scornfully. "No, my lord. You may rise. You challenged me to meet you, and I have received your fire. Your lordship is now probably content. I might try to make terms now, but I should be sorry to take so pitiful an advantage. There is your pistol, my lord. I wish you good day."

Lord Maudlaine had risen as Brace addressed him, and mad with shame and confusion, he stood listening to his rival's words; but when Brace handed him the undischarged pistol by the butt, the old fiendish rage took possession of his soul, lending fire to his eye, and nerve to his arm. He took the weapon and held it to his side; but as Brace turned and walked down the path, he dashed after him.

"Stop!" he cried, hoarsely; "not yet—you have not yet escaped!" when, as Brace turned, startled at the change that had come upon his rival, the young man's heart quailed for a few moments, for he was standing within six paces of the Viscount, who was taking deadly aim at his breast.

Another second, and the aim might have proved mortal; but, as the pistol exploded, a heavy body seemed to dart from the bushes beside the Viscount, who was thrust aside, and the bullet grazed the bark of a huge beech-tree a dozen yards in advance.

"Weel done, Peter, my lad!" cried a voice—"that was weel jumpit. Why, ye murderin' loon, to shute at an unairmed man like that; and is it the like of thee as is to have the Castle? Gude-sake, Maister Norton, dinna ye hold me. I could shock all the braith out of his coward's bodie, I could. Oh! ye may weel go," he cried, loudly, as the Viscount hurried away. "We saw it all, Mr Brace, Peter here and me; but not soon enow to stop the first shot. We saw him go doon, and for a wee my hairt was in my mooth, for I thocht ye'd kilt him. But that was a bonny leap of the lad's here, and disarrangit his aim, or, sir, I believe he'd have hit ye. But Sir Mooray shall know what a viper he's got under his roof before he's an hour older."

"No, not a word—not a single hint of this must be given to him!" exclaimed Brace, firmly. "I will not win my way forward by such means. Mr McCray, I ask it as a favour: let this be all buried."

"And it was verra like that ye were to being buried yersel'," grumbled the old Scot; but after a good deal of arguing, Brace carried the day by the use of Isa's name, and for her sake it was settled that the proceedings should be kept as their own secret, unless Lord Maudlaine should think proper to give a garbled account, in which case, in his own defence, Brace might find it necessary to speak, when McCray promised that he would "bear witness to the truth."

"I'll answer for the laddie here, sir," said McCray; "and noo we must goo, for it winna do for us to be seen speaking to ye. Ye're a proper lad, but I'm Sir Mooray's sairvant, and we mustn't foregather at all. I think I see how matters air; but I'm going to talk it ower with the gudewife, and then I shall have the scales cleart frae my een. Gude day, sir. Noo, Peter. Ah! laddie, ye shouldna ha' ta'en that sovereign; but there, I dinna ken but what ye're right. Ye savit the laddie's life; and I think that its warth mair than a gowd sovereign to him."

The next minute Brace Norton, now almost giddy with excitement, strode away. He had had a most narrow escape of his life, but he told himself that he could afford to be generous, for had not Isa that morning owned how painful it was to pass a day without seeing him? He was more and more, too, in her confidence, and she had told him of her fathers morose looks, and of how she found that he knew of their interviews, although he had not spoken a word, but, as was his wont at times, shut himself up from all intercourse, leaving her entirely to the persecution of her detested suitor.

"I cannot help leaving the house all I can," she had said, naïvely. "If he would only go, see my dislike, or be generous, I would not care; but I believe he proposed to my father when we first encountered him in Italy, and my father acceded to his propositions."

Then they had talked about the future, and forgetting what he had since gone through, Brace recalled all: how he had whispered comfort to her, and told her to hope. Of how he fully expected that the day would come when the old enmity of her father would be swept away, and that in spite of all the black clouds around them now, the sun would shine forth at last.

"This old mysterious story must have a solution," he had said; "but there, I will not revert to it!" Then they parted, and thinking upon it all more deeply than ever, Brace's musings were interrupted as we have seen by the coming of the man upon whom his thoughts had turned.

Tangled

Two days—four days, and a week passed, and Brace did not see Isa. He sought all her favourite rides, and waited about for hours, but she did not come. He felt sure that something was wrong, and wondered again and again whether that something was connected with the meeting with Lord Maudlaine. As the days passed, Brace's mind was incessantly tortured by imaginings of garbled accounts, of insidious attempts to poison the ear of Isa, and at length his anxiety became almost unbearable. If he had made some arrangement by which he might have sent a letter, he would not have cared, but, under the circumstances, he felt that to write would only be to insure the return of his note, and he dared not send.

A fortnight had passed and no news, when Brace Norton's heart leaped as, at breakfast, Captain Norton unlocked the letter-bag, and passed over a couple of letters to his son, one of which was in a handwriting he had never before seen, but whose authoress his heart told him, as, unable to control himself, he rose from the table and sought his room.

The note was but short, and contained exactly what he had anticipated, but none the less it made him sink on a chair by his dressing-table, cover his face with his hands, and groan in the bitterness of his heart.

It was precisely as he had conjectured. Sir Murray had angrily commanded his daughter to refrain from meeting the reader any more. He had told her that she must learn to school her heart, for such a union, for family reasons, was absolutely impossible; and, besides, he had passed his word that she should be the wife of Lord Maudlaine, who had, during the past fortnight, been most assiduous in his attentions, driving her, Isa said, to taking refuge in her own room for hours every day. She told him that they must meet no more; that she was very unhappy; but that Jane, the housekeeper, her old nurse, had spoken comforting words to her, telling her that perhaps, after all, the old troubles between the two houses might be swept away.

"I would not, on any account, my child, advise you against your papa's wishes," Jane had said; "but you must not marry Lord Maudlaine while your poor little heart is another's. I have seen too much misery amongst those you know for that to take place. You must wait, my child—you must wait—wait."

The letter concluded:—

"But how can I wait, when papa insists? Do not be angry with me, for I am very, very unhappy, and very weak. I am no heroine of romance, and cannot see how all this will end; but I pray hourly for your happiness, for that will be the happiness of Isa Gernon."

He had never written a line to her, and this was her first letter to him, breathing in every word the simple, guileless love of her pure young heart. There were no passionate protestations—no vows of sincerity and faith— nothing but a fond belief in him, and his power to save her from the fate which threatened to be hers. And what could he do? How could he save her?

These were questions that would take time to solve; and perhaps, he thought, bitterly, then he would be too late.

There was one thing, though, that, in spite of his misery, he could not help remarking: the utter absence of any reference to the meeting; and it soon became evident that his lordship had thought good to keep all secret. But what a fate for that poor girl, to become the wife of a man so cowardly and devoid of honour!

"It shall not be!" exclaimed Brace, excitedly. "She looks to me for help and protection, and I supinely sit and grieve when I should be up and doing!"

He strode up and down the room, turning over in his mind a score of schemes, one and all useless, some even absurd; but all seemed to resolve in one idea, and at last he uttered his thoughts aloud, exclaiming:

"That shall be the last resource—all failing, I will bear her off!"

"No, Brace," said the soft, gentle voice of Mrs Norton. "That would be as dishonourable as it is wild. You are half mad with disappointment. Why not wait wait patiently? I cannot but think that Isa, with all her gentleness, is too much of a true woman to give up, even under coercion. Wait and be hopeful."

"Mother," said Brace, bitterly, "I have thought over the past till my brain has grown confused; and still I have gone on groping in the dark to try and find a way out of this difficulty. Time goes swiftly now, and before many days are past I must join my ship for a two years' cruise. You tell me to be patient, and wait; but it makes me recall the sufferings of another, and I see myself coming back some morning to hear the chiming of old Merland's bells, while there is nought left for me to exclaim but those two bitter words: 'Too late!'"

"Bitter, then, my son," exclaimed a deep voice; "but time has happiness in store for us all."

Brace Norton turned hastily to see his mother sink sobbing in his father's arms.

Lover and Father

"Noo, leuke here, young man, I wadna speake to ye at all but for your cloth, for my ain brither wore the true-blue, and was lost at sea in a Kirkcaldy herring-boat, and so I always feel disposed to foregather with ane who sails the ocean. Noo, ye've stoppit me oot here in the lane, speerin' aboot the auld times. I was Sir Mooray's gairdener then, fresh up frae the North Kintree—frae Galashiels, and spak the Scottish dialec then, only lang-dwelling in furren pairts has made quite a furrener o' me. But I was gaun to say, Sir Mooray wud be sair angered wi' me if he knew I so much as spak to ye, and I must do my duty by him."

"But just answer me a few questions!" cried Brace, eagerly.

"Na, na!" said McCray, as he leaned against a gate and took snuff. "I'm sorry for ye—I am indeed, for I ken a' aboot it. I had it frae the gudewife, who nursed the bairn oop yinder, ever sin' she was a babe—at a time, too, when my ain hairt was sair. Ye lo'e the sweet flower weel, I've nae doot; but it canna be, young man—ye must goo awa' and try and forget her. There's a sair black pit atween ye twain, and I canna see that it will ever be filled up or bridged ower. Ye must try and bear it all as weel's ye can."

"But do you believe the story, McCray?" exclaimed Brace.

"I dinna ken—I winna say. All I can say is, I wush ye micht put a' reet and win the sweet lassie; for yon loon wi' the title—There, dinna say anither wurd to me, Meester Norton, for I'm forgetting whose sairvant I am. Tak' my advice: join your ship, and go try and forget it a'; for it's an awfu' black affair a'thegither, and I'm sair afraid that the mair ye try to put it reet the waur ye'll mak' it.

"He'd ha'e made her a bonnie jo," muttered McCray, as he went off, shaking his grey head. "And he's a fine, fair-spoken young fellow; but Sir Mooray hates him like poison, and it can never be."

He turned once, to see Brace Norton standing against the gate; and his heart swelled, as he thought of the days of old and his own misery.

"Puir lad—puir lad!" said McCray, as he strode on. "There was a wee bit of hope for me, but it's a sair case for him, and for her too—bless her bright e'en! for I fear she lo'es him weel!"

Brace Norton never stirred for an hour, but leaned there, in one of the most secluded lanes round Merland, trying to form some plan of action, but in vain. He had determined to see McCray, and had long watched for the opportunity; while now, that he had had his interview, what had he gained? If he could obtain an interview with his wife, he might perhaps learn something of her; but how could he do it? Writing was such poor satisfaction. Could he do it by other means?—could he depute some one to question Jane McCray—one who would possess sufficient influence to gain from her some information? For he felt that it was only by constant search that the clue could be obtained—for that there was a clue, and that the mystery might yet be cleared up, he felt sure.

The answer to his question came in a way he little expected, for just then he heard the sound of a horse's feet, and his heart bounded, as slowly round a bend of the lane, the chequered sunshine playing upon her riding-habit, came Isa Gernon. Her head was bent, and her lithe, graceful form swayed in gentle undulations to the well-trained pace of her highly-broken mare.

Would she pass him? Would she ride on without a word?

It almost seemed that she would, for, buried in thought, Isa Gernon had not seen the figure by the green lane bank; when moved by an uncontrollable impulse, Brace darted to her side, to catch her gloved hand in his, and stand at her saddle-bow gazing up into her face.

"There was the groom, some fifty yards behind, but he told himself it was no business of his. He knew Sir Murray disapproved of it all; but Sir Murray never asked him to put a stop to it; while, if he was a sailor, Mr Brace Norton was a thorough gent, and free with his 'arf-crowns as could be. It wasn't for him to interfere with what my young missus did. All he— Peter Barlow, young lady's groom—knew was, that if he'd been Miss Isa, he'd sooner have had Mr Brace Norton than a dozen Lord Maudlaines. Lord, indeed! as professed to 'unt, and to know so much about 'osses, and sat across one like a sack o' chaff, while Mr Norton had as pretty a seat as ever he see a man have out of the profession—for, of course, you couldn't expect gents to ride like a groom.

"Don't speak, Isa dear—Isa, my own sweet love!" whispered Brace, his voice growing soft, and his words trembling with tenderness—"do not say a word! I know all: that you are forbidden to see me; that there is a ban upon our family; and that the past reveals a sad—sad story of misery and broken hearts. But this meeting is not of your seeking—you cannot help yourself. See, dearest! I am holding this soft, gentle hand in mine—I am forcing you to listen to me; for, oh! Isa, sweet love, I am mad with grief and misery. You know the story of my father's—your poor mother's broken heart: is ours to be the same fate? Do not think me cruel in bringing up these tales of the past; but is it not our duty to try and clear away the mystery? My life upon it!" he exclaimed, excitedly, "there is a clue to be found, in spite of the time that has fleet; for do you for a moment think I will ever credit a word of the cruel calumnies that stain our family names? They are all false—false and unworthy! but they must be cleared away. And now listen, dearest: do not weep, for we must be up and doing; it is no time for tears. I love you too well, Isa, ever to give you up; Heaven giving me strength, I will fight with my last breath to win you, and you must help me! See Jane McCray, your housekeeper; question her closely—learn all you can; and if you can trace a fact worthy of attention, contrive to send me word. Your silence I will take to mean that your efforts are without avail. I will be honourable: I will not ask you to write to me—I will not write to you. While this stain is upon me, I feel that I am unworthy to stand even in your presence; but it is the last time, Isa, until I come, proudly, in the strength given me by the knowledge that those foul cobwebs are swept away from the shield. I do not ask you to bind yourself to me in any way; for, to me, your sweet, pure heart is too true—too generous to give me cause for doubt. Isa, I am yours—yours only, in this world, I hope, if not in another. A few days longer, and I shall be with my ship, on the blue sea, Isa, and I can do but little, save think and pray for the future; and I shall go without a dread—without a feeling that I shall be supplanted, even at your father's command. Shall I tell you why?"

"Yes," said Isa; and her tears fell fast upon his upturned face, as she bent lower and lower.

"Because I know that your hand will go with your heart, and that the heart is in my keeping. Watch and wait, dearest. Remember your mother's— my mother's words: 'True-blue!' It is the colour I sail beneath, darling, and under it I shall watch and wait."

Isa's tears fell faster and faster. She would have spoken, but her emotion choked her utterance; and still she bent lower and lower towards the hand that held hers so tightly. The graceful palfrey she rode tossed its head and shook its curb impatiently, but moved no step forward. The groom had evidently made up his mind that utter ignorance of all that was passing would be pleasing to his mistress, and that some one else might reward him with five shillings; so having settled his saddle and girths to his satisfaction, he took to examining his horse's mane and tail, such proceedings necessitating his back being turned, an attitude he meant to maintain until summoned.

A glance had shown this to Brace Norton; and no doubt it was very wrong, but the lane was so retired and shady, Isa Gernon was so very beautiful, and she had laid bare the secret of her young, ingenuous heart to his gaze. He was too frank a sailor—unskilled in etiquette and formality. He only knew then—he could think of nothing else—that he loved the fair girl before him very dearly; that she was weeping bitterly for his sake; and that, but for untoward fate, she might have been his. Who, then, can be surprised that one hand should rest lightly upon the soft, handsome neck, crushing, as it did so, the massive braids of her glorious dark hair; that that head should, in obedience to Love's command, bend lower and lower, without thought of resistance flashing across the gentle girl's mind, until, for the first time in her life, her lips were pressed in a long, sweet kiss, that to her seemed given in token of farewell?

"I must have you now, Isa," said Brace, sadly, as with a deep blush she shrank from his embrace, though her hand was still tightly clasped in his. "I bind you by no promises, I ask nothing, but I go away contented, for the day shall come when all these sad obstacles shall be swept away, and—There, I can say no more," he exclaimed passionately. "Go now; I am cruel to you in keeping you like this, placing you at the mercy of even your groom's tattling tongue. I shall make you in your calmer moments almost to think meanly of me for this clandestine meeting; but what can I do, Isa, when my appearance at the Castle would only be the signal for rude expulsion? Once more Good-bye!"

He gave the mare's head a caress, and then shook the bridle as he spoke, forcing the interview to an end, as the graceful animal softly bounded forward in answer to his touch, its mistress's head turned back till a bend of the lane hid her from Brace's longing gaze, when, placing his hand in his pocket, he prepared to purchase the groom's silence, but, to his surprise, that individual dashed past him at a smart canter, and on turning to seek the explanation of his strange conduct, Brace Norton's eyes fell upon the fierce, wrinkled countenance of Sir Murray Gernon.

He could not doubt for a moment that the baronet had witnessed, at least, the latter part of the interview, and Brace's brow flushed as he recalled the scene so sweet to him, and full of solace to his aching heart. What should he do: turn and avoid the angry father? No, he could not do that; he would meet him boldly, and listen to all he had to say, giving for answer the sole reply that he loved Isa, and that the meeting was unpremeditated.

Sir Murray's lips were white with passion as he strode up to the young man, and the stick he carried quivered in his strong hand as he held it half raised, as if about to strike. He stopped short in front of Brace, glaring at him fiercely, but for a few moments, as he gazed in the young man's calm, dispassionate face, he did not speak. At last, though in a voice choking with wrath, he exclaimed, as he pointed with his stick in the direction taken by Isa:

"Like father—like son. You know, I do not doubt, the history of twenty years ago—a history that you, pitiful, contemptible slave that you are, compel me to revert to. You know how my happiness was blasted. You know that, urged by his necessities, your father dishonoured himself for ever, in the eyes of gentlemen, and became a thief."

"I know that to be utterly false, Sir Murray Gernon," said Brace, calmly.

"You know how, afterwards, he played upon the weakness of a fickle woman, till she fled with him," continued the baronet, without seeming to hear the interruption.

"I know, too, that that is false, Sir Murray," said Brace still calmly; "and that my father is as pure-minded and honourable a man as ever breathed."

"Insult—robbery—disgrace!" continued Sir Murray, without heeding him. "Everything, in his revenge for my unhappy marriage, he heaped upon my head. Twice, for long spaces of time, I exiled myself; till now, when, after twenty years, I come back to spend the rest of my days in peace in my old home, I find my enemy's son grown up and ready, the moment I plant foot upon the English shore, to waylay me, and accost Miss Gernon with his impertinent persecution. I warned you—I sought in every way to discourage you; your own heart must have told you that every word addressed to that girl was an insult to me, and that, even would I have stooped low enough to have permitted it, any union was impossible; and, still finding in her her mother's weakness—the weakness your vile parent betrayed— you persevered. You knew, too, that she was engaged—that I had made arrangements for a suitable marriage; and, doubtless, you found in that a good lever for moving her—telling her that she was the victim of paternal persecution. Dishonour, dishonour, dishonour! in every step dishonour, trickery, and deceit; winning upon her, by clandestine meetings, till I find that she has stooped so low as to suffer, here in a public thoroughfare, in the presence even of a menial, a low groom, what I myself witnessed—what has, before now, become the ribald jest of the servants in the Castle. I do not ask you to refrain; that, I know, is useless. I do not ask you to plead the excuse you have ready—the paltry drivellings of your *love*, as you would doubtless call it. Son of a base and cowardly trickster, you inherit all your father's villainy, and I would horsewhip you as I would some base groom, only that I look upon you as too low—too contemptible even for that!"

He paused for a few minutes, as if for breath, scowling the while at Brace Norton, who, with flushed face and set teeth, stood bearing it all, whispering that one name again and again, as a talisman to guard him from forgetting himself, and, in some furious outburst of passion, striking down to his feet the lying denouncer of his family.

"I know that it is in vain to appeal to you as I would to an honourable man," continued Sir Murray, pale with rage, "and here you drive me to my last resource; for sooner than that weak, drivelling girl should be your wife, I would see her in her coffin! But I have no need for that: plastic as wax in your hands, she can be plastic as clay in mine. I can mould her to my wishes, in spite of all you have done. I can treat you in the same way, even to making you give her up—now, at once, before you leave this ground. I have kept this shaft for the last, wishing to try all else first; and had I had to deal with an honourable man—with an officer and gentleman," he said sarcastically, "this shaft would never have been loosed."

"Look here, Sir Murray Gernon," exclaimed Brace, now thoroughly roused, "I am a frank, plain-spoken sailor. The deck of a man-of-war is no school for polish and etiquette; but I tell you this to your teeth, that you know that what you have said to me this day is a base, calumnious tissue of cruelty, such as no gentleman should have uttered. Nay, it is my turn now; I listened to you in silence, you shall hear me. You know my father to be an honourable man; you know, too, that my love for your child has been the result of no plotting and planning, but of circumstances alone. You know how accident has thrown us together, and before Heaven I vow that man never loved woman with a purer—a holier love. I say it now before you, without shame, without fear, for I am proud of it—proud, too, of knowing that my love is returned. Do you, with all your pride, imagine that young hearts are to be directed here or there according to your wish or whim? You know better; and that we cannot govern ourselves in such matters. I leave here for sea in a few days' time, and I tell you what I have told her; that I bind her by no promises, that I ask nothing, merely time—time to clear away these clouds that overshadow our youth—"

"Have you nearly finished?" exclaimed Sir Murray, interrupting him; and his old mocking smile appeared upon his face.

"Yes," said Brace, sadly; "I have done, Sir Murray. I hope some day that you will know me better. But I tell you this: that so long as life is in me I'll never give her up; and, what is more," he added fiercely, "I know she will be true to me, even without the tie of promise or troth!"

"I told you that this was my last arrow, and I fly it reluctantly," hissed Sir Murray, as he leaned towards the young man; "before I loose the string, I ask you will you give up all pretension to the hand of that child?"

"No!" exclaimed Brace.

"It is an arrow whose flight will be sharp and aim sure, young man. I warn you that it will quiver in your heart, and its barbs will rankle there for life. Once more, will you give her up, and come here no more?"

"No!"

"Will you not for your mothers sake? But there, I know the baseness of your heart. Isa Gernon, and the prospect of Merland Castle and its many acres, are not to be given up so easily. I knew your answer; but, in a fit of madness, I thought I would give you, as you are young, one chance of playing the honourable man. You will not give her up, then?"

"No—*no*! Are you a demon? Why do you tempt me like this?" cried Brace.

"Yes," said Sir Murray, leaning closer and closer towards the young man, whose hot words he did not seem to have heard, so drawn and strange was his aspect—"yes, you will give her up, and I will tell you why: I hate her—yes, bitterly as I hate you; but I have some feeling yet left in me, and I will not see this wrong done. Look here: your path is across the sea; go, and at once. Yours is an honourable calling; try and root out all the base, and be an honourable man. Do not come near Merland again for years; but before you go, write to Isa, and tell her that you give her up, that all is at an end, and that a union is impossible. You have influence with the weak child: tell her, then, as your wish, that she should raise no objection to the match I propose."

"Are you mad, sir?" exclaimed Brace.

"No, young man," said Sir Murray; "but I have suffered enough to make me so. Do as I tell you, since she never can be yours, for—"

He leaned forward, laying one trembling hand upon Brace's shoulder, his face the while drawn and distorted, as he whispered, for a few moments, in the young man's ear.

They were few words to which Sir Murray Gernon's lips gave utterance; but they sent a flash of rage through Brace Norton's heart, as, catching the baronet by the throat, he exclaimed:

"How dare you utter so base—" He said no more; but his hands dropped to his sides, as he seemed to read in the baronet's livid and distorted features the truth of his utterance. For a few moments the young man stood motionless, a sob of horror and despair rending his breast as he struggled for utterance; the next minute, with the same blind, groping pace—the same aspect of misery seen a quarter of a century before on his father's face—an aspect that might have betokened the judgment for a father's sin descending upon the son—Brace Norton, broken-hearted and half-stunned, hurried away.

Against Hope

Father—mother? Whom could he fly to for advice at such a time? Brace Norton asked himself. To neither. He knew what his father's counsel would be, and that his mother, while sympathising, could not help him. Reveal the words spoken to him by the baronet he could not. After the first few hours of agony—of bitter agony—that he had suffered, he would not even revert to them himself. He could not but think that Sir Murray had felt what he said to be true; but, for himself, he felt that it was monstrous. He believed that his mother had told him all she knew, and he was ready to cast his life upon the honour and truth of his father. There was no failing of confidence between them, and he reddened with shame at having, even for a moment, credited the baronet's assertion. Give up Isa? No; not while he had life! His course was plainly enough marked out; he could see it now: it was to be his duty to clear up the mystery that had long hung over Merland Castle, and he would do it. Happiness might yet be the result for him; but even if it were not, there was in the eyes of many yet living a stain upon his fathers fair fame. That stain he would wipe away, even to the convincing of Sir Murray Gernon.

He must, he felt, keep every thought and act from those who were dear to him—the subject was too painful even to be broached in their hearing. Where, then, should he commence?—for his time was but short ere his vessel would be refitted, and he must join. The old steward, McCray? No; he had found him close and reserved. Jane—Mrs McCray: the woman of whom Isa always spoke so tenderly—who had nursed her from a child, and had been Lady Gernon's confidential maid? She could help him, perhaps; but would she? He could try, without waiting for Isa.

Brace Norton pondered long as he strove to contrive a plan for seeing Jane, but only to decide at last that he must write.

He wrote a long, earnest appeal, such as he felt he could write in safety to so staunch a friend of Isa's. He told, in frank, earnest terms, of his love, of his sorrow for the dense cloud that existed between the two houses, and of his determination to pierce it. His letter breathed throughout his firm faith in his father's honour—words which, of course, to Jane McCray, would convey the young man's faith in her mistress, though her name was not mentioned; and Brace concluded by imploring Jane to tell him all she knew, keeping back nothing that might aid him in his endeavours to find a clue that should bring to light the causes of the sorrows that had so long overshadowed the houses of Gernon and Norton.

He sent his letter, and waited one—two—three days; on each of which he had the misery of seeing Isa at a distance riding out, accompanied by Lord Maudlaine.

On the fourth day, though, an answer came, written in very guarded language, but all the same, whispering of pity and a plainly-expressed hope that for Isa's sake Mr Brace Norton might be successful in his quest; but help, Mrs McCray said, she could give him none—she had nothing she could tell more than was known already by Mrs Norton. Simple facts, these; and with one exception—that of Jane's suspicions—Brace was already well-informed, every word being treasured deeply in his heart.

Brace Norton's brow knit as he thought over again and again the narrative of his mother. If his father would but take counsel with him, and they together tried to investigate the matter, he felt that all would be well; but he dared not broach the subject in his presence, and once more he turned to himself for aid.

There was the disappearance of that cross: what could have become of that? The answer was plain enough—his parents' and his own suspicions must be correct: Gurdon, the old butler, must have stolen it. Sir Murray had accused him of it; and if proper search had been made, no doubt it would have been found. Twenty years transportation he was to suffer, and that period must be up now some time; was it possible that, upon a promise being given him that no further prosecution should follow, and a bribe were supplied, he would afford such information as should prove to the satisfaction of all what had become of the cross?

No doubt he would—*if alive!*

Brace determined to try and trace Gurdon—to see if he had returned to this country; and, leaving home, he sought out the proper official place at which to apply, and learned that John Gurdon had completed his term of servitude, and had then been set at liberty. That was all. He had been set at liberty twelve thousand miles from England; nothing further was known.

"I shall meet him, perhaps, during my cruises," muttered Brace, bitterly; and he returned home utterly disheartened.

Then he turned his attention to the disappearance of Lady Gernon. What had become of her? Elopement was out of the question. Had she, moved thereto by Sir Murray's harsh treatment and cruel suspicions, fled, to pass the rest of her life somewhere at peace? If so, without doubt, in the course of twenty years, she must have been heard of. That supposition was not likely, and he dismissed it, to give place to a dread fear that, sick of life, she might have sought rest in direct opposition to the divine canon. But Brace could not harbour that thought. Lady Gernon had always been painted to him as too pure-minded, patient, and suffering a woman to fly to such a refuge; she was rather one to suffer and pray for strength to bear it.

"Of what are you thinking, Brace?" said Mrs Norton, tenderly, as, entering his room, she found him brooding over a new suspicion that had entered his mind.

He started as she spoke to him, and tried to drive away his thoughts, and to speak to her cheerfully; but the same dire suspicion came again and again, and at last, as she urged him to speak—to confide in her—he said, almost in a whisper:

"Mother, I was wondering if it were possible that Lady Gernon was murdered!"

Mrs Norton shuddered as she recalled the visit of Jane McCray, and the disclosures she had made—every word of which, in spite of the great lapse of time, now seemed to occur to her as plainly as if they had been spoken but a few hours since.

"Hush, Brace!" she whispered, her face assuming an aspect of horror. "The idea is too dreadful. Think, too, of what it embraces."

"Yes—yes, I know," he exclaimed, impetuously; "but, mother, this must be cleared up. I will have all brought to light. I should have said nothing but for your questions, rather choosing to pursue my own course."

"But think, Brace—think of Isa. Suppose such a revelation as you seek to make, how then?—consider how it would affect her. My son, had you not better suffer than bring such a charge against her father?"

"Her father—Sir Murray Gernon? I never suspected him of so foul a crime. Mother, you have something you keep back from me. You have suspected him of this, then, perhaps years ago."

Mrs Norton said nothing, but her agitated countenance spoke volumes; and rising from his seat, Brace exclaimed, bitterly:

"Oh! mother—mother. Is there an evil fate hanging over us? Everything seems to militate against my prospects of happiness. If I had never seen her—if I had never seen her!" he groaned.

"Brace, my son, be a man!" exclaimed Mrs Norton, her eyes the while swimming with tears. "You are young yet, and women's hearts are not so frail as novelists would paint them. Wait on and hope. Live in the happy thought that Isa loves you; and, if she be her mother's child, no threat, no persuasion will tempt her to give her hand without her heart. You are young, very young yet, and time may prove all—may lay bare the secrets of the past. I did suspect him. Promise me that you will hold my words secret as the grave, and that you will make no use of them, for Isa's sake, and I will tell you."

"Mother," said Brace, bitterly, "I would cut off my right hand sooner than speak a word that would injure any one belonging to her. Say what you will, you cannot alter what I see already. It is all plain enough. My hands are chained, and I must, as you say, live on and hope."

"Yes," he said, after Mrs Norton had told him of Jane's visit, "it is possible that all may have been her hallucinations; and it is as possible that—there—no, it is impossible, and I will not harbour the thought. Mother dear, you must teach me your old resignation, that I may wait patiently for the good time when all shall be made plain; for I will wait, you helping, though,"—he said, with a sad and mournful smile—"that time may not be on this side of the grave!"

A Visitor to his Lordship

Lord George Maudlaine had been making rather a long stay at Merland; but things were, he told himself, going on very satisfactorily. Brace seemed to have been driven off, and in a few days would be at sea. Sir Murray was all that could be desired, and favoured more strongly than ever the matrimonial projects of his lordship, telling him, with a grim smile, that he need fear no rival now. In fact, at times, his lordship thought him almost too eager, and tried to make out whether, by any means, he was going to be what he called "taken in." He was lying one morning about nine o'clock, indolently going over the matter in his not very logical mind. He had had a cup of coffee brought him by his valet, and had added to the dense odour he had already imparted to the pale blue satin hangings of his bed, by smoking a cigar, and spilling the ash about the delicate linen in which he lay.

"Let me see," said his lordship, yawning, and going over the matter for the twentieth time. "I don't think I can get anything more out of it. I can't see how it can prove a 'sell.' She's very pretty and lady-like, and well-bred, and all that sort of thing. Don't much care for me, but then, that don't matter. The Castle, and every penny the old man has, comes to her at his death, and he comes down handsome as to marriage settlements. Why, there can't be anything wrong, though the more she hangs away, the more he pushes the matter forward. I'd run back in a moment if I thought I was being 'done'; but, then, I don't see how I can be; and, besides, it was my own seeking at first. It's all right, and in a few months I shall be able to shake myself clear of those precious Hebrews. Come in! Well, Willis?"

"Gentleman wishes to see your lordship on important business."

"Must be some one wants his little bill," thought his lordship. "Tell him I'm particularly engaged," he said, aloud. "What the deuce does he mean by coming at such an hour as this? Know who it is?"

"Yes, my lord," said the valet, meaningly, for as his own salary was regularly paid, and his perquisites were many, he had a very profound contempt for all duns. "Think it's Mr Braham, my lord."

"What?" exclaimed his lordship, completely thrown off his equanimity, for he had judged the visitor to be one of the tradesmen of the little town—one of the unfortunates whom he had favoured with his orders. "You don't mean to say—"

"Come down to Marshton last night, m' lord, and driven over this morning."

"Has—has any one—has Sir Murray seen him, do you think?"

"Can't say, m' lord, but he drove up to the grand entrance quite cheeky, in as wretched an old gig as ever your lordship see—saw," added the valet, correcting himself.

"You'd better show him up," said his lordship, with a blank look of misery in his face, as he first threw off, and then replaced, his silken night-cap. "Say I'm ill, Willis."

"Yes, m' lord," said the valet, and he went out with his tongue in his cheek. "I heered him say as he'd hold the string, that day he went away from us in town, and it strikes me as he's come to pull it now. Step this way, sir, if you please," he continued, entering the breakfast-room, where he found Mr Braham making himself perfectly at home with some coffee and "devilled" chicken, breakfast being a meal that strangers at the Castle took at their pleasure. The meal was prepared, and allowed to remain in the breakfast-room for a couple of hours, ready for those who liked to partake thereof. Hence, Mr Braham, being hungry from his early ride, judged himself to be one who would like to partake, and acted accordingly.

"I'll have another cup of coffee first, my man," he said, coolly. "Lordship quite well?"

"Well, no, sir," said the valet; "but if you'll step up, he'll see you in his bed-room."

And, for his own sake, having his lord's future somewhat at heart, the servant could not refrain from displaying his eagerness to get the inopportune visitor away from the breakfast-room, lest Sir Murray or some guest should encounter him.

"It's all right, my man—never mind me. I'm hungry, and if Sir Murray Gernon does come, I'm only his lordship's confidential man of business, d'yer see?"

The valet nodded, and stood staring while the early visitor displayed his vigorous appetite.

"That the young lady I met in the hall?" said Mr Braham, coolly.

"Young lady, sir?" said the valet, inquiringly.

"Now, look here, my fine fellow," said the money-lender: "take my advice. Keep friends with me, and, I think, it will be better for you in the long run. I might find it necessary to write and ask you a few questions, and I should expect satisfactory answers. I dare say you have a pencil—haven't you?"

The valet nodded, while the visitor busied himself with his pocket-book.

"Look here, then! here's a scrap of paper for you to make memorandums on, ready to tell me anything I want, specially keeping in mind any movements his lordship may make. You see, he's forgetful, and don't write to me, and a long journey like this, to find him gone, would be rather a nuisance, do you see? Ah! I see you understand; and, I dare say, when you've fairly worn out that piece of paper, I can find you another."

Now, as the said piece of paper was a five-pound note, Mr Willis, his lordship's valet, had no difficulty at all in promising to make the necessary memoranda. It was strange, too, how very much Mr Braham appeared to change in his sight. It would be a queer thing, thought the valet, if his lordship's confidential man of business couldn't have a bit of breakfast after his journey; so, requesting the visitor to ring when he was ready to go up to his lordship's room, he prepared to leave.

"No, don't go, my man," said Braham, "I've just done. That was the young lady, I suppose?"

"Yes, sir; that's her," said Willis.

"Ah! Nice girl. Thanks—yes, you in ay open a bottle of claret. Fine place this, my man. If I were you, I should stick to his lordship. Money is tight in the city, sometimes—eh? Ha—ha—ha! We know—eh? But it will all come right; and if I were you, I should go in for the butlership. It'll come to that by-and-by, I dare say."

Mr Braham condescended to wink at the servant, and the valet made bold to wink in reply; and, at last rising, Mr Braham was ushered into Lord Maudlaine's room.

"De do, Mr Braham?" said his lordship, languidly; and then, as the door closed on the valet: "Con-found you! what the deuce brought you here?"

"Customary conveyance, my lord," said the Jew, coolly.

"But what could induce you to come down here and spoil all?" exclaimed the Viscount.

"Your honourable lordship's extreme want of punctuality," said the unwelcome visitor.

"Punctuality!—what do you mean?" said his lordship, fiercely.

"Nothing—nothing," said the Jew, nonchalantly, as he lolled back in his chair, after helping himself to one of the cigars on the table, and preparing to smoke. "I see from your lordship's freedom of conversation, that you possess the happy independent spirit given by money. I see you are quite prepared."

"Prepared—prepared for what?" gasped the recumbent debtor.

"Oh! only to meet my demands! I did wait a week; but as I did not hear from you, I was obliged to come and remind you."

"Remind me of what?" exclaimed the Viscount.

"Oh! only that time's up!"

Lord Maudlaine sank back upon his pillow, half stupefied.

"Impossible," he pondered: he had made no memorandum—he never did of these disagreeable transactions; but it was impossible that six months could have elapsed, and he said so.

"Six months, my lord? Why, what put it into your head that the paper had six months to run?"

"Why, I asked you to make it six months, and you said you would try."

"Well, I did try, my clear lord. But you astonish me! Did you not read the bills over, when you put your name to them?"

"Confound you! you know I did not!" cried the Viscount, angrily. "They were only for three months, then?"

"That's all, my lord. But there—what does it matter? Give me a cheque for the amount, and have done with it. There will be so much weight off your mind."

Lord Maudlaine grinned in a manner that indicated how gladly he would have liked to wring his tormentor's neck, but he crushed down his wrath.

"Well, what's to be done? I can't pay."

"Very sorry, my lord—but you know the result, without Sir Murray Gernon would—"

"Hang you, be quiet!" exclaimed the other, fiercely. "He knows that I am poor; but would you upset all, now that matters have gone so far? You must renew again."

"But the cost to your lordship will be ruinous," expostulated the Jew.

"What do you care for that? Look here, Braham: all is going on as well as possible—I only want time. If you clap me in a sponging-house now, you will not get a penny, for Sir Murray's pride would never get over it. I could never show myself here again. You must renew."

"Can't," said Braham, shaking his head—"can't, indeed. Money is more and more valuable every day."

"So is time to me," said his lordship, grimly. "Now, look here, Braham: is such a chance as this to be played with?"

"Thousand pities to lose it."

"Thousand pities—yes!" exclaimed the Viscount, excitedly. "Yes, I'd give a thousand pounds sooner than be thrown off now."

"Well," said the Jew, "I don't want to be hard. On those terms—terms, mind, that you offer yourself—I'll renew for another three months; but mind this: I'll have the money to the day, or you know the consequences. If the money is not paid, you will be taken, even if it is at the church door."

"Terms!—what terms?" stammered the Viscount. "I offered no terms."

"Your lordship said that you would give a thousand pounds for three months' reprieve," said his visitor, coolly.

"Pooh! absurd! You are mad," said the Viscount.

"Oh! I beg pardon," said Braham, rising. "I understood you to say so. As your lordship pleases."

"Sit down there, for Heaven's sake, Braham. What are you thinking about?"

"Nothing—nothing, my lord; but pray excuse me. Time is nothing to you; it is everything to me."

"By George! what a position," muttered the unhappy Viscount. "There, look here: you'd let me off for another three months, on the same terms as the last—eh?"

The Jew shrugged his shoulders and shook his head. His hand was already upon the door, he opened it, and had passed out, when, half mad with the prospect before him, the Viscount shrieked:

"Braham! Here! Stop! I agree;" and the Jew slowly re-entered the room.

"No, my lord, I think it would be better not," he said. "You are already too deeply in debt. My conscience would not allow me to make such terms."

"I can't stand it—that cant, Braham," said the Viscount, hoarsely. "You have the paper and stamps in your pocket—there are pens and ink; draw them up, and let me sign the bills, and let's have an end to it. I'm not very clever, but it is plain enough to me how you pull the string, for you have me fast enough. Make much of it, though, for I would not consent but that you have me in a corner."

"Now, don't be hard," grinned Braham, as, without a minute's loss of time, he drew out the requisite slips of paper, and held them, when ready, for the Viscount to sign. "Look at the risk I run," he added, as he took a fresh clip of ink, and held the pen to his lordship, placing the writing-table by the bedside, ready to his hand.

"Take them, and make much of them. You came down meaning to make a good bargain out of me, and I hope you are satisfied?"

"Quite—thanks, my lord," laughed the Jew, as he placed the bills in his pocket-book. "Never mind, my lord; you will settle down soon, and cease kite-flying; but mind this: three months only, and then—no mercy!"

"Good morning," said the Viscount, shortly; and unwilling to display his rage, he turned round in bed, and dragged the clothes over his shoulders.

"Good morning, my lord," said the Jew, with a grin of triumph; but the hour of success had not yet arrived for either: incubation was proceeding apparently in the most satisfactory manner, but until Isa Gernon's hand was his, Lord Maudlaine's prospect of getting out of debt was small indeed.

A Night's Adventure

"Surely my heart would have told me, and the nature within me have revolted from such a sense of passionate love, had his cruel, his base words been true," said Brace Norton, as he stood one evening by Merland Park palings, watching the lights fade one by one at the Castle; for the hour was late, and, reckless and wretched, the young man had strolled down from the Hall, to have his evening cigar, as he had told his anxious-eyed mother, but really to take a last farewell of the casket which contained his treasure.

"I cannot give her up, mother," he had said to her, sadly. "I am not ashamed to tell you how dearly I love her, and shall continue to love her, even while all hope is at an end for me. But I cannot help it. We do not make ourselves. They talk of schooling, or ruling, one's heart, but what poor idiot could first have said that! He must have been heartless himself, and never have known what it is to love."

And what could Mrs Norton say? She could but recall the past, and the long bitter years she herself had had before she enjoyed the fruition of her love. She lamented, grieved for the unfortunate attachment, but her heart yearned towards the sweet girl. All the old affection of her nature which she had felt for the mother was now given freely to the child. But she had never been made the receptacle of her son's full confidence; there was one thing, one bitter sentence whispered—nay, hissed in his ear, by Sir Murray Gernon, that the young man never again suffered to pass his lips, as, after long battling with self, he felt convinced it was untrue.

And now he leaned lingeringly upon those park railings, watching the light, far distant as it was, that he believed to be that which shone from Isa's chamber, till at last it was extinct, and it was like the crushing out of hope from his aching breast. For what was his fate? The next day must see him far away from Merland, leaving one whom he knew to love him, at the mercy of father and favoured suitor. True, there was the frequent sense of her sweet kiss, the dear confession of the love of her pure young heart, yet upon his lip; but what would they say to her—how would they impress her with the impossibility of a union? With no friend and adviser but that true-hearted Jane McCray, what could the poor girl do?

Brace Norton sighed—a sigh that was almost a groan, as he felt what must be the end; and recalling the past—the old story told him by his mother—he seemed to see such another wedding scene as Merland church had once before witnessed. But no; he thought he would be far away, chained by duty to his vessel; and he should return at last, a broken-hearted, aimless man. He would not blame her, for she would, he knew, be forced into it, and there was no help—none!

An hour must have passed away as he stood there that dark night, thinking of his journey on the morrow, and of his utter distaste now for the sea life he had loved so well. Promotion, the hope of commanding his own vessel, all the ambition of his nature, had given place to the passionate love which pervaded his soul; and at last, after an intense, longing gaze at the dark mass of buildings seen against the sky in front, he was about to turn and leave the shadow of the clump of trees that overhung the palings where he stood, when he started, and his heart began to beat heavily, he knew not why, at the unwonted sound of a heavy step coming down the lane. For this was but a by-way, and no one but a keeper, or a late-returning servant from the village, would be likely to take that path so late at night.

"I had better not be seen," thought Brace, and his face flushed with annoyance at having to play such a hiding rôle, as he drew farther back into the shade.

The step came nearer, and then suddenly grew indistinct, as the new-comer stepped on to the turf at the lane side; but there was a faint rustling amongst the fallen leaves, which told of whoever it was coming nearer and nearer.

"One of the servants," muttered Brace; and then as his thoughts wandered to the morrow—"could I not prolong my stay? could I not get increased leave of absence? To torture myself more bitterly," he muttered the next instant fiercely; and then he was brought back to the present by the footsteps becoming more audible, and at last stopping close by where he stood.

Brace Norton remained motionless, as from the shade he could indistinctly make out the figure of a heavy-looking, muscular man, in rough clothes, pressing forward, as it were, and gazing right in his face.

"Discovered watching here," he thought, bitterly, "and all to be conveyed to the baronet and my lord, as a means of disparagement, in her hearing. Shall I bribe the scoundrel to be silent? No," he thought, "I will not. Let him bear his pitiful news; and, if it comes to her ears that I was watching, like a thief at midnight, she will know why. Her poor heart will interpret my feelings, and give one beat for me."

Brace Norton's thoughts, it must be owned, were of a romantic tendency, but, perhaps, it was excusable at such a time; and, nerving himself, he stood perfectly motionless, waiting for the man, whoever he was, to speak.

But it was dark; and, had it been possible, Brace Norton, as he stood there, for some few minutes, with the new-comer apparently gazing full in his face, would have seen that the man's gaze was vacant and strange, and that his eyes failed to pierce the gloom around.

"At last!"

Those two words seemed to be breathed, as it were, close to Brace Norton's ear, as, almost brushing him, the figure came close to where he stood, listened, apparently, for a few moments, and then, drawing himself up, climbed the low oak palings, and began to thread his way amongst the trees.

"At last!" What did that mean? Who was this? No servant or keeper, evidently. Was he poacher? He had no gun, and he was alone, which fact also militated against his being burglar.

There is no concealing the fact: Brace Norton was glad of the excuse for getting once—even but for a few minutes—close to the house, with the hope of seeing if only her window; and, telling himself that this nocturnal visitor could mean no good towards the inhabitants of the Castle, he, too, softly climbed the palings, and tried to follow the figure.

If he could only have some opportunity given him of showing his zeal—of rescuing somebody from danger! Or could it be—was this to be—an endeavour to carry off Isa? His heart beat swiftly, and his breath came thick and fast for a few seconds, till his better sense prevailed, and he smiled at the silly romance that, he told himself, he had allowed to obtain entrance to his breast.

But, meanwhile, he had pressed cautiously on, peering anxiously before him, and trying hard to make out the direction the figure had taken. In vain, though: the dark shadow had passed amongst the trees, and was gone. He tried in different directions, but with only one result—ill-success; and, for a moment, as he stood upon the grass, listening eagerly, he felt disposed to place all to imagination. He knew, though, that it was not; and determining to go nearer to the house, he drew forth his watch, and tried to make out the hour.

That, however, was impossible; so, opening it, he passed his fingers over the hands, to find that it was after one.

Would they be sitting up for him at home? He could not help it. This was his last night, it might be, for years—as he should try, on a certain event happening, to avoid the place—perhaps for ever.

Suddenly a thought struck him. If the man he had seen was some wrong-doer, and sought the house, he must, he knew, cross the bridge; for Brace had from a distance often studied the configuration of the grounds, and knew that from the side where he stood the bridge road was the only way up to the mansion.

Young and active then, he started off over the short crisp turf at a sharp run, purposely making a slight circuit, and arrived cautiously at length by the bridge end, to find that he was too late to see the figure pass, for he was already on the bridge, his step sounding hollowly upon the old worn planks.

What could it mean—at that hour, too? Brace Norton hesitated no longer; the thoughts of risk, and of being better on his way homeward, were dismissed, and using all the caution he could, he tried to follow the man.

But in vain the darkness prevented him from even catching another glimpse; but that he was in the right track he knew, by coming suddenly upon a pair of boots upon the grass, against one of which he kicked.

This seemed to point to the fact that it must be some one who well knew the grounds, or he would not have trusted to the finding again of his boots in the darkness. But what could it mean? Was there some nefarious design afloat?—a robbery, for instance—and was this man in league with more in the house?

These, and many such questions, troubled Brace Norton, as, momentarily growing more and more excited, he strode on, avoiding flower-bed and rustic vase, cautiously leaping gravel paths; and, at last, after passing along two sides of the great square mansion, standing thoughtful and discomfited.

On the side where he stood, there was on his left the old moat—the moat which, in the front, had been expanded into the lake, advantage having been taken of a low-lying tract of land by the baronet, to have it flooded. The water, then, except on one side, shut in the pleasure grounds, a wall enclosed them on the other; and, unless some door happened to be open—which was unlikely at such an hour—the stranger was either somewhere about the grounds, or had returned by way of the bridge.

This last idea Brace dismissed at once, and determining that the stranger must be on the other side of the house, he began to retrace his steps, when his ear was saluted by a faint rustle, as of a body passing amongst dry twigs.

Cautiously making his way in the required direction, Brace crept over the grass for perhaps twenty yards, and then he stopped, listening eagerly, but only to hear the loud, laboured beating of his own heart.

It must have been something more than a simple desire to satisfy his curiosity, or to gaze up at some window which he might imagine was that of Isa Gernon. Had he been asked, he would have owned to a strange feeling of attraction, drawing him on and on to what proved the most exciting adventure of his life. He knew, though, that he ran great risks, and that, if seen, his visit was sure to be misinterpreted; but another minute had hardly elapsed ere, like his sire in bygone days, he could only yield to the intense desire of affording help where he believed others were in peril.

For suddenly, from a corner of the house, where a dense mass of evergreens made more black the shade, came a strange, low, grating noise—a sound that he had never before heard, but which he attributed to the right cause upon the instant; and then, going down upon hands and knees, he tried to govern into regularity his laboured, panting breathing, as he crept cautiously towards the spot from whence the sound had arisen.

"That's it at Last"

Brace Norton's heart told him truly: the noise was the grating of a diamond over glass, and it was repeated four times. Then there was a pause, ere at the end of a few minutes came a dull, snapping noise, and one faint tinkle as of falling glass upon the ledge of a window.

He stopped, listening attentively, for he seemed by instinct to know what would follow; he almost seemed to pierce the black darkness ahead, and to see an arm passed through a cut-out pane of glass—a fastening thrust back. Yes, there was the dull snap, and now the raising of the sash. No, it could be no sash, for there was a dull creaking as of the rusty hinges of an old iron lattice casement. Then came a soft rustling. Yes, that was the stranger drawing himself up, and passing through the window.

Would he fasten it after him?

No; it was evidently left open, and all was still. It must be some one who knew the place. What should he do? try and alarm the house? No; he did not fear one man. There was some mystery here; and at the thought of that word mystery, as it seemed to come with a dull impact upon his heart, that heart throbbed and beat still more rapidly, for a strange influence connected mystery with mystery; and Brace Norton, mad almost with excitement, followed to where he had heard the sound, felt in the intense darkness for the window, found it as he had expected—open, and drawing himself up, he leaned in, and listened, half feeling that it was but to receive a fierce blow upon the head; but, no: all was still.

"I'll risk all," muttered Brace. "My position as an officer, and my word of honour that I was impelled by good motives, must be sufficient to clear me from all blame."

The next minute he was in a small lobby—so he judged it to be—and feeling gently along the wall, he soon found the open door, and stood in what seemed to be a long stone passage—the passage, in fact, though he knew it not, which led from the servants' offices to the grand entrance of the house.

Should he turn to right or left? All was dark and silent; but that a robbery was in progress he felt now sure. If, he thought, he could seize the burglar at his work, there would be some claim again on Sir Murray Gernon's generosity; but if he tried now to alarm the inmates, and the burglar took flight, there was nothing but his own word to clear him from what would look to suspicious eyes like a clandestine entry to the Castle for reasons of his own.

Brace wavered for a few moments as he stood there listening in the black darkness; but directly after a strange impulse moved him to proceed; and cautiously feeling his way along, he stood at length at the foot of the grand staircase, irresolute as to the next direction he should take.

For a few seconds he could hear nothing but the loud tick of a clock somewhere close at hand, but directly after came a slight grating, which he knew to be a key turning in a lock; and gliding in the direction, he found an open door, through which he passed in time to hear a faint ejaculation, as some one brushed against a light chair. Then came once more the sound of key in lock, and Brace suspected that he must be in a suite of rooms, leading one from the other.

There was furniture all around, but by means of exercising great caution he was enabled to creep on slowly till his hand rested upon an open door, against the edge of which he nearly struck his forehead. On trying to the left, he found that his hand rested on a chiffonnière, his touch displacing a china cup and saucer standing upon the marble top. The sound was very slight, but it seemed to have alarmed the burglar, for as Brace stood motionless behind the door, there was a faint, very faint rustling sound, and a hard breathing coming nearer and nearer, till, as he shrank slightly back, he could hear the dull throb, throb of another beating heart, and he held his breath till the oppression was fearful.

He had but to stretch forth his hand to seize this midnight visitor, but something restrained him, and after a few minutes' pause, the rustling and gliding sound recommenced; then came the faint rattle of a door-handle, and this time the slight creaking of hinges.

Brace crept round the door, and passed cautiously into another room, his every step measured with the greatest care, till, after traversing some distance of what seemed an endless journey amongst crowded furniture, he was almost in despair, regretting that he had not seized the man when within his reach, for he could find no door; but a minute later, and there was a soft rattle on his right—a sound as of some one lifting fire-irons from their place and laying them upon a soft rug; and, guided by the sound, Brace felt his way to another open door, and stood upon the long-piled carpet of another room, where he could again hear the hard breathing. There was a faint click, and what sounded like the fall of a standard, and then once more utter silence for full a quarter of an hour.

But at the end of that time, measured out by a chiming pendule upon the chimney-piece, the rustling again commenced; and, as Brace cautiously stepped two paces nearer, he could, mentally, see all that took place, as, with nerves strained to their greatest tension, he eagerly drank in each sound.

The rough visitor was upon his knees, moving the fender aside. Then there was the rustling, as of the removal of paper-shavings from the grate, and directly after the click, click of iron-work.

What could that be? What did it mean? The man must be at work at the grate. Was he a workman, in a state of insanity or somnambulism? This could be no burglar.

Yes, there it was again, the clicking rattle of the iron plate of a register-stove, followed by a faint puff of air, laden with that fine, impalpable soot from an unused chimney; and, as the excitement began to fade, Brace smiled bitterly, with something like contempt, for the pitiful conclusion of this romance. The man was, evidently, trying to ascend or reach up the chimney, for he could hear him groping about behind the iron-work; there was the rustle of little bits of falling mortar. The hard breathing had ceased, but there was the rustling noise of the man's lower limbs, as he seemed to be straining hard to reach something, and at last came the sound as of his struggling down.

Brace, on smiling at the pitiful termination of his knight-errant's quest, had crept closer and closer, until now he stood guardedly upon one side of the fire-place, for there could be no doubt respecting the sounds he had heard. The rustling continued for a few moments, and then the hard panting noise recommenced, followed by an unmistakable stifled sneeze, and directly after a voice muttered:

"Cuss the sut! But I've got it at last, though."

Got what? Brace's heart began to increase its rate, and the excitement, he knew not why, rapidly returned, as there was the sound of an opening box, a scratching, and a faint line of light appeared upon the fender.

"No go," muttered the voice, and again there was the opening sound, and the scratch of a match upon the stone this time, for it commenced burning with its faint blue fluttering light before the splint caught fire.

At the same moment there was the sharp blowing, as of some one puffing dust from some object—the sooty dust, light as air, being wafted right in Brace's face. Then the splint caught fire, and blazed up for an instant, but only to be quenched the next, as there fell, upon the young man's ears the softly-muttered words:

"That's it at last!"

The Cross

That faint flash of light, instantaneous as it was, sufficed to pierce one of the veils that had for many years shrouded the mysteries of the past. Brace saw in that brief interval the meaning of the nocturnal visit, the caution observed, and as plainly as if the words had been uttered in his ears, he knew the man's name. It was clear enough now: when that scoundrel had left the conservatory, he must have entered this room—the blue-room, it must be—the room which, for twenty long years, had held a secret unsuspected by a soul. And he, Brace Norton, had now at his mercy the cause of the long, cruel suspicions which rested upon Lady Gernon and his father. He had him at his mercy, with the proof of innocence in his hand—the proof which, after twice failing, he had, after twenty years' transportation, returned to drag from its hiding-place. But not to establish the innocence of the living, or of her who had so mysteriously disappeared; it was for his own aggrandisement: Brace could feel that, as, with an intense desire upon him to strangle the cause of so much cruel misery and heart-burning, he leaned forward.

For in that one brief flash—brief as the time that these thoughts had taken to dart through his mind—Brace Norton had seen lying, in a soot-grained hand, flashing in wondrous beauty, the magnificent true-blue sapphire cross described by Mrs Norton; and as the light was quenched, Brace had sprung forward, clutching glittering gems with one hand, and the marauder's throat with the other.

There was a howl of rage and astonishment from the man he clutched, as, with his impetuous bound, Brace Norton drove him backwards, but the next instant the struggle going on was fierce and desperate. Capture and escape were forgotten in the intense desire to hold the cross. On the one hand, there was the valuable object panted for during twenty long years of punishment. On the other, there was fair fame, and also the hope of reconciliation and future happiness; and, as Brace Norton nerved himself for the fight, he mentally vowed that he would die sooner than be conquered.

It was time now to rouse the house, and as, for an instant, he struggled uppermost he uttered a long, loud cry for help, one which went echoing through the house, followed by the crashing of slight drawing-room furniture, the overturning and wrecking of what-nots laden with rare and curious china. The frail chairs were fallen over and snapped, and once the man, who fought so fiercely, fell over the fender that he had dragged from its place, but only to bound up again, and for the struggle to become more fierce than ever.

It was the battle between youth and activity and the iron muscles of one who had lived a long and abstemious life of toil, and more than once Brace Norton could have groaned, as he felt himself gradually growing weaker and weaker. But he still clutched the cross tightly, in spite of the furious blows dealt him in the face by his adversary, whose hot breath came upon the young man's flushed temples now, as, in a determined effort, he grasped him round both arms in a deadly hug that threatened to crush his ribs, whilst the next moment Brace felt himself lifted from the floor and hurled back, his foe falling upon him with all his weight.

The sense was almost driven from his bruised body by this fierce onslaught; but in spite of his despair, Brace was still determined. He could not fight now, he was too much exhausted; but he could defend the treasure, which grew in value as he seemed to be about to lose it.

So far he had grasped the cross with but one hand; now he placed over it the other, holding it to his breast, and pressing his chin upon his hands.

"Leave go!" hissed his enemy, and blow after blow was rained upon poor Brace's face, his foe now seating himself upon his chest, and by turns striving to unlace his fingers, and striking him brutally with his bony hands.

"Will help never come?" thought Brace. "Am I to give up life and the cross as well?"

The next moment he had exerted his little remaining strength, and with a fierce plunge partly dislodged his foe and turned himself half round upon his face, so that now he held the cross beneath him, gaining a few more minutes, in the hope that help might come, when, with a cry of rage, the man again struck him furiously.

Then there was a moment's reprieve, and half-stunned and totally helpless, Brace listened; but for a few seconds he could only hear a horrible singing in his ears. Then he shivered, for the man was doing something, and Brace's sharpened senses told him that a knife was being opened by teeth grasping the blade; then he gave a faint, shuddering struggle, but only to lie passive, as a strange blow fell upon his unprotected shoulder—a hot, burning blow, accompanied by a deadly, sick sensation.

It was his last effort, as, struggling round, a light flashed into the room, and in that one second he saw above his breast the upraised knife of his adversary. The next instant there was a loud report, followed by the noise as of thunder in his ears, and then all was blank.

The Doctor's Answer

It was with a sense of waking from a dream that Brace Norton opened his eyes to gaze upon lights and faces dancing around him; but it was long before he could collect his thoughts sufficiently to reply to questions that were asked. By degrees, though, he could make out that it was Sir Murray Gernon who was speaking, and then there arose a loud, wailing woman's cry, followed by a voice Brace recognised.

"Ye're reet, lassie—it is, sure enew. It's Jock Gurdon come back to get his deserts."

"Blast you!—a doctor—I'm—I'm dy—Here, quick!—a doctor, or I shall bleed to death!" groaned the wretched man.

"Has any one gone for a medical man?" said a stern voice.

"Yes, Sir Mooray, I've sent for a doctor and the police, too. It's gude for us that the loons were quarrelling over the spoil."

"Isa, my child, this is no place for you!" exclaimed Sir Murray.

"That's right," cried Lord Maudlaine, who was also present; "I've been asking her to go. My dear Miss Gernon—Isa—what are you about? Don't go near him!"

Lord Maudlaine might well exclaim, for Isa Gernon, pale and scared, was slowly advancing towards where Brace Norton lay. The eyes of love were more piercing than those of the bystanders; and in those swollen and bleeding features Isa had recognised those of the man who had told her again and again of his love.

"Brace!" she cried, in a low, husky voice, as, falling upon her knees at his side, heedless of all present, she laid her hands upon his; for this could be no burglar, as they had told her—there must be some horrible mystery here.

"Isa!" he whispered, as his eyes met hers for an instant, ere they closed.

"Quick!—quick!" cried the agitated girl. "Father—dear papa—oh, what is this? You have shot him, and he is dying. Oh, quick!—quick!—a doctor!"

Her cries seemed to drive away the fainting sensation that oppressed Brace Norton; and as Sir Murray—astounded at his daughter's words—hurried to her side, the young man's eyes again unclosed, for his lips to part in a faint smile.

"No, no," he whispered—"not shot—that man—Gurdon—I followed him—stabbed, I fear—perhaps to death—the cross, Sir Murray; look! Lady Gernon's—my father's innocence—left for me to prove—I know—old story—take it, Isa, love—if I pass away, recollect—not—son—dishonoured man—saved—"

"The brae laddie has fainted, and, Gude save us! it's young Brace Norton. Here, quick!—some water, and don't all stand staring like daft fules!" cried McCray. But, at the same moment, with his mind a chaos of wild thoughts, Sir Murray Gernon had sunk upon his knees by the young man, whose hands still clutched the sparkling cross, the jewels glittering brightly yet, though partly encrusted with soot. It was some few minutes, during which he had been striving to stanch the young man's wound, before he could arrange his thoughts into something like their proper sequence.

This man, then—this Gurdon—had, indeed, stolen the cross; picked it up the night of the great party—more than twenty years ago—and concealed it here, behind the stove; for it was plain enough from whence it had been taken. Here, then, was the key to Gurdon's attempted burglaries—the man who, with the knowledge of a hidden treasure, had never been able to take it from the spot where it had been placed. Had he, then,—he, Sir Murray Gernon,—been wrong in his suspicions, and was this young man's father, after all, innocent? No; impossible! he was clear of one foul stain, but the other mystery was unsolved.

The unwonted feeling of gentleness that had come upon him, for a few minutes, as he knelt by the injured man, soon passed away, and the old, hard frown came fiercely back.

There was no one there he could speak to, and say that he was glad the jewels were found, and that he hoped the other mystery might be cleared up; but he rose, with a half-shudder, from his knees, as Jane McCray came forward, pale and trembling, her eyes fixed on his; and as the recollection of the past came back, he would have turned and left the room. But Jane's hand was on his arm, and, in a voice that was only heard by Isa, she said, beseechingly:

"Oh, Sir Murray, don't be hard upon your poor child, as you were on my own dear lady! I'll never say a word—I'll take all with me to the grave; only, now that it has pleased Heaven to make all this clear, and to show you what you would never believe, try and repent, and ask forgiveness of those you so cruelly wronged! You can't do much now—it's too late; but oh! Sir Murray—dear master—do something! Twenty years and more ago, now, since the wrongs were done; and yet, you see, how judgment comes at last for the wicked. You know now how cruelly wrong you were; there it all is. You thought, between them, there had been something done with that cross, and now you see. I hoped that man had died repenting, in a far-off land; but it was to be his fate to come and clear this up first—to show you how ill you treated my poor, sweet lady—to show you her innocence and—"

"Loose your hold, woman!" whispered Sir Murray, hoarsely.

"No," she said, holding his arm tightly—"not yet. You know how I promised her, Sir Murray, that I'd be, as far as I could, a mother to that child; and I've tried to. Haven't I, for her sake, sealed my lips, and kept hid a secret that has made the white come in my hair? Am I not an old and faithful servant? After what I have done, can you not trust me when I say that I will carry all I know to the grave? But, Sir Murray, you will try—you will make right what you can. Don't break their hearts. Look at that brave boy. You know how he loves her; you know how you injured his father. Promise me that you will repent of it all, and try to make them happy."

"Confound the woman!" cried Sir Murray, angrily—"she is mad! Lord Maudlaine, this is no place for your betrothed; take her away. Ha! here is the doctor at last."

As Jane McCray covered her face with her hands, and fell back with a groan, Lord Maudlaine advanced to where Isa, who had heard all that had passed, still knelt by Brace Norton's side.

"Miss Gernon—Isa," he said, anxiously; "let me lead you away. Sir Murray wisely says that this is no place for you."

"No place!" she cried, her soft eyes flashing into light. "Is it not a woman's place beside the man she loves, when he is stricken down and helpless? Keep back, sir! I do not require your forced attentions!"

The aspect of Lord Maudlaine's face was a mingling of the ludicrous and the enraged; but no one seemed to heed it, for, evidently violently agitated, Sir Murray had left the room, while all eyes were now directed to the doctor, whose ministrations were rapid, and orders issued sharply, as if he meant to have them obeyed.

"Gude-sake, sir!" said McCray, at last, unable to restrain his feelings, for he had read the anxiety in his young lady's countenance—"Gude-sake, sir, tell's how they all are!"

"Burglar—bad shot through shoulder, but not dangerous; Mr Norton—serious stab, knife pierced the—"

"Gude-sake, sir, never mind that!" exclaimed McCray. "Tell's the warst at once: is he likely—"

McCray did not finish his sentence in words, but with his eyes; while, with an anxious troubled look, the doctor glanced towards the figure of Isa Gernon, before he replied:

"Well, McCray, I—There, I'll give you my opinion to-morrow."

Crushed Down

Die? What, with those sweet imploring eyes bidding him live?—with hope telling him that now one part of the mystery was cleared the other must soon be swept away?—with his own heart whispering energy, and patience, and desire for life? No; his spirit had well-nigh been drained away by that cruel stab, but Brace Norton smiled at the pain he suffered, and fought back the black shade that bade him succumb.

They bore him from the Castle to his own home; for as soon as the news spread of the late adventure, Captain and Mrs Norton, who had passed an anxious night, had themselves driven over to the Castle, and, in spite of the doctor's remonstrance, insisted upon bringing their son away.

"I cannot help it, Challen," said Captain Norton—"the risk must be run. You must do your best to avert danger, for he cannot stay here."

"As you will," said the doctor; and he proceeded to superintend the young man's removal to the carriage.

Sir Murray Gernon knew of their coming, but he did not meet them. He shut himself up in his study, and as Brace was being placed in the carriage, McCray came forward, and handed a note to Captain Norton, who started as he saw the cipher on the great seal.

He tore it open and read the following lines:

"Sir Murray Gernon feels it to be his duty to apologise to Captain Norton for having done him *one* grievous wrong. The Sapphire Cross was stolen by Sir Murray's butler, and is once more in its owner's hands.

"Sir Murray Gernon asks Captain Norton's pardon."

Without a word, Captain Norton handed the note to his wife, who read it; and then, with the proud blood rushing to her temples, she handed it back, watching him to see what he would do.

There was a look almost of passion in Captain Norton's eye, and the great broad scar looked red and angry, as he stood there biting his lip for a few brief instants before he spoke.

The library door was ajar, and every word of his sharp, military speech was plainly heard by the occupant, as, drawing himself up, Captain, Norton turned to McCray.

"You are Sir Murray Gernon's confidential servant," he said. "I will not write, but tell him this from me: he asks my pardon for a wrong, and I have waited over twenty years till the truth should appear. I go now to wait for the fellow-letter to this; when he shall ask my forgiveness for another wrong, then I will send him my reply."

He turned and walked slowly and proudly down the great steps of the main entrance, while their owner cowered in his room, shrinking back into the far corner, as he watched and saw through the window that Isa was at the carriage-door, holding one of Brace's hands in hers, as she looked appealingly in Dr Challen's face. His brow darkened as he saw it, for it seemed as if his efforts were to be set at nought, and that the more he battled against the stream of events the more it swept him back. But he did not hear his child's plaintive words, as she spoke to the doctor.

"Pray—pray tell me!" she whispered: "Is he in danger?"

"Danger? Well, yes, of course he is," said the doctor, taking her in his arms and kissing her as he would one of his own children. "But there, bless your bright little face, go in, and don't fidget and make those eyes dull with crying, and I'll cure him right off for you. Now, Captain Norton," he continued, lightly—"slow march for the horses—two miles an hour—with the windows all down, and I must ride inside."

Brace fainted as the carriage-door was closed, but it was with the sense of his hand being kissed by two soft, warm lips, ere all became misty and confused; and then it was that Dr Challen's light, flippant manner gave place to a quiet, serious aspect, as he plied restoratives, and prepared for the battle that his experience told him was imminent.

It was a long and fierce fight, but youth, with hope shining now in upon the young man's heart, prevailed; and though no encouraging letter from Isa—no communication came from the Castle but a formal inquiry or two made on the part of Sir Murray—Brace daily grew stronger, telling himself that he would yet, perhaps, see the day when all would be made plain. There was a feeling of exultation that came upon the young man, when he saw the proud, happy bearing that seemed to have come upon his father? and more than once there was a fond blessing from her who had held faith when all the world disbelieved. This exultation did more than all Dr Challen's medicaments, but the doctor took to himself the credit, all the same.

Brace's ship sailed without him, and he could not but rejoice at the time afforded him for further investigation, while he prayed earnestly that accident might again favour him, though at times his heart sank, as rumours came of the state of affairs at the Castle. For though he had dismissed them as impossible, utterly refusing them credence, at times charging Sir Murray Gernon with subterfuge, at others giving him the credit of believing the words he had whispered, they began now, as he approached convalescence, to make a deep and lasting impression upon him. He had not seen her—he had not heard from her, and the gap between the families seemed almost to have widened since the discovery of the cross; but there was no Lord Maudlaine at the Castle now: he had taken his departure, and Brace was hopeful that it was for good; when one day, when he had regained his strength, his heart leaped tumultuously, for he saw Isa approaching him, on her favourite mare, attended as usual by Peter Barlow.

It might be wrong, but he could not help it, and he hurried forward to meet her, his hands outstretched, and face bright and eager, but to his utter despair she touched the mare with her whip, averted her head, and cantered by, leaving him, almost giddy with misery, by the road-side.

Why Isa Gernon Avoided Brace

Lord Maudlaine had indeed left the Castle, but not for the reason Brace Norton had hoped. The time was getting on, and a hint or two to that effect from his friend in London had induced him to seek an opportunity for speaking to Isa alone.

The opportunity was soon afforded him, for Sir Murray, guessing his wish, and himself anxious that the marriage should take place, left them one evening together in the drawing-room, while he sought his study, where, a quarter of an hour after, the Viscount came to him.

"What! so soon?" said Sir Murray.

"Utter refusal—appeal to my feelings—impossible to accept me—and all that sort of thing," said the Viscount, angrily. "I'm being played with, Sir Murray Gernon," he exclaimed, bitterly—"led on and trifled with!"

"Are you willing to take her as she is—to risk all?" said Sir Murray, quietly.

"Quite—yes, of course," said his lordship.

"Stay here, then, till I return," said Sir Murray.

He went to the drawing-room, where he found Isa, vainly striving to keep back her tears.

"Come here and sit down, Isa," he said, in quiet, measured tones. "There, don't tremble," he said, as he took her hand. "I'm not very angry with you, and I'm not going to scold and play the tyrant. You have just refused Lord Maudlaine, when you know that for months past it has been an understood thing that he was to be your husband. I do not ask you why you have done this, because I know. While we were in Italy there was no opposition shown upon your side; since we have returned you have often made me blush for the coldness—almost rudeness—with which you have treated him."

"Oh, papa!" exclaimed Isa, appealingly.

"You must hear me out," he said sternly. "I will tell you why you are cold to him: it is because you think that you love this Brace Norton; and, irrespective of the feeling between our houses, were he a man of honour, he would, after my words to him, have ceased his persecution."

"Your words!" faltered Isa.

"My words," he said sternly. "I saw him, and I have appealed to him in every way, but only to meet with an obstinate refusal. Then I brought to bear means that at the time I believed to be effectual. This is no silly romance of love, my child, but stern fact, that I have to deal with. I have chosen Lord Maudlaine to be your husband. You will be a titled lady, and some day wear a Countess's coronet. You will both be wealthy, and let me tell you that it is an alliance to be proud of. Now, promise me that, if I send him in, you will accede to his proposals."

Isa was silent.

"You hear me, Isa," he said, gently—"why do you not reply? You will accede to his wishes, will you not?"

"I cannot," said Isa, in a whisper. "It would be a mockery!"

"Absurd, silly, romantic nonsense, my child! You must accept him, and at once. I wish to have your marriage off my mind before I return to Italy; for I cannot stay in this place."

"Let us go, then, together!" said Isa, eagerly. "Why do you trouble about this matter at all?"

"It is my wish to see you married, and to Lord Maudlaine," he said, firmly. "I cannot live with the constant harass of this man's pretensions. I tell you, on my honour as a gentleman—since you set at nought my word as your father—that a marriage between you and Brace Norton is an impossibility. I told him—lowering myself even to giving him the reasons; and the man's character is such that—here, look, I have his letter to you, and which I refuse to let you read. I tell you, Isa, that in spite of my moroseness at times, I have a love for you from the way in which you recall your mother; but I would see you in your coffin sooner than the wife of this man!"

"But, papa—dear papa," sobbed Isa, "you are prejudiced—you are cruel! You do not know how good, and brave, and true he is, and I love him so—so dearly!"

She threw herself, sobbing, upon his breast, hiding her burning cheeks; while, apparently softened, he held her to him—a sad, wild, pained look in his face, as he kissed and smoothed her long, dark tresses.

"My child," he said, sadly, "I own I hate father and son with a fierce, undying hatred; but it is not that alone which makes me tell you that Brace

Norton can never be your husband. Can you not believe me when I tell you that every word I utter is solemn truth?"

"Yes—oh yes!" sobbed Isa.

"Then you will see Lord Maudlaine?"

"Indeed—indeed, I cannot!" sobbed Isa. "I—"

"Hush!" said Sir Murray, sternly, as, rising, he stood holding her hand. "In plain terms, you must. Hearken to me, Isa. You know me only as a cold, harsh, and bitter man; an unhappy life has made me what I am. Proud I was always: but I might have been amiable—loving and loved—but it was not to be. I have still some traces of better feeling left; and I ask you—I implore you—not to force me to make revelations that shall prove the impossibility of your wedding Brace Norton. I might look over his father having been the bane of my life, and, did I see that it was for your happiness, give way; but once again, I tell you that it is impossible. Will you take my word?"

Isa looked up into his face with an aspect that was pitiable.

"Can you feel no pity for me?" she whispered.

"Yes," he said, gently; "I am having pity on you, though you cannot see it, and are obliged blindly to take my word. And now I ask you, can you not have pity on me?"

Isa sat as if stunned, while, throwing her hand from him, Sir Murray strode for awhile up and down the room. Then, returning to her, he again seated himself by her side.

"Look here, Isa," he said, "Lord Maudlaine wishes this affair to take place at the end of this month. I may tell him that you consent, may I not?"

"No!" she said, her spirit rising at the thought of being forced into accepting a man she despised. "I will not consent."

"You are blind, Isa—blind!" he said, sadly; and then a groan seemed to tear itself from his breast, as he bent over her, speaking in low, hoarse tones.

"I would have spared you," he said; "for whatever you might have felt for this young man, Isa, you had the one good excuse, that you had obeyed me in accepting Lord Maudlaine. Time will not allow that the wedding should longer be deferred. It is his wish that it should take place at once—and mine; for my life is a burden to me here. I lead the life of one haunted by the past; and it was only when, moved by some strange impulse that I could not counteract, I returned, to find, what?—misery, and disappointment, and scenes that remind me of what should have been my happier days. But, once more, do you force me to this avowal? I ask you again to spare yourself and me, taking it for granted that what I tell you is right. May I refrain, and then tell Lord Maudlaine to come to you?"

"I cannot—indeed I cannot!" imploringly exclaimed Isa.

Sir Murray rose, his face working and his whole aspect speaking of the careworn, broken man. Then waiting a few moments, he stood with one hand shading his eyes, before again speaking.

"Isa," he said, "Jane McCray has acted the part of a mother to you, at your own mother's wish; and I have ever kept her at your side. Go to her now, and ask her why I have never shown you a father's love—a parent's tender care; and though she will utter a strenuous defence of the dead, you may read in her words my reason for saying that Brace Norton can never be your husband. You will know yourself that it is impossible that such an union can take place; for, before Heaven, my child, I believe every word I utter to be true!"

With Trouble Looming

"Dinna be fashed with me, lassie, I ainly say what I think and feel, and I do believe that it is perhaps better things should tak' their course. If ye could ha' married the man ye chose, Jenny, first aff, I dinna think, my lassie, there'd ha' been this nice, smooth auld face under your cap, and the grey ainly sprunk lightly among your hair, just like to set it aff. Why, your e'en are bright as ay they were, when I had a sair heart aboot Jock Gurdon, who's got well again, and Sir Mooray is na gane to prosecute him; but, Jenny, lassie, he's na sae bad a man, aifter all, Sir Mooray is na, for there, lassie—there they air, ten new crisp five-pound notes, and all for Jock Gurdon, to take him ower to America, and start life as a new man."

"Heaven bless Sir Murray for it!" said Jane, fervently.

"Amen to that, lassie; and I hope Jock Gurdon will mend his ways. And I've been thinking, lassie, that if I tak' the money, it will rise up some of the auld anger in the man, so ye shall e'en do it yer ainsel', and give him a few words for his benefit; for ye're a gude woman, Jane, and Heaven was verra kind to me when He gave me sic a wife."

Jane McCray did not speak, but her comely face was raised to her husband's, and a few bright tears fell from her eyes as she returned his loving kiss.

"I should be a happy woman if it were not for that poor bairn," said Jane. "She believes it, though I scolded her, and told her how cruel and false it all was, and that my own dear, sweet lady—"

"Hoot, lassie! ye're getting excited. The puir child has said 'yes' to his lordship at last, and they're to be married. Marriages air made in heaven, lassie, so let's hope it's all for the best."

"For the best!" sobbed Jane McCray, wringing her hands. "Oh! Alexander, dear husband! can't we stop it, for I foresee all sorts of misery and unhappiness for them both in the days to come; and it's cruel—cruel to force the poor child!"

"Nay, my lassie, but it is na force. She is only giving way to Sir Mooray's wishes, and if my laird here were a proper man, I wad na say a word. But there, he's gane to town for some days—till the wedding time, noo—and the sooner its ower the better. Peter tells me that the puir bairn met young Norton, when they were oot laist, and he tried to speak to her, but she turned her head, and cantered on."

Jane groaned, and wrung her hands. "I wish I was in my grave, sooner than see it all come to pass," she sobbed.

"Weel, it's perhaps a sair potion to swaller, Jenny; but be a woman. What does the puir bairn say?"

"Say? Nothing; only goes about the place pale and wan, with her poor heart breaking," said the housekeeper; "and when that creature—"

"Hoot, lassie! what creature?" said McCray.

"That popinjay lord," said Jane scornfully. "When—"

"Gude save us, lassie! dinna ye ken yer catechism: 'order yersel' lowly and reverently to a' yer betters;' and that's na ordering yersel' lowly and reverently."

"When I've seen him take hold of her, as if she was his property that he had bought, and stroke her hair and kiss her, the poor thing has shuddered; and once she struggled from him, and came to me to take care of her— for she only sees him with me in the room—and as soon as he'd gone she sobbed, as if her heart would break."

"Puir bairn," said McCray; "but he's gane noo, and she'll ha'e a respite."

"Respite, indeed!" said his wife angrily. "It puts me in mind of the old time—over five-and-twenty years ago—when my poor dear lady was all low and desponding because, at the wish of old Master and Mrs Elstree, she had accepted Sir Murray; and there she was with her cousin, Mrs Norton, you know, sobbing her poor eyes—I mean heart—away. I declare, whether it's wrong or right, Alexander, that if that poor young man—no! poor? nonsense: he's better off a deal than my fine lord, and as brave as he's high—"

"That's a true word, lassie," said McCray, who was having his evening pipe and tumbler of whisky and water, his day's duties being ended.

"If that Mr Norton came to me and asked me to help him to run away with the child, I'd help him to the best of my power."

"Nay—nay—nay! your tongue's gane wild, lassie."

"Wouldn't you, then?" said Mrs McCray.

"Weel, I'll na say," said the cautious Scot. "Ye see, lassie, there's for and against; and in spite of a' ye say about crule suspeeshons, I think, as I said before, that it's our duty to all we know to haud our peace and let matters tak' their course."

And matters were taking their course rapidly; for as time passed on, Brace Norton roamed the lanes like the ghost of his former self; but never once did he meet poor Isa.

The wedding-day was fixed, and the dresses were ordered, and once more Merland was to be the scene of festivity and rejoicing. After the wedding Lord and Lady Maudlaine, people said, were to start for the Continent, and Sir Murray intended to go alone to Italy to reside, while the Castle was to be the home of my lord and my lady.

"And you'll have fine doings there, I suppose," said one of two strange men who had come down to stay at old Chunt's inn—surveyors they said they were, perhaps connected with the working on the marsh.

"Yes," said Chunt, who was stout now, and hardly ever left his chair; "the Castle will be again what it ought to be, for the new master, they say, can make the shiners fly. I see he's come down again."

"Yes," said one of the men, taking his pipe from his month; "I see he's come down."

"Ah, you know him, do you?" said Chunt.

"Know him? Well, so far as having him pointed out to me goes, I know him. Fine thing for him, they say."

"Bless you," said Chunt, "I believe there's no end to the money he'll have; but I hope it'll be a happy marriage, that's all I've got for to say." And in spite of people trying to draw Chunt out, that *was* all he had to say, and he tightened his lips for fear another word should escape. "Wanted, eh?" said Chunt—"I'm coming," and he waddled out to speak to a new-comer.

"How do, sir? Post-chaise and pair, sir. Oh, yes, sir; any time you like. You'll give your orders? Thanky, sir."

Mr Chunt waddled back as his visitor departed, and one of the frequenters of the bar asked who that gentleman was.

"That gent?" said Chunt. "Oh! that's Master Brace Norton."

Preparations

The day before the wedding, and traces everywhere at Merland village of the grand doings to come, even a score of white-smocked navvies, with their rolled-up trousers, great laced boots, and huge stolid faces, stopping to stare about, after a morning's freak, consisting of four hours' neglect of work, and the consumption of endless pots of beer and pipes of tobacco in Chunt's tap-room; but they were soon off to their work cutting the great drain through the peat, where the wind and horse mills were busy pumping out the water.

"Some people's allus a' enjoying o' themselves, and having feasts," growled one peat-stained giant.

"Ah!" said another, taking his pipe out of his mouth to spit. "I should just like to come back and spoil all their fun!" But half an hour after, like the rest of his fellows, he was delving away, cutting the soft peat in great bricks, and heaving them out of the cutting, as he worked off his superabundant beer.

But there was misery at Merland Castle, and more than once Jane McCray, sobbing, told her husband that she had thought it would have broken her heart when she saw poor dejected, wounded, pale John Gurdon, and gave him the money, and wished him a happy future, when he broke down, and cried like a child at receiving treatment he said he had never deserved; but it was nothing to this, seeing that poor wasted child waiting for the hours to pass before she was condemned to what would be like a death in life.

For half-hysterical at times, an impression seemed to have come upon Isa Gernon that she would be fetched away, that even against her own will she would be saved from the fate that awaited her, and she started up, and listened, and looked from her window again and again for what did not come. Dresses were tried on, trunks were packed, presents poured in, bouquets, jewels, everything to give éclat to the proceedings; but Isa seemed to see nothing but one upbraiding face ever before her, reproaching her for her cruelty—a cruelty which she nerved herself by saying was but duty.

Brace Norton knew all, even the time at which the wedding would take place; but he uttered no complaint, only wandered about hour after hour, telling himself that to-morrow all would be at an end, ending by reproaching himself for his inaction. Towards afternoon, he strolled out towards the marsh, and smiled bitterly a fierce, angry smile, as he saw the men busily cutting their way with the great drain towards the pit, from which he had saved the bride of the ensuing day.

"Would we had died there together," he said, bitterly; and then he stooped, and picked a bunch of the forget-me-nots so abundant there, and tied them with one of the thin rushes from the mass at his feet. An hour after, enclosed in an envelope, they were laid on Isa's dressing-table, where she found them, and as had wept of old her mother, she had wept, for she guessed from whence that simple bouquet had come. She kissed them, held them to her breast, and then sank upon her knees, sobbing hysterically for the love she felt that, in spite of all revelations, she could not crush down, for she thought she was alone. But it was not so, for Jane McCray had entered unperceived, and started and turned pale as she saw the tiny flowers and the envelope in which they had arrived.

"True-blue," she said aloud, for her thoughts had reverted to the past; and then, trembling with superstitious dread, "Miss Isa," she said, "throw those flowers away—they're fatal, and bring nothing but misery and despair to those who wear them. All those long years ago, and it seems only yesterday that your poor mamma brought a bunch from the marsh. If he has sent you those, it was cruel and heartless of him, at such a time."

And angry with the maid who must have brought them, Jane made as if to take them from her mistress's hand; but she stopped half way, trembling more than ever, as she saw Isa press the simple blossoms to her breast with both hands, her head thrown back, her blue-veined eyelids closed, and her lips moving rapidly—for there, on her knees, she was invoking Heaven's blessing on the sender, and praying for strength to carry her through her trials.

Jane's anger had passed away, when, after a few minutes, she assisted Isa to a couch; for there was something in the poor girl's face that troubled her, and kept her hovering round as from a strange kind of fascination.

Was she going to be ill? Had her poor nerves been drawn too tightly? And would they snap beneath the unfair tension? At one time it seemed to Jane McCray, when Isa started up as if listening, that there would be no wedding the next morning.

But the preparations went on, and Sir Murray entertained a select party at dinner. My lord, the Viscount, was in excellent spirits, and paid frequent visits to the decanters. Certainly, a week had passed since the money was due, but then he had written to Braham, telling him of the day of the wedding; and the money-lender had sent a congratulatory reply, to say that it was "all right," and that he very much regretted his inability to attend himself.

The second course was on the table, and McCray was busy handing the wine to the various guests, when a footman, who had just entered the room, pulled him by the sleeve.

"Gude-sake, man!" he exclaimed, testily, "ye'll make that wine as thick as mood!" when, hearing the man's whisper, he set the decanter down upon the floor, and ran out.

Isa had sent to excuse herself, for she was, indeed, too ill with excitement; and, at Jane's earnest solicitation, she had gone to lie down, to fall into a broken slumber, filled with troubled dreams, and all connected with the coming day. Again and again she was being led to the church, when Brace seemed to snatch her away and hold her to his breast: but when she tried to clasp him in return, he faded, as it were, away, and there was nothing there: then they were wandering together by the marsh, picking the true-blue forget-me-nots; but each flower seemed weeping for their sorrows; and at last the soft, treacherous earth seemed to give way, and they were plunged together in the black, strangling water, to sink lower, lower, lower, till all was blinding and dark; but his arms were tightly round her now, his lips were to hers, and he was breathing words of love—of love, and holy love—to her, telling her that they would part no more; that there should be no more misery, no more watching and weeping; but that their parents' sorrows should be succeeded by the sunshine of their joy; and, returning his caresses from the depth of her heart, she shrieked aloud, for she was rudely awakened to the misery of the present; for, apparently wild with excitement, Jane rushed into the room, caught her for a moment in her arms, to kiss her, almost fiercely, and then throwing her rudely back upon the couch—

"Lie there, my child—lie there!" she exclaimed. "She gave you into my charge, and I have been faithful. Sleep, if you like, but let it be in peace, for there will be no wedding to-morrow!"

Was she mad? Was she crazy? Isa asked herself those questions, as she heard the door closed and locked upon her; then, unable to restrain her tears, she sank back weakly weeping.

"They're Bringing My Lady Hame"

Alexander McCray, in his excitement at being told that Brace Norton was in the hall, set down the decanter upon the carpet, where it was directly after kicked over by the under-butler. But McCray hurried out, lest Sir Murray should hear who had arrived—his dread being that there would be a *fracas* brought on by the young man's imprudence. He looked for the visitor, though, in vain, and turned back to enter the dining-room, when the glass door looking out upon the carriage-drive was thrown open, and Brace, pale and wild-looking, appeared.

"Gude save us! and how can ye be sae foolish, laddie?" exclaimed McCray, hurrying to him. "Ye'll mak' sair wark of it a', and do naebody any gude. If ye lo'e the puir bairn," he said, with a touching simplicity, "gang yer gait, and let her be in peace, for ye'll break her puir sair hairt if ye mak' a dust noo!"

"What?" whispered Brace—"has she not told you?"

"Told me?" exclaimed McCray. "Ah! stop, then! Gude save us, the lassie's mad! Jenny! wife!—here, stop!"

But Alexander McCray's words might have been true, from the way in which the housekeeper rushed into the dining-room, exclaiming, "Sir Murray—Sir Murray!"

The pent-up excitement of years upon years was struggling for exit, and, heedless of all present—of the confusion her presence created as the baronet rose, glaring at her with a mingling of fear and anger—Jane darted towards him.

"Where is McCray? Take this woman out?"

"No—no," she shrieked, excitedly. "Let no one dare to touch me! I knew the truth would out some day; and now it has come—come in time to stop this cruel wedding. It has been hidden from the eyes of man all these years, but Heaven would not suffer that it should rest longer. No!" she cried, as, clinging to Sir Murray, he tried to shake her off—"it has come home to you at last. I will not leave go. You know how I have kept my lips sealed; and now the time is come when they should be opened. Sir Murray—my poor lady—has—"

Jane McCray's words became inaudible, as, dizzy with excitement, she reeled and then fell, to lie insensible upon the carpet. The visitors looked from one to the other; some sought to assist the housekeeper, others made for the door; while, trembling himself, Lord Maudlaine hurried to Sir Murray's side.

"In Heaven's name, what does it all mean?" the Viscount whispered.

"I don't know—I—I—What, you here?" exclaimed Sir Murray, as Brace Norton appeared in the doorway.

"Tell him, McCray," said Brace, in a low voice. "Speak to him gently."

Pale and scared-looking, his ruddy, open countenance speaking the sense of the painful duty he had to perform, McCray moved slowly towards Sir Murray.

"What is it?" the latter said, in a strangely incoherent way. "Is Miss Gernon ill or—or—in Heaven's name, speak!" he cried, as if forcing the words to leave his lips—"*has she fled?*"

"No, Sir Mooray," said the old Scot, in a low voice, as he spoke almost tenderly, watching the change in his master's countenance the while, and catching him by the wrist; and, as if foreseeing what would happen, he placed his arm round him. "Sir Mooray," he whispered now, as the baronet's eyes assumed a fixed and ghastly expression, "*they're bringing my lady home!*"

McCray's foresight was needed; for at those words—words that Sir Murray Gernon seemed to have expected—he raised one hand to his cravat, and then his knees gave way beneath him, and he would have fallen but for the stout supporting arm of his old servant.

"It's apoplexy! Sir Mooray was seized so before. There, for Gude-sake, my laird, don't stand glowering there like that, but rin and send a groom for the doctor. Fetch pillows, will ye? and, ladies and gentlemen, in Sir Mooray's name I ask ye all to gang hame; for this is a sair nicht at the Castle!"

At the same moment there was seen through the darkness of the autumn evening the flashing of lights in the park avenue, then they slowly approached the bridge, passed over it, and a few minutes after there were steps upon the gravel drive, and, headed by Captain Norton, hat in hand, men bore softly into the great hall a hastily-contrived litter. Then, guided by McCray, the litter was borne into one of the nearest rooms, and slowly and in silence the men went out on tip-toe, leaving present only Brace Norton, his father, and the old major-domo.

No word was spoken, but McCray softly stole to the door and closed it, as, suddenly, Captain Norton fell upon his knees, resting his hands for a few moments upon the litter, covered as it was with a white sheet; and then, taking the hand stretched out to him by his son, he tottered from the room; and those who looked upon his pale face saw that great scar standing out plain and red, and that his eyes were wet with tears.

The weakness was but of a few minutes' duration; and as they stood in the brightly-lighted hall once more, Captain Norton's voice was sharp and short in its utterance, as he inquired of the state of Sir Murray Gernon.

"I left them bathing his face, sir," said McCray; and he led the way into the nearly deserted dining-room, where, breathing stertorously, Sir Murray still lay; Jane McCray having been assisted to her own room.

"But ye no think there was foul play, sir?" whispered McCray to Brace Norton. And the young man shook his head, as, eagerly watching his fathers acts, he laid his hand upon the old steward's lips.

For, going down upon one knee, Captain Norton threw more open the stricken man's neck-band, raised his head slightly, and stayed for a few moments holding one of Sir Murray's hands in his.

"Brace," he said, in a low tone, as, alone now with the old steward, he looked up in his son's face—"Brace, McCray, you know all from the first. Fate dealt hardly with us both; but at any time, I could have held out my hand to him, and said, you do me wrong. But, Heaven help him! for he has suffered much. He is more to be pitied than blamed!"

There was the sound of wheels upon the gravel once more, and Captain Norton rose to his feet, just as the door was hastily opened, and Dr Challen entered, raising his hands and eyes first to Captain Norton and then to Brace, as if exclaiming, "Good heavens, what a night!"

"The old seizure," he said, after a few minutes; and then he beckoned to McCray to help him.

"Gude-sake, sir, it's a sair nicht!" exclaimed the old steward, after a few minutes. "Ye maun let me go; for at the glint I got just noo through the open door, there's something wrang wi' my Laird Maudlaine and Mr Brace; and this is no time for mair troubles."

"Go, in the name of all that's sensible!" said the doctor, "and ask them if they are mad. Why, they're scuffling already!"

Dr Challen was wrong; for though Lord Maudlaine had followed the young man and his father to the hall, and had gazed at Brace with a look in which bitterness, disappointment, and hatred struggled for mastery, he spoke no word, till suddenly the glass door was opened, and two men entered, one pressing right to the back, the other stepping in front of his lordship.

"Our orders were, my lord, to take you as you left the church to-morrow morning," said the latter; "but as it seems there'll be no church-work, why, we do it now, unless, of course, your lordship's prepared with the stiff."

With a fierce oath, Lord Maudlaine started back; but the man was as active.

"Suit of Lewis Braham, m' lord, as I dare say you know—eight thousand four hundred and forty-five pounds six and eightpence. Does your lordship pay?"

"Surely this is not necessary on a night like this!" exclaimed Brace, indignantly; and taking the sheriff's officer by the arm, he swung him away.

"Don't resist the law, sir," exclaimed the man, in the well-known words; and the next minute the two officers had hurried their capture to a fly waiting at the door; and the next morning Viscount Maudlaine was on his way to durance vile.

At Last

Brace Norton, on his return from the marsh, had been wandering about in a strange, restless fashion; which troubled those who, unknown to himself, had been watching him keenly day after day. For the eyes of father and mother had met, for each to read the other's thoughts, as they recalled a scene which took place in a pine wood directly after a wedding, many years ago.

"I don't fear it of him," said Captain Norton, quietly; "but if you wish it—"

"How can you read my thought so well?" said Mrs Norton, sadly. "It is indeed my wish. He has now just taken the direction of the marsh again."

"I will not leave him again until he seems calm and resigned to his fate," said Captain Norton.

"Calm—resigned," said Mrs Norton, mournfully. "Then there is no hope for him, poor boy?"

"Hope? Not in that direction, I fear," said the Captain; and he strode after his son.

It required no great exertion to overtake the young man; and, ready to suspect danger, Captain Norton viewed with anxious heart the strange, vacant look in his son's face.

"Off for another walk, Brace?" he said, cheerfully, as he clapped him on the shoulder.

"Yes," said Brace, drearily.

"Be a man, Brace," said his father, in a low, earnest voice; and he stood for a few moments clasping his son's hands in his own. "I, too, have suffered, Brace!"

"I know it—I know it!" said Brace, in the same sad, listless way, "and I'll try and bear it; but oh! father, my heart feels desolate!"

"Come, I'm going to see how the works progress. You'll go with me: to-morrow we'll start early, and go away for a few days."

Brace allowed his father to take his arm, and he walked with him mile after mile, listening, apparently, to his descriptions of the progress of the drain, till, evening drawing on, they came round by the old pine grove, crossed it at one end, where the evening breeze was sighing with a low, murmuring noise amidst the boughs over head—a sound as of waters breaking upon a distant shore.

In spite of Captain Norton's efforts to be cheerful, he felt now that he had made a grievous mistake in the route he had chosen; for the solemn whisperings of the gloomy old pine wood had their influence even upon him; and, as his heart beat painfully, he shudderingly recalled the past. So strong were the impressions made by memory, that he had not a word to say in opposition when Brace gently disengaged his arm, and seated himself upon one of the fallen trunks, to bury his face in his hands. Captain Norton even felt that he could have followed his son's example, as, like spectres of the past, came trooping by the thoughts and scenes of the bygone, as the old pine wood grew more and more dim and sombre, for the sun had just dipped below the distant horizon.

There was the old scene at the church porch; the encounter at the rectory; the walk over the moor; his madman's acts; and, lastly, his awaking to the fact that the devoted woman who had followed him was lying bleeding at his feet—perhaps breathing her last sighs. Then came a change, and he saw again Marion, his old love, returned from abroad; the meeting in his own garden; the scene at the party; the disappearance of the cross; the blow stricken by Sir Murray Gernon; and, lastly, the news that Lady Gernon had, in one short hour, as it were, passed from this life. And now, here was his son—apparently persecuted by the same sad fate—crouching before him, heart-broken and despairing. What was in the future for them both?

He asked himself the question; and then, as if electrified, he started, and stood listening.

"What was that, Brace?" he cried, excitedly.

"Nothing but the men leaving work," said the young man drearily.

"Nonsense!—rouse yourself!" cried the Captain, "and come on: there is something wrong. Hark at the hurried buzz of voices! The dam must have burst! Let us go."

"It is only the wind in the pine-tops sighing as if all the sad spirits of the air were there in debate," said Brace. "I like staying here, father; for it is as if one was once more at sea, with the heralds of the coming storm whispering through the rigging, and telling the news of the fierce winds, soon to shake spar and cord. Father," he said dreamily, "I ought not to have stayed at Merland so long."

"There is something going on out there!" cried the Captain, who had not heeded his son's words. "Come, Brace—once more be a man, and let us go and see."

The young man started up, and together they hurried to where the navvies had been at work, to find that, half-drunken, they had neglected to see to the security of a dam, beneath which they were working, and it had burst, sweeping all before it, tearing down and scooping out the sides of the drain; and Brace and his father arrived in time to save the lives of two of the men, whom the water had swept some distance down.

But no lives were lost, and soon, the water having passed, the men collected where they had been at work, one angrily blaming the other as being the cause of the mischief.

"Are you all here?" exclaimed Captain Norton in his sharp, short, military way. "Count up!"

"Seventeen, eighteen, nineteen. Where's Joe Marks?" cried the ganger, counting.

"Here, all right!" growled a wet savage, who was vainly trying to ignite his pipe with some sodden matches.

"Where's Sol Dancer?" cried the ganger, after another spell at counting.

"Oh! he's over there," said another with a grin. "You couldn't drownd he, if you was to try."

"We're all right, sir!" said the ganger. "We was going to work another hour, as they lost a lot o' time this morning; but it's all over now for to-night. Nice job to get straight again in the mornin'. But, hallo! what's that?"

He was about to step forward, through the soft peat mire, when he was pressed back by Captain Norton, to whom and to his son had come in one and the same instant, the revelation of the second part of the Merland mystery; and together they leaped down into the great cutting, to wade through up to their waists in the black, decayed bog vegetation. They needed no words for explanation; the tufts of little forget-me-nots and silky cotton rush growing around, and yet untouched by the navvies' spades, told all; for there, in the side of the great drain, where the rush of water had, in its fierce eddy, scooped out a vast mass of peat, stood, perfectly upright, with hands clasped together as if in prayer, her head thrown back, as if to give the last glance upward, towards the haven of rest, the body of Marion Lady Gernon.

Foul play? Treachery there was none, save that of the deceitful moss spread over the soft peat—a verdant carpet over black relentless death from which there was no escape. Even yet, tightly clasped within her fingers, were the remains of the specimens she must have been gathering when the moss gave way, and she sank, apparently without a struggle, from the eyes of the world.

There was no horrible decay here—no frightful repelling change; the peat had the strange preservative character within it of holding unaltered that which it took to itself; and as the body of a poor Saxon woman was once found, after probably fifteen hundred years' immersion, so was found that of Marion Lady Gernon.

The truth at last—the dread truth, proclaiming itself, trumpet-tongued, for all men to hear—proclaiming innocence, and wronging suspicion, suffering, and death. The last veil was lifted from the past; and as the truth shone forth, clear and bright, foul suspicion and lying scandal shrank away abashed from the bright light to the dark shades where they had been engendered.

"The truth at last!" groaned Philip Norton, elderly and grey now, as he stood, with clasped hands, gazing at the silent dead—"the truth at last, and now he will believe."

The navvies shrank back in half dread at the strange sight for a few minutes; and when, recovering, they would have advanced, Brace motioned them back, and he alone heard his father's words.

"At last—at last! what I have prayed for so long. At last! Oh Heaven! I loved her too well to have sullied her even in thought!"

He stood motionless for a few minutes, and then, by a fierce effort, he started back into life.

"Let no hand but ours rest upon her, Brace," he whispered; and then, of the woodwork near, a litter was hastily contrived, and on a bed of the heather and rush, amidst which she had loved to linger, the sleeping figure was slowly borne towards the village, till, as they neared the Park, Brace left his father to prepare those at the Castle for the awful visitation.

At One

Two months elapsed, and Merland village had almost ceased talking about the grand funeral from the Castle—"the strange berryin'"—when, after twenty long years, Lady Gernon was borne to the family vault, with the Nortons, at Sir Murray's wish, for chief mourners. For he lay as he had been stricken down, a broken, helpless man, tended ever by his two old, faithful servants; McCray watching his every glance, and often and often sitting at his bedside, to read to him, in a strong Scottish twang, the news of the present and the future. But for a long while there was a strange, uneasy aspect in Sir Murray Gernon's face whenever Jane McCray was in the room. And that uneasy look was at last interpreted by the housekeeper, who, as she smoothed his pillow, asked him of his thoughts—for he had, as it were, questioned her with his eyes—while she held bottle and medicine-glass in her hand.

"She never but once tasted it," said Jane McCray, "I changed it every time."

His words came now only in broken utterances, so that only his regular attendants could comprehend his wishes, but that time, plainly and loudly came the words:

"Thank God!"

Few knew the bitter fight that took place in that proud man's breast, as, humbled now, he saw clearly the way in which he had taken suspicion to his breast, nurturing it and preparing the soil for its lasting stay, until the foul roots had laced and interlaced—until it was like tearing his heart to pieces to drag them forth. But it had to be done, and he did it manfully, in those long hours, when he lay helpless and alone. How he could read now the past by another light; his own weakness, the bitter sufferings of the true-hearted woman who had striven to bear the cross that had fallen to her lot. How all his wealth and possessions had been but so much dust and ashes, and his life, so far, one dreary blank. But there was the future!—and for awhile his face brightened, and he looked elate; there was his child—there was Philip Norton's child. Should not they possess the happiness that had never been his? But then his brow became overcast, as he thought of how he would have to humble himself before his old rival and enemy.

It was a bitter fight; but help came, as Isa glided into the room, and knelt beside his pillow, placing her little hands in his; and the weak tears rolled down his furrowed cheeks, as he prayed for strength to root out the last foul thread that seemed to canker his breast. He could see it all now—all so plainly, that with him rested the happiness of many around; and as he took those hands and held them to his brow, he prayed earnestly as man ever yet prayed, that the past might be forgiven, and a new heart granted to his suffering breast.

That prayer must have been heard, for the next day Brace Norton and his father were at the Castle, seated by the sick man's bed, till Sir Murray made a sign to McCray, who whispered in Brace Norton's ear, and they two left the room.

No eye saw—no ear heard what took place in that bed-chamber; but when, at last, alarmed at the long silence, Brace and Isa stole in, Sir Murray's eyes were closed, and Captain Norton's head was bowed down, while Brace felt his heart leap and the tears rush to his eyes, as he saw that their right hands were tightly clasped together.

Captain Norton started to his feet as the young couple entered, but it was no display of shame at his weakness, for he clasped Isa directly to his breast, and Brace saw that the hand his father had dropped was feebly held out to him. And then, though no words were spoken, a strange peace, hitherto unknown, stole upon every heart there present.

After a Lapse

"I ha'e been thinking, Jenny," said Alexander McCray, one afternoon, when, during intervals of taking pinches of snuff, he had mixed himself a tumbler of whisky and water, wherein floated the transparent discs of half a sliced lemon—"I ha'e been thinking, Jenny, if it wasna for Sir Mooray wanting my airm noo he's oop again, and liking it better than that three-wheeled chair thing, I'd give oop the stewardship, and go back to my gairden."

"Nonsense!" said Mrs McCray, smiling.

"Weel, lassie, ye may ca' it nonsense, but I ca' it soun' sense, for it's quite hairt-breaking to see the way that man neglects the floor-beds. There's no floors noo in the gairden like there was in my day."

"Alexander!" exclaimed his wife, jumping up, and turning him round so that he could see through the low window out into the pleasure-grounds— "you are getting in the habit of talking nonsense! Did you ever see such a flower as that in the grounds in your day?"

"Gude save us—no," said Sandy, putting on his glasses, and a smile dawning on his rugged face—"Gude save us—no, lassie! Ye're reet, for she's a bonnie floor, indeed; and look at the sweet tendrils of the thing, and how she clings to the brae stake that's goin' to support her. Eh, lassie! but they're a brae couple, and Heaven be gracious to them!"

"Amen!" said Jane, softly, as, with dewy eyes, she rested upon her husband's shoulder, and continued to gaze at the sight before them.

"They say it's a vale o' sorrows, this warld, Jenny lassie," said McCray, taking off and wiping his spectacles; "but to my way of thinking, it's a verra beautiful gairden, full of bright floors and sweet rich fruits. But ye ken, lassie, that there's that de'il—muckle sorrow to him—a'ways pitching his tares and his bad seeds ower the wall, for them to come oop in weeds; and gif ye no keep the hoe busy at wark, and bend your prood neck and stiff back to keep tearing them oop by the roots, Auld Sootie's rubbing those hands of his at the way in which his warks run on. Perhaps ye'll just put the whusky near by my haund. I thank ye, lassie. Winna ye tak' a wee soopie?"

Mrs McCray declined; and after refreshing himself with a goodly draught, the old Scot continued:

"Ye're reet, lassie; the gairden has got its breet floors aifter all; and I think I'll e'en stay as I am. Heaven bless them! And there's that gudely vine of the Captain's coming to them, leuking as she desairves. Gude-sake, Jenny, I believe gif there's a better woman on this airth than thee, it's Mrs Norton; but she's na ye're equal in soom things, lassie. She mak's a gudely lady, but she wad ne'er ha' fitted in your station."

There was another sip of "whusky" before McCray spoke again, when, as two fresh figures passed slowly by the window:

"Eh, lassie!" cried Sandy; "but leuk there—that's the thing that wairms my hairt better than e'en the whusky or the glint o' yer twa e'en. It mak's me think o' whaat Dauvid says aboot brethren living together in unity. Leuk hoo the puir laird hangs on the Captain's airm, and hoo he listens to his wards. They're like brithers indeed noo; and the Captain's always reading to him. Boot—eh, lassie?—it strikes me they're gaun doon to the church again."

McCray was right, for, arm in arm—Captain Norton, upright of bearing, Sir Murray Gernon bent and feeble, walking with the shuffling step induced by his last seizure—they were bound on the frequent pilgrimage they made, a visit never paid by either alone—a pilgrimage to a shrine most holy in their eyes—for it was to the grave of the woman they had both loved.

The stormy epoch was past; and a gentle time of calm had come. Brace Norton had just returned from a two years' cruise, an impatient time, but one which he had passed in peace, for at every station he knew that long and loving letters awaited him. But now he was returned, and but few days more were to elapse before words were to be pronounced that should make two hearts one.

But Merland village was greatly dissatisfied; the couple, they said, were capitally matched, and young Lieutenant Norton would be 'most as wealthy as Sir Murray himself; but it did seem hard on the poor lord, who was said to be picking up a living anyhow at the foreign gaming-tables. Then, too, there were no grand preparations, and the wedding was to be quiet as quiet, and no open house at the Castle; and the general opinion seemed to be that times were not as they used to be—a declaration to which old Chunt cordially assented.

Still, people were more lenient, and many a blessing was showered on the blushing girl, who was led—nay, who led herself, feeble, broken Sir Murray Gernon—into the church, while, when the service was over, a deep hush fell upon all, and people held back with reverence; hats were doffed, and words were spoken in whispers, for when, leaning upon her husband's arm, Isa Norton came slowly through the porch, it was seen that she bore a wreath of tiny flowers, and, to the surprise of all, she stopped.

There was no fierce hand, though, to pluck them from her; and people whispered more and more as they saw the tears standing brightly in her eyes—tears of sorrow and happiness—thankfulness, too, for the bliss that was theirs. The bells would have struck up, but whispered words stayed the ringers; children would have flung flowers in the bride's path, but, for a few moments, their little hands were arrested; for, leaning upon Captain Norton's arm, both suffering strongly from the emotion evoked from the past, Sir Murray Gernon now appeared, to stand by his daughter's side; and the halt was by Lady Gernon's resting-place, the family vault of the old family—the spot where, years before, broken-hearted, mad almost, Philip Norton stood waiting the coming of the bridal party.

Even the whispers now were stayed, for the Merland people felt that something unusual was about to take place, and they were right; and for long years after it was talked of, and handed down: for, with trembling hand, Isa raised the wreath—the forget-me-not wreath—she held, and laid it, her simple offering, upon the grave of the dead, where they stood awhile, with bended heads, and then passed on. Then came the silver chiming of the old—old bells; the children cast their flowers; and long and hearty cheers rang out for the bridal pair; there was the hurrying of footsteps, the trampling of horses, and the rush of wheels, and the wedding procession swept away; but the simple wreath remained where it had been placed—remained for people to say, again and again, that the act was strange; but it was the token that Marion Gernon's memory was fresh in every heart, and the colour of that wreath, wet with her child's tears, was *True-blue*!